A GRADED FRENCH GRAMMAR

By

The Modern Language Staff
of Skerry's College

LONDON
SIR ISAAC PITMAN & SONS LTD.

First published 1954
Revised and reprinted 1964

SIR ISAAC PITMAN & SONS LTD.
PITMAN HOUSE, PARKER STREET, KINGSWAY, LONDON, W.C.2
THE PITMAN PRESS, BATH
PITMAN HOUSE, BOUVERIE STREET, CARLTON, MELBOURNE
22–25 BECKETT'S BUILDINGS, PRESIDENT STREET, JOHANNESBURG

ASSOCIATED COMPANIES

PITMAN MEDICAL PUBLISHING COMPANY LTD.
46 CHARLOTTE STREET, LONDON, W.I

PITMAN PUBLISHING CORPORATION
20 EAST 46TH STREET, NEW YORK 17, NEW YORK

SIR ISAAC PITMAN & SONS (CANADA) LTD.
(INCORPORATING THE COMMERCIAL TEXT BOOK COMPANY)
PITMAN HOUSE, 381–383 CHURCH STREET, TORONTO

MADE IN GREAT BRITAIN AT THE PITMAN PRESS, BATH
F4—(F.130)

FOREWORD

THIS book is divided into two Parts. In the first, the manner of instruction is designed to smooth the path of those who are unfamiliar with the grammatical terms often used in text-books, and those whose knowledge of English grammar is not very thorough. The second Part provides a revision of the grammar, condensed to meet the needs of students who require to brush up quickly what they once knew. For many years we have prepared students in both groups, and this book seeks to pass on the benefits derived from this extensive and varied experience in teaching French.

In addition to the grammar, graded passages are included to provide practice in both translation and comprehension. There are also Vocabularies and a useful Verb Table.

It is confidently believed that this novel approach to the study of French grammar will appeal strongly to both students and teachers.

Those who are taking up the study of French later in life will find this an admirable book for their purpose. It anticipates and removes the many "snags" which so often hinder success in the early stages of study.

FOREWORD

CONTENTS

PART I

PASSAGES FOR TRANSLATION

VOCABULARY

PART I

LESSON 1

The Definite Article (The Word "the")

Masculine		Feminine	
Le chocolat	*the chocolate*	**La** limonade	*the lemonade*
L'étudiant	*the student*	**L'**eau	*the water*

The plural is always **les**—

Les étudiants   *the students*

There are only two genders in French, the masculine and the feminine.

Present Indicative of "désirer," to want

je désire	*I want*	**nous désirons**	*we want*
tu désires	*thou dost want*	**vous désirez**	*you want*
il désire	*he wants*	**ils désirent**	*they want*
elle désire	*she wants*	**elles désirent**	*they want*

VOCABULARY FOR EXERCISE 1

le thé, *the tea*	la mère, *the mother*
le café, *the coffee*	la soupe, *the soup*
le lait, *the milk*	la crème, *the cream*
le sucre, *the sugar*	aimer, *to like*
le chocolat, *the chocolate*	détester, *to hate*
le vin, *the wine*	préparer, *to prepare*
le bébé, *the baby*	refuser, *to refuse*
l'enfant (*m.* or *f.*), *the child*	accepter, *to accept*
l'homme, *the man*	admirer, *to admire*
l'oncle, *the uncle*	crier, *to cry out*
le père, *the father*	protester, *to protest*

EXERCISE 1

A. *Insert the Definite Article in each of the following Sentences*

1. Je prépare . . . thé. 2. Tu désires . . . lait. 3. Il aime . . . sucre. 4. Elle refuse . . . crème. 5. Il déteste . . . limonade. 6. Elle

accepte . . . eau. 7. Nous aimons . . . café. 8. Vous aimez . . .
oncle. 9. Ils aiment . . . chocolat. 10. Elles admirent . . . bébé.

B. *Translate into English*

1. J'aime le café. 2. Tu aimes le thé. 3. Il aime le sucre. 4. Elle
aime le lait. 5. Vous aimez le père. 6. Nous aimons la limonade.
7. Ils aiment la mère. 8. Elles aiment l'oncle. 9. Le bébé aime le lait.
10. Je désire la crème.

C. *Translate into English*

1. La mère prépare la soupe. 2. Elle prépare le thé. 3. L'homme
refuse le chocolat. 4. Il accepte le vin. 5. Les enfants refusent l'eau.
6. Ils acceptent le lait. 7. Nous aimons le chocolat. 8. Vous admirez
le bébé. 9. Les enfants crient. 10. Vous protestez.

D. *Translate into French*

1. She prepares the coffee. 2. We refuse the wine. 3. The mother
accepts the water. 4. She refuses the lemonade. 5. The father likes the
milk. 6. He accepts the cream. 7. I protest. 8. She wants the cream.
9. We want the sugar. 10. The baby screams.

LESSON 2

The Indefinite Article (The Word "a")

Un pain	*a loaf*	**Une** pomme	*an apple*
Un abricot	*an apricot*	**Une** orange	*an orange*

Present Indicative of "être," to be, and of "avoir," to have

je suis	*I am*	**j'ai**	*I have*
tu es	*thou art*	**tu as**	*thou hast*
il est	*he is*	**il a**	*he has*
elle est	*she is*	**elle a**	*she has*
nous sommes	*we are*	**nous avons**	*we have*
vous êtes	*you are*	**vous avez**	*you have*
ils sont	*they are*	**ils ont**	*they have*
elles sont	*they are*	**elles ont**	*they have*

VOCABULARY FOR EXERCISE 2

le beurre, *the butter*

le fromage, *the cheese*

le légume, *the vegetable*

le cahier, *the exercise book*

le crayon, *the pencil*

l'ami (*m.*), *the friend*

l'amie (*f.*), *the friend*

le fils, *the son*

la fille, *the daughter*

le Français, *the Frenchman*

la France, *France*

l'Anglais, *the Englishman*

le livre, *the book*

en, *in*

l'Angleterre, *England*

la plume, *the pen*

la tante, *the aunt*

la montre, *the watch*

la côtelette, *the cutlet*

la viande, *the meat*

la confiture, *the jam*

la cerise, *the cherry*

fermer, *to close*

donner, *to give*

marcher, *to walk*

toucher, *to touch*

et, *and*

EXERCISE 2

A. *Insert the Indefinite Article in the following Sentences*

1. J'ai . . . montre. 2. Il a . . . cahier. 3. Elle a . . . plume. 4. Tu as . . . crayon. 5. Nous avons . . . ami. 6. Elles ont . . . amie. 7. Vous avez . . . oncle. 8. Ils ont . . . tante. 9. Le père a . . . fils. 10. La mère a . . . fille.

B. *Translate into French*

1. We have the bread and the butter. 2. She has a loaf. 3. You have an apple. 4. The uncle has one orange. 5. They have the cheese. 6. The friend has the jam. 7. I have a cherry. 8. A man has the meat. 9. The father has an apricot. 10. The mother has a cutlet.

C. *Translate into French*

1. The baby cries. 2. He wants the milk. 3. He touches the cream. 4. She walks. 5. The man shuts a book. 6. The Frenchman is in France. 7. The Englishman is in England. 8. I want an apple. 9. They give an orange. 10. You want a watch.

LESSON 3

The Word "à"

1. **à** generally means *at, to,* or *in*—

à Paris, *at Paris, to Paris,* or *in Paris*

2. To say *to the*, always look at the noun after the word *the*—

Masculine
Nouns

> **au** père   *to the father* (consonant)
> **à l'**oncle   *to the uncle* (vowel)
> **à l'**homme   *to the man* (mute "h")
> **au** héros   *to the hero* (aspirate "h")

(Observe that one does not put "à le.")

Masculine
plural
forms

> **aux** pères   *to the fathers*
> **aux** oncles   *to the uncles*
> **aux** hommes   *to the men*
> **aux** héros   *to the heroes*

(Note **aux** for *to the* before any plural noun.)

Feminine
Nouns

> **à la** mère   *to the mother*
> **à l'**amie   *to the friend* (fem.)
> **à l'**histoire   *to the history*
> **à la** haine   *to the hatred*

The plurals all take **aux** for *to the*—

> *aux* mères, *to the mothers*

The Perfect Tense

j'ai donné	*I have given*	**nous avons donné**	*we have given*
tu as donné	*thou hast given*	**vous avez donné**	*you have given*
il a donné	*he has given*	**ils ont donné**	*they have given*
elle a donné	*she has given*	**elles ont donné**	*they have given*

This tense is made from the present tense of **avoir**, *to have*, and the past participle of the verb **donner**, *to give*, obtained by putting **é** instead of **er**. So—

> *I have accepted* is **j'ai accepté**
> *I have prepared* is **j'ai préparé**
> *I have refused* is **j'ai refusé**

VOCABULARY FOR EXERCISE 3

Londres, *London*
Édimbourg, *Edinburgh*
Douvres, *Dover*
l'argent (*m.*), *the money, silver*
la femme, *the woman*
le professeur, *the teacher*
la ville, *the town*

demeurer, *to live*
prêter, *to lend*
emprunter, *to borrow*
remercier, *to thank*
parler, *to speak*
préférer, *to prefer*

EXERCISE 3

A. *Insert the French form for "to the" in the following Sentences, and Translate them into English*

1. J'ai donné la montre (*to the*) homme. 2. Tu as parlé (*to the*) hommes. 3. Il a parlé (*to the*) femmes. 4. Nous avons donné l'argent (*to the*) femme. 5. Vous avez parlé (*to the*) oncle. 6. Ils ont parlé (*to the*) oncles. 7. Le héros a parlé (*to the*) ami. 8. L'étudiant a parlé (*to the*) professeur. 9. Les professeurs ont parlé (*to the*) étudiants. 10. Les étudiants ont donné l'argent (*to the*) professeur.

B. *Translate into English*

1. J'ai accepté le chocolat. 2. Elle a préparé la soupe. 3. Il a refusé le thé. 4. Elle a accepté la crème. 5. Tu as préféré le lait. 6. Nous avons désiré le café. 7. Vous avez accepté l'eau. 8. Ils ont protesté. 9. Elles ont crié. 10. Nous avons aimé la limonade.

C. *Translate into French*

1. I live in Paris. 2. You live in London. 3. She lives in Glasgow. 4. We live in Newcastle. 5. He lives in the town. 6. I have lived at Dover. 7. She has lived in Liverpool. 8. She likes Liverpool. 9. They like Edinburgh. 10. I like the town.

D. *Translate into French*

1. I have lent the watch. 2. He has given the money. 3. She has thanked the man. 4. You have thanked the woman. 5. We have borrowed the pen. 6. She has borrowed the pencil. 7. We have given the lemonade to the students. 8. She has given the milk to the baby. 9. I have given the money to the mother. 10. They have lent the money to the man.

LESSON 4

The Word "de"

1. Generally **de** means *of*—

le livre **de** Jean, *the book of John*, i.e. John's book

2. To say *of the* correctly, always look at the word after *the*—

Masculine Nouns	**du** père	*of the father*	(consonant)
	de l'oncle	*of the uncle*	(vowel)
	de l'homme	*of the man*	(mute "h")
	du héros	*of the hero*	(aspirate "h")

(Observe that one must not put "de le.")

Masculine plural forms	**des** pères	*of the fathers*
	des oncles	*of the uncles*
	des hommes	*of the men*
	des héros	*of the heroes*

(Note **des** for *of the* before any plural noun.)

Feminine Nouns	**de la** mère	*of the mother*
	de l'amie	*of the friend (fem.)*
	de l'histoire	*of the history*
	de la haine	*of the hatred*

The plurals all take **des**—

des mères, etc.

The Perfect Tense of "avoir" and "être"

j'ai eu	*I have had*	**j'ai été**	*I have been*
tu as eu	*thou hast had*	**tu as été**	*thou hast been*
il a eu	*he has had*	**il a été**	*he has been*
elle a eu	*she has had*	**elle a été**	*she has been*
nous avons eu	*we have had*	**nous avons été**	*we have been*
vous avez eu	*you have had*	**vous avez été**	*you have been*
ils ont eu	*they have had*	**ils ont été**	*they have been*
elles ont eu	*they have had*	**elles ont été**	*they have been*

VOCABULARY FOR EXERCISE 4

le repas, *the meal*	avaler, *to swallow*
la pomme de terre, *the potato*	sucer, *to suck*
le petit garçon, *the boy*	et, *and*
manger, *to eat*	

EXERCISE 4

A. *Insert the French form for "of the" in the following Sentences, and translate them*

1. La montre (*of the*) père. 2. La plume (*of the*) mère. 3. L'argent (*of the*) héros. 4. Le lait (*of the*) bébé. 5. La limonade (*of the*) étudiants. 6. Le thé (*of the*) femmes. 7. Le café (*of the*) hommes. 8. Le pain (*of the*) étudiant. 9. La tante (*of the*) ami. 10. L'oncle (*of the*) amies.

B. *Translate into English*

1. J'ai eu le beurre et le fromage. 2. Vous avez eu les légumes. 3. Elle a eu le pain et la confiture. 4. Elles ont eu la viande. 5. Nous

avons été à Paris. 6. Elle a été à Londres. 7. Vous avez été à Newcastle.
8. J'ai été à Liverpool. 9. Tu as été à Édimbourg.

C. *Translate into French*

1. I have eaten the meat and the potatoes. 2. John has eaten the
apples and the cherries. 3. The lemonade of the students. 4. We have
swallowed the coffee. 5. The baby has sucked the milk. 6. The boy's
watch (the watch of the boy). 7. The woman's pen. 8. The uncle's
money. 9. The aunt's apples. 10. We like Liverpool and Newcastle.

LESSON 5

Three Ways of Translating the Word "some"

1. **Un peu de.** 2. **Quelque** (plural, **quelques**). 3. **Du (de
la, de l', des).**

un peu de beurre	*a little butter*
quelques pommes	*a few apples*

Un peu de is used with singular words—

un peu de lait	*some milk*
un peu de fromage	*some cheese*
un peu de patience	*some patience*

Quelques is generally used for plural articles—

quelques pommes	*some apples*
quelques plumes	*some pens*

The remaining form can be used with singular and plural—

du fromage	*some cheese*
de la farine	*some flour*
de l'huile (*fem.*)	*some oil*
des amis	*some friends*

Even if the English passage omits the word "some," it must
be inserted in French—

I have friends	j'ai **des** amis

Note that the word "some" must be repeated before each noun—

> *I have apples and bread*   j'ai **des** pommes et **du** pain

Negative Forms of the Verbs

je n'ai pas	*I do not have*
je ne suis pas	*I am not*
je ne donne pas	*I do not give*
je n'ai pas eu	*I have not had*
je n'ai pas été	*I have not been*
je n'ai pas donné	*I have not given*

VOCABULARY FOR EXERCISE 5

français (adjective), *French*
anglais   „   , *English*
monsieur,   *Sir*

EXERCISE 5

A. *Translate into English*

1. J'ai des amis français. 2. Vous avez des amis anglais. 3. Elle a des amies. 4. Ils ont des plumes. 5. Je n'ai pas le pain. 6. Vous avez un peu d'eau. 7. Nous avons quelques pommes. 8. Il a eu un peu de fromage. 9. Elles ont eu des cerises. 10. Un peu de patience, monsieur.

B. *Translate into French*

1. I do not like. 2. He does not give. 3. We do not accept. 4. I have not had. 5. She has not been in Paris. 6. We have not been in London. 7. They have not refused. 8. He has not protested. 9. I have not accepted. 10. We have not had the money.

LESSON 6

The Word "some"

After a negative, translate *some* or *any* by **de,** before any noun, singular or plural—

> je n'ai pas **de** pain   *I have not any bread*
> je n'ai pas **d'**amis   *I have no friends*
> je n'ai pas **de** farine   *I have not any flour*

Position of Adjectives

The following adjectives generally come before the noun they qualify—

Examples

bon	*good*	un **bon** petit garçon
mauvais	*bad*	un **mauvais** petit garçon
méchant	*naughty*	un **méchant** chien (*dog*)
jeune	*young*	un **jeune** homme
vieux	*old*	un **vieux** livre
beau	*fine*	un **beau** cadeau (*present*)
joli	*pretty*	un **joli** livre
laid	*ugly*	un **laid** petit garçon
vilain	*ugly*	un **vilain** homme
gentil	*nice*	un **gentil** petit chien (*little dog*)
meilleur	*better*	un **meilleur** prix (*prize*)
premier	*first*	un **premier** effort (*effort*)

Most others follow the noun.

Interrogative Verbs

A question is expressed in English by saying *do you?* or *are you?*, e.g. *Do you give?* or *Are you giving?*

Note that the French merely put **donnez-vous?**

There are no special words for *do you?* or *are you?*

Note the **t** in **a-t-il**, *has he?*, for euphony. A question may be put by saying **Est-ce que vous donnez?**

Sometimes this form conveys the idea, *Do you mean to say that you are giving?*

NEGATIVE INTERROGATIVE

Are you not giving?, *Do you not give?* are conveyed by **Ne donnez-vous pas?**, **Est-ce que vous ne donnez pas?**

Have you given?, *Did you give?* are conveyed by **Avez-vous donné?**

Have you not given?, *Did you not give?* are conveyed by **N'avez-vous pas donné?**

EXERCISE 6

A. *Translate into English*

1. Je n'ai pas de beurre. 2. Vous n'avez pas de fromage. 3. Il n'a pas de lait. 4. Nous n'avons pas de thé. 5. Elles n'ont pas de café. 6. Ils

n'ont pas de limonade. 7. Avez-vous du pain? 8. Je n'ai pas de pain.
9. N'avez-vous pas l'argent? 10. Je n'ai pas d'argent.

B. *Translate into French*

1. A good boy. 2. A young man. 3. A bad book. 4. A fine book.
5. A better friend. 6. The first effort. 7. A pretty present. 8. An old
dog. 9. A naughty boy. 10. A little friend.

C. *Translate into French*

1. Do you lend? 2. Have you lent? 3. Did he give? 4. Has she
given? 5. Did you eat? 6. Have you swallowed? 7. Have they eaten?
8. Did she accept? 9. Have they refused? 10. Did he like?

D. *Translate into English*

1. N'avez-vous pas aimé Paris? 2. N'avez-vous pas admiré la ville?
3. N'avez-vous pas accepté le cadeau? 4. N'a-t-il pas mangé le repas?
5. N'ont-ils pas avalé le thé? 6. N'a-t-elle pas mangé les pommes?
7. N'ont-elles pas prêté l'argent? 8. N'as-tu pas emprunté le crayon?
9. N'avons-nous pas emprunté l'argent? 10. N'ai-je pas admiré
Édimbourg?

LESSON 7

The Word "some"

1. When *some* is before an adjective, consider carefully where
the adjective would be in French, e.g. *some good friends, some
English friends.*

Now, in French, **bons** goes before the noun **amis,** but
anglais, being an adjective of nationality, follows **amis.**
Hence—

de bons amis
des amis anglais

Adjectives of *nationality, religion, colour, shape,* generally follow
the noun; hence—

des amis français	*some French friends*
des étudiants juifs	*some Jewish students*
des livres verts	*some green books*
des tables rondes	*some round tables*

But remember to translate *some* by **de** if the adjective precedes the noun in French—

de beaux livres	*some fine books*
de jolis gants	*some pretty gloves*
de vieux amis	*some old friends*

Past Tenses
THE IMPERFECT

j'étais	*I was*	**j'avais**	*I had*
tu étais	*thou wert*	**tu avais**	*thou hadst*
il était	*he was*	**il avait**	*he had*
nous étions	*we were*	**nous avions**	*we had*
vous étiez	*you were*	**vous aviez**	*you had*
ils étaient	*they were*	**ils avaient**	*they had*

je donnais	*I gave, I was giving, I used to give*
tu donnais	*thou gavest, etc.*
il donnait	*he gave, etc.*
nous donnions	*we gave, etc.*
vous donniez	*you gave, etc.*
ils donnaient	*they gave, etc.*

Generally, this tense is formed from the Present Participle **étant, donnant,** etc., by cutting off the **ant** and adding the endings—

-ais, -ais, -ait, -ions, -iez, -aient

This tense is used to translate the English—

(*a*)	was . . . ing	e.g. I was accepting **j'acceptais**
(*b*)	were . . . ing	we were giving **nous donnions**
(*c*)	used to . . .	I used to prefer **je préférais**
(*d*)	continuous action	I lived in Paris **je demeurais à Paris**
(*e*)	repeated action	I often lived in Paris **je demeurais souvent à Paris**
(*f*)	would = used to	I would often refuse **je refusais souvent**

VOCABULARY FOR EXERCISE 7

la cité, *the city*
l'invitation (*f.*), *the invitation*
allemand (*adjective*), *German*
écossais   ,,   , *Scottish*

EXERCISE 7

A. *Translate into English*

1. J'ai des amis anglais. 2. Ils sont de bons amis. 3. Ils demeurent à Liverpool. 4. Nous avons des livres verts. 5. Vous avez de bons amis. 6. Ils ont des amis français à Paris. 7. Elles ont des amis écossais à Édimbourg. 8. Tu as des amis allemands à Berlin. 9. Jeanne a de jolis gants. 10. Alfred a de beaux livres.

B. *Translate into English*

1. J'étais à Londres. 2. Tu étais à Douvres. 3. Papa était à Liverpool. 4. Marie était à Newcastle. 5. J'avais un ami. 6. Nous avions de bons amis. 7. Je donnais souvent des livres à Alfred. 8. Il donnait souvent des livres à Jeanne. 9. Elle donnait souvent de l'argent à Marie. 10. Ils donnaient du pain et du beurre aux hommes.

C. *Translate into French*

1. I was accepting the invitation. 2. You were admiring the city. 3. She was swallowing the milk. 4. I used to lend some money to the friends. 5. He used to borrow the money. 6. We often lived in Paris. 7. They would often refuse. 8. I used to protest. 9. We used to like the meals. 10. They were not accepting the money.

D. *Put in the word for "some" in the following phrases*

1. (Some) friends. 2. (Some) good friends. 3. (Some) English friends. 4. (Some) green books. 5. (Some) Jewish students. 6. (Some) round tables. 7. (Some) fine books. 8. (Some) pretty gloves. 9. (Some) old friends. 10. (Some) good butter.

LESSON 8

The Plurals of Nouns and Adjectives

1. Nouns and adjectives generally form their plural by adding **s** to the singular—

le petit chat	*the little cat*
les petit**s** chat**s**	*the little cats*

2. But nothing is added if the noun or adjective ends in **s**, **x**, or **z**—

le bois	*the wood*
les bois	*the woods*
la noix	*the nut*
les noix	*the nuts*
le nez	*the nose*
les nez	*the noses*

3. Nouns and adjectives ending in **au** and **eu** generally add **x** in the plural—

le beau cadeau	*the fine present*
les beau**x** cadeau**x**	*the fine presents*
le neveu	*the nephew*
les neveu**x**	*the nephews*

4. Nouns and adjectives ending in **al** generally change **al** to **aux** in the plural—

l'anim**al**	*the animal*
les anim**aux**	*the animals*

NOTE: In the adjectives **aux** is the masculine plural only—

égal (*m.*), égale (*f.*)	*equal (singular)*
égaux (*m.*), égales (*f.*)	*equal (plural)*
les garçons sont égaux	*the boys are equal*
les femmes sont égales	*the women are equal*

EXCEPTIONAL CASES

1. Nouns ending in **ou** normally add **s** in the plural. But the following take **x**—

le bijou	les bijou**x**	*jewels*
le caillou	les caillou**x**	*pebbles*
le chou	les chou**x**	*cabbages*
le genou	les genou**x**	*knees*
le hibou	les hibou**x**	*owls*
le joujou	les joujou**x**	*toys*

Do not be misled into thinking that all nouns ending in **ou**
take **x** in the plural. Cf.—

le clou   les clou**s**   *nails*

2. The adjective **bleu** takes **s** in the masculine plural—

les gants bleu**s**   *the blue gloves*

VOCABULARY FOR EXERCISE 8

dans, *in*
l'arbre (*m.*), *the tree*
le pommier, *the apple-tree*
qui, *which, who, whom*
le cerisier, *the cherry-tree*
deux, *two*
oui, *yes*

non, *no*
la poire, *the pear*
la fleur, *the flower*
la glace, *the ice-cream*, or *the ice*
le poirier, *the pear-tree*
intéressant, *interesting*

EXERCISE 8

A. *Translate into English*

1. Les petits chats et les petits chiens sont intéressants. 2. Les bois
verts ont des noix. 3. Les nez des femmes. 4. Avez-vous accepté les
beaux cadeaux? 5. Non, j'ai refusé les bijoux. 6. Les neveux admir-
aient les animaux. 7. Les étudiants sont égaux. 8. Avez-vous mangé
le repas? 9. Oui, nous avons eu de la viande, des pommes de terre et
des choux. 10. Les bois ont des hiboux.

B. *Translate into English*

1. Dans les bois vous admirez les arbres. 2. Le pommier est l'arbre
qui donne les pommes. 3. Le poirier est l'arbre qui donne les poires.
4. Le cerisier est l'arbre qui donne les cerises. 5. Nous admirons les
fleurs dans le bois. 6. Aimez-vous les fleurs? 7. J'aime les pommes, les
poires et les cerises. 8. Les étudiants aiment la glace. 9. Je désire une
glace. 10. Avez-vous mangé la glace?

C. *Translate into French*

1. The two tables are equal. 2. I like the fine presents. 3. The
women like the pretty jewels. 4. The owls are in the wood. 5. Have
you eaten the nuts? 6. I have eaten the two apples. 7. Do you want an
ice? 8. We want two ices. 9. The cat and the dog are (some) fine
animals. 10. The men are equal.

D. *Translate into French*

1. Did you not admire Paris? 2. Did you not like London? 3. Did you
not accept the invitation? 4. Did she not eat the ice-cream? 5. Did

they not eat the pears? 6. I used to give an apple to the boy. 7. He used to give some cherries to the students. 8. He was admiring the book. 9. In the woods I used to admire the flowers. 10. They would often lend some money to the friends.

LESSON 9

The Feminine Form of Adjectives

1. Always make the adjective agree with the noun it qualifies. You have two points to watch—

    (*a*) Is the noun plural?   e.g. **les petits chats**
    (*b*) Is the noun feminine?   e.g. **les jolies fleurs**

This rule is most important, because many marks are lost in an examination by students who fail to observe it.

2. The feminine of most adjectives is made by adding **e** to the masculine—

l'oiseau bleu	*the blue bird*
la fleur bleu**e**	*the blue flower*
les oiseaux bleus	*the blue birds*
les fleurs bleu**es**	*the blue flowers*

3. If the adjective ends in a mute **e**, do not add any **e** for the feminine—

le jeune chien	*the young dog*
la jeune femme	*the young woman*

4. But if the adjective ends in **é**, then add **e** in the feminine—

un homme âgé	*an aged man*
une femme âg**e**	*an aged woman*

VOCABULARY FOR EXERCISE 9

haut, *high*
grand, *big, tall*
content, *happy, pleased*
travailler, *to work*
étudier, *to study*
le jardin, *the garden*
la maison, *the house*
aussi, *also*

le tableau, *the picture*
le piano, *the piano*
le miroir, *the mirror*
la chambre, *the bedroom*
la salle, *the room*
la salle de classe, *the class-room*
souvent, *often*

EXERCISE 9

A. *Translate into English*

1. Les fleurs du jardin sont jolies. 2. J'admire aussi les arbres du jardin. 3. Nous avons un beau poirier dans le jardin. 4. Nous sommes contents dans la maison. 5. Elle est contente dans le jardin. 6. La maison est haute. 7. Les jardins sont petits. 8. Ah! Les jolies fleurs! 9. Ah! Les jolis bijoux! 10. La chambre est petite.

B. *Translate into English*

1. Les étudiants sont contents. Ils travaillent. 2. Ils étudient dans la classe. 3. Les jolis livres sont intéressants. 4. Jeanne a une grande maison et un petit jardin. 5. Alfred avait un grand chien et un petit chat. 6. Admiriez-vous les jolies fleurs dans le jardin? 7. J'admirais les beaux tableaux dans la chambre. 8. Nous admirions les jolis miroirs et le beau piano. 9. Jeanne a une glace; elle est contente. 10. Marie a un livre intéressant.

C. *Translate into French*

1. An aged man and an aged woman were in the garden. 2. They were admiring the pretty flowers. 3. The young students have worked in the class-room. 4. The young women are pleased; they have accepted some fine presents. 5. The young men are happy; they have accepted some interesting books. 6. We have a fine piano, two mirrors, and some interesting pictures in the room. 7. The young man has refused the present of the aged man. 8. Oh! what pretty gloves! 9. Oh! what pretty flowers! 10. Oh! what a pretty house!

D. *Translate into French*

1. Have you not accepted the pretty picture? 2. No, I have refused the picture and the two mirrors. 3. I like the fine piano. 4. I admire the little flowers in the garden. 5. The birds in the trees were happy. 6. The owl was not happy. 7. He hated the birds. 8. The boys liked the birds in the woods. 9. They used to accept some bread. 10. The books were often interesting.

LESSON 10

The Feminine Form of Adjectives (cont.)

1. Adjectives ending in **-al** add **-e** in the feminine.

2. But those ending in **-el, -il, -ol, -ul,** double the **l** before adding **-e,** generally—

> Les femmes sont éga**les** (*equal*)
> Les femmes ne sont pas crue**lles** (*cruel*)
> Les femmes sont genti**lles** (*nice*)
> Elle est fo**lle,** *She is mad (masculine* **fou**)
> nu**lle** réponse, *no reply*

3. Similarly, adjectives ending in **-ais, -as, -eil, -et, -ien, -on, -os,** and **-ot**—

> une réponse ne**tte**   *a distinct reply*
> une paire parei**lle**   *a similar pair*
> la bo**nne** farine   *the good flour*
> La femme est so**tte**   *The woman is foolish*
> La chaise est ba**sse**   *The chair is low*
> La neige est épai**sse**   *The snow is thick*
> l'ancie**nne** amie   *the former friend*
> la gro**sse** figure   *the big face*

VOCABULARY FOR EXERCISE 10

la vie, *the life*
las, *tired*
le mur, *the wall*
général, *general*
la semaine, *the week*
le jour, *the day*
amusant, *amusing*
quotidien (*adj.*), *daily*
immortel, *immortal*
frapper, *to knock*
apporter, *to bring*
aujourd'hui, *today*
hier, *yesterday*
le mois, *the month*
l'année, *the year*
dimanche, *Sunday*
lundi, *Monday*

mardi, *Tuesday*
mercredi, *Wednesday*
jeudi, *Thursday*
vendredi, *Friday*
samedi, *Saturday*
janvier, *January*
février, *February*
mars, *March*
avril, *April*
mai, *May*
juin, *June*
juillet, *July*
août, *August*
septembre, *September*
octobre, *October*
novembre, *November*
décembre, *December*

EXERCISE 10

A. *Translate into English*

1. Les femmes ne sont pas égales. 2. Marie n'est pas cruelle. 3. J'ai

crié. Nulle réponse. 4. La petite femme est gentille. 5. Il m'a donné
une réponse nette. 6. Elle a admiré les gants. 7. Marie a une paire
pareille. 8. La bonne femme a refusé le cadeau. 9. Elle n'est pas folle.
10. La neige est épaisse dans le jardin.

B. *Put in the Feminine Forms for*

1. Bon. 2. Général. 3. Immortel. 4. Sot. 5. Ancien. 6. Bas.
7. Gros. 8. Nul. 9. Las. 10. Quotidien.

C. *Translate into French*

1. The daily life. 2. The tired woman. 3. The low wall of the garden. 4. The high walls of the house. 5. The immortal heroes of Paris.
6. The general efforts of the men. 7. I have knocked—no reply.
8. I have brought some presents. 9. Yesterday I have accepted the
house. 10. Today he has accepted the invitation.

D. *Translate into English*

1. Les jours de la semaine sont lundi, mardi, mercredi, jeudi, vendredi,
samedi et dimanche. 2. Les mois de l'année sont janvier, février, mars,
avril, mai, juin, juillet, août, septembre, octobre, novembre et décembre.
3. Nous n'aimons pas les lundis. 4. Nous aimons les vendredis. 5. Les
samedis sont amusants. 6. Les dimanches sont intéressants. 7. Nous
travaillons le mardi et le jeudi. 8. Nous travaillons aussi le lundi, le
mercredi et le vendredi. 9. Au mois de janvier, la neige est épaisse.
10. Au mois de juillet, les fleurs sont jolies.

LESSON 11

The Feminine Form of Adjectives (cont.)

1. If an adjective ends in **-ier**, the feminine ends in **-ière**—

f**ier**   *proud*   f**ière**

2. If an adjective ends in **-x**, the feminine ends in **-se**—

jalou**x**   *jealous*   jalou**se**
heureu**x**   *happy*   heureu**se**

Exceptions are—

dou**x**   *sweet*   dou**ce**
fau**x**   *false*   fau**sse**

3. If an adjective ends in **-f,** the feminine ends in **-ve**—

furti**f**   *furtive, stealthy*   furti**ve**

4. Watch the following adjectives which have a double form in the masculine singular—

	un **vieux** livre	*an old book*	(consonant)
	un **vieux** héros	*an old hero*	(aspirate "h")
but:	un **vieil** homme	*an old man*	(mute "h")
	un **vieil** ami	*an old friend*	(vowel)

The feminine has only one form, **vieille**—

une **vieille** lettre	*an old letter*
une **vieille** haine	*an old hatred*
une **vieille** histoire	*an old story*
une **vieille** amie	*an old friend* (feminine)

NOTE. In the masculine plural, **vieux** is used before any noun—

de **vieux** livres
de **vieux** héros
de **vieux** hommes
de **vieux** amis

In the feminine plural, **vieilles** is used before any noun—

de **vieilles** lettres	de **vieilles** histoires
de **vieilles** haines	de **vieilles** amies

The following adjectives follow this rule—

mou, *soft*; **nouveau,** *new*; **beau,** *fine*; **fou,** *foolish*
mol, molle; nouvel, nouvelle; bel, belle; fol, folle

VOCABULARY FOR EXERCISE 11

pourquoi, *why*	le fer, *the iron*
le métal, *the metal*	le plomb, *the lead*
précieux, *precious*	le cuivre, *the copper*
utile, *useful*	la mine, *the look, mien*
l'or, *the gold*	la classe, *the class*
payer, *to pay for*	

EXERCISE 11

A. *Translate into French*

1. A jealous woman. 2. A happy house. 3. A proud mother.

4. A stealthy look. 5. An old friend (*masculine*). 6. An old book. 7. An old story. 8. Old friends (put *some* before *old*). 9. Old pictures (put *some* before *old*). 10. A fine friend.

B. *Translate into English*

1. J'ai de beaux tableaux dans la maison. 2. Nous avons de beaux livres. 3. Une nouvelle maison; de nouveaux amis. 4. Les vieux amis sont bons. 5. Au mois de juin nous admirons les bois. 6. Au mois de septembre nous aimons les pommes. 7. Les poires sont bonnes; les pommes sont mauvaises. 8. La mère est fière. 9. Les étudiants sont heureux dans la classe. 10. Les nouveaux étudiants ont des amis dans la classe.

C. *Translate into French*

1. The days of the week are Monday, Tuesday, Wednesday, Thursday, Friday, Saturday, and Sunday. 2. The months of the year are January, February, March, April, May, June, July, August, September, October, November, and December. 3. We like the months of July and August. 4. We do not like the months of December and January. 5. We hate the month of November. 6. Sunday is a fine day. 7. Monday is a bad day. 8. Old friends are good friends. 9. Old books are often good books. 10. We are happy in the garden.

D. *Translate into French*

1. Why did you refuse the invitation? 2. Why did you not accept the fine presents? 3. The new students like the students in the class. 4. She has lent the new pen to Marie. 5. They have borrowed some pencils. 6. I have paid for the two ices. 7. We often lived in London. 8. The precious metals are (the) gold and (the) silver. 9. The useful metals are (the) iron and (the) lead. 10. (The) copper is also a useful metal (translate the word *the* in brackets).

LESSON 12

The Feminine Form of Adjectives (cont.)

1. Some adjectives have an irregular feminine form. Watch the following—

Frais, *fresh*; feminine **fraîche**

Be careful not to put "fraise"; **la fraise** is *the strawberry*.

Sec, *dry*; feminine **sèche**

Sec can mean *lean*—un homme **sec**, *a lean man*.

blanc	white	feminine	blanche
franc	frank	,,	franche
favori	favourite	,,	favorite
long	long	,,	longue
public	public	,,	publique
bénin	good, kind	,,	bénigne
malin	evil	,,	maligne
grec	Greek	,,	grecque
turc	Turkish	,,	turque

To remember which adjective has the "c" in the feminine, some students say there is a "c" in Greece, none in Turkey.

2. The main adjectives of colour are—

bleu	blue	brun	brown
blanc	white	vert	green
rouge	red	noir	black
gris	grey	jaune	yellow
marron	chestnut	rose	pink

VOCABULARY FOR EXERCISE 12

la rose, *the rose*
la violette, *the violet*
l'aubépine (*f.*), *the hawthorn*
l'herbe (*f.*), *the grass*
la couleur, *the colour*

le lis, *the lily*
le muguet, *the lily of the valley*
le pavot, *the poppy*
le cheval, *the horse*

EXERCISE 12

A. *Translate into English*

1. Dans le jardin nous avons de belles fleurs. 2. Les roses sont rouges et blanches. 3. Les muguets sont verts et blancs. 4. Les pavots sont rouges. 5. Les violettes sont bleues. 6. L'aubépine est rose. 7. L'herbe du jardin est verte. 8. La poire est verte; la pomme est rouge. 9. Les cerises sont noires et rouges. 10. La fraise est fraîche.

B. *Write down the Feminine Form of the following Adjectives*

1. Sec. 2. Blanc. 3. Gris. 4. Jaune. 5. Favori. 6. Long. 7. Public. 8. Grec. 9. Turc. 10. Malin.

C. *Translate into French*

1. The blue pencils. 2. The black pens. 3. The yellow gold. 4. The red copper. 5. The pink flower. 6. The white rose. 7. The green grass. 8. The brown books. 9. The white lily. 10. The chestnut horse.

D. *Translate into French*

1. We like the white house and the green garden. 2. The birds like the brown woods and the green grass. 3. Jeanne likes the red flowers. 4. She detests white flowers. 5. The flowers are not fresh. 6. Tom's favourite pencil is blue. 7. Marie's favourite pen is green. 8. The old men are kind. 9. The Greek woman is speaking to the Turkish woman. 10. The grey colour of the houses.

LESSON 13

Comparative and Superlative of Adjectives

The forms for comparative and superlative of adjectives are as follows—

utile, *useful*; **plus utile,** *more useful*; **le plus utile,** *the most useful*

1. Le chien est **plus utile** que le chat. *The dog is more useful than the cat.*

Le cheval est **le plus utile** des animaux. *The horse is the most useful of the animals.*

(a) Un **beau** livre	*a fine book*
Un **plus beau** livre	*a finer book*
(b) Un livre **intéressant**	*an interesting book*
Un livre **plus intéressant**	*a more interesting book*
(c) **Le plus beau** livre	*the finest book*
Le livre **le plus intéressant**	*the most interesting book*

Note that the position of **plus** depends on the position of the adjective.

Observe that **plus** is used in French, whether English uses -*er* or *more*, -*est* or *most*.

2. Elle est **aussi riche que** Jeanne. *She is as rich as Jeanne.*
Elle n'est **pas si riche que** Jeanne. *She is not so rich as Jeanne.*
Note the use of **si** with the negative comparison.

VOCABULARY FOR EXERCISE 13

intelligent, *clever*	trois, *three*
stupide, *stupid*	la jeune fille, *the girl*
le bonnet, *the cap*	mais, *but*
la plante, *the plant*	triste, *sad*
diligent, *hard-working*	autre, *other*

EXERCISE 13

A. *Translate into English*

1. Jeanne est riche, Marie est plus riche, et Yvonne est la plus riche des trois. 2. Alfred est intelligent, Louis est plus intelligent, et Georges est le plus intelligent des trois. 3. Les jeunes filles sont plus diligentes que les garçons. 4. Mais elles ne sont pas si intelligentes que les garçons. 5. Yvette est plus jolie que Jeanne. 6. Tom est plus méchant que Pierre. 7. Le livre vert est plus épais que le livre jaune. 8. La petite chaise est plus basse que la grande (*one* is left to be understood by the French). 9. Le cheval est plus vieux que le chien. 10. Le chat n'est pas si beau que le chien.

B. *Fill in the Adjectives of Colour in the following Phrases*

1. Le livre (green). 2. Le bonnet (blue). 3. La fleur (red). 4. La plante (yellow). 5. Le mur (grey). 6. La noix (brown). 7. L'homme (black). 8. L'homme (white). 9. La fleur (pink). 10. Le cheval (chestnut).

C. *Translate into French*

1. (The) gold is more precious than (the) silver. 2. (The) iron is more useful than (the) lead. 3. Jeanne is more beautiful than Marie. 4. (The) copper is not so precious as (the) gold. 5. Pierre is more diligent than Tom. 6. Henri is more diligent than Tom. 7. The garden is not so beautiful as the house. 8. The rose is more lovely than the poppy. 9. The tree is thicker than the plant. 10. The girls are more intelligent than the boys.

D. *Translate into French*

1. The boy was taller than the girl. 2. The girl is as clever as the boy.

3. (The) lead is as useful as (the) iron. 4. She was richer than Jeanne.
5. I was not so happy as Tom. 6. He was sadder than Marie. 7. She
was more hard-working than the other girls. 8. Tom was happier than
the other boys. 9. Jacques was not so rich as the other boys. 10. The
new students were cleverer than the other students.

LESSON 14

Comparative and Superlative of Adjectives and Adverbs

1.

the most	le **plus**
a most	un **très**
most	**très**

Note that **plus** is not always the translation of *most*.

If the word *most* is preceded by *a* or by nothing, use **très** for
most—

   a most interesting book, un livre **très** intéressant.
   The book is most interesting. Le livre est **très** intéressant.

2. Irregular comparatives and superlatives—

Adjectives

bon, *good*; **meilleur,** *better*; **le meilleur,** *the best.*
mauvais, *bad*; **pire,** *worse*; **le pire,** *the worst.*
petit, *small*; **moindre,** *less*; **le moindre,** *the least.*

3. The corresponding adverbs are—

Adverbs

bien, *well*; **mieux,** *better*; **le mieux,** *the best.*
mal, *badly*; **pis,** *worse*; **le pis,** *the worst.*
peu, *little*; **moins,** *less*; **le moins,** *the least.*

POINT I. Do *not* put **plus** before the above.
POINT II. It is possible to use **plus mauvais,** instead of **pire**;
plus petit instead of **moindre,** and **plus mal** instead of **pis.**

POINT III. A good way to distinguish **meilleur** and **mieux, pire** and **pis, petit** and **peu** is as follows—

1. Generally speaking, with **être**, use **meilleur**.
2. Most other verbs use **mieux**.
3. Before a noun, use **meilleur**—
    (i) Elle est meilleure que Jeanne.
    (ii) Elle travaille mieux que Pierre.
    (iii) La meilleure femme.

POINT IV. The word *in* after any superlative is generally translated by **de**—

le garçon le plus intelligent **de** la classe, *the cleverest boy in the class.*

VOCABULARY FOR EXERCISE 14

chanter, *to sing*	le bal, *the dance, the ball*
jouer, *to play*	(plural, **les bals**)
danser, *to dance*	le ciné, le cinéma, *the cinema*
l'acteur, *the actor*	le théâtre, *the theatre*
l'actrice, *the actress*	l'élève (*m.* or *f.*) *the pupil*
le frère, *the brother*	la sœur, *the sister*
l'erreur (*f.*), *the error*	

EXERCISE 14

A. *Translate into English*

1. Elle chantait mieux que l'autre femme. 2. Il jouait mieux que l'autre garçon. 3. Elle est meilleure que l'autre femme. 4. Alfred joue pis que Jeanne. 5. Il est pire que Jeanne. 6. Jeanne travaille plus que Marie. 7. Marie travaille peu, Yvonne travaille moins, mais Agnès travaille le moins. 8. Jeanne est petite, Yvonne est plus petite, et Agnès est la plus petite des trois sœurs. 9. Vous travaillez moins que les autres élèves. 10. Elle danse mieux que les autres jeunes filles.

B. *Insert the French for the Words in Brackets in the following Sentences*

1. Un (little) oiseau chante. 2. Il travaille (little). 3. Elle danse (little). 4. Elle est (little). 5. Les frères chantent (well). 6. Les sœurs chantent (better). 7. Elles sont (better) que les frères. 8. Elle travaille (less) que vous. 9. Elles travaillent (the least). 10. La (least) erreur.

C. *Translate into French*

1. Pauline sings better than the other girls, but they dance better than

Pauline. 2. The most interesting book. 3. A most interesting book.
4. The book is most interesting. 5. The most beautiful flower. 6. A
most beautiful flower. 7. The flower is most beautiful. 8. Most
amusing! 9. The dance is most interesting. 10. (The) gold is most
useful.

D. *Translate into French*

1. He studies better than the other students. 2. She works better than
the man. 3. The best student in the class. 4. The most beautiful flower
in the garden. 5. The loveliest tree in the wood. 6. The most useful
metal of the three. 7. The cinema was most amusing. 8. The theatre
was most interesting. 9. The actors spoke well. 10. The actresses sang
and danced well.

LESSON 15

The Cardinal Numbers

0   **zéro**

1	**un** (*feminine*, **une**)	21	**vingt et un**
2	**deux**	22	**vingt-deux**
3	**trois**	30	**trente**
4	**quatre**	31	**trente et un**
5	**cinq**	40	**quarante**
6	**six**	50	**cinquante**
7	**sept**	60	**soixante**
8	**huit**	70	**soixante-dix**
9	**neuf**	71	**soixante et onze**
10	**dix**	80	**quatre-vingts**
11	**onze**	81	**quatre-vingt-un**
12	**douze**	90	**quatre-vingt-dix**
13	**treize**	91	**quatre-vingt-onze**
14	**quatorze**	100	**cent**
15	**quinze**	101	**cent un**
16	**seize**	200	**deux cents**
17	**dix-sept**	201	**deux cent un**
18	**dix-huit**	1,000	**mille**
19	**dix-neuf**	1,001	**mille et un**
20	**vingt**	2,000	**deux mille**

POINT I. The *only* number between 0 and 100 to take **s** is 80, **quatre-vingts**—

quatre-vingts hommes, 80 *men*; but **quatre-vingt-trois** hommes, 83 *men*.

POINT II. Note that **-ze** = *-teen*; and **-te** = *-ty*.

Thus if you feel tempted to translate **quinze** by 50 instead of 15, you have an automatic check.

POINT III. Note that *no* hyphens are used with **et**. Observe that it is 81, 91 and 101 which have no **et**.

POINT IV. If **cent** has a number only on its left, add **-s** to **cent**, e.g.—

trois cents hommes, 300 *men*

But if it has a number on its right do not add **-s** to **cent**, e.g.—

trois cent trois hommes, 303 *men*

POINT V. Distinguish **deux mille,** 2,000; and **deux milles,** two miles.

VOCABULARY FOR EXERCISE 15

la gare, *the station*	situer, *to situate*
la ferme, *the farm*	compter, *to count*
l'âge (*m.*), *the age*	la taille, *the height*
quel (*fem.* quelle), *what?*	le pied, *the foot*
l'an (*m.*), *the year*	le pouce, *the inch*
le mille, *the mile*	le village, *the village*

EXERCISE 15

A. *Translate into English*

1. La maison est située à trois milles de la ville. 2. La gare est située à sept milles du village. 3. La ferme est située à deux milles de la gare. 4. Quel âge avez-vous? 5. J'ai seize ans. 6. Jeanne a quinze ans et Louis a treize ans. 7. La femme a cinquante ans. 8. L'homme a soixante ans. 9. Le professeur a quarante-deux étudiants dans la classe. 10. Le plus jeune des étudiants a dix-sept ans.

B. *Write down the French for*

1. 80 men. 2. 81 women. 3. 15 boys. 4. 50 girls. 5. 500 students. 6. 505 books. 7. 1,001 days. 8. 2,000 weeks. 9. 2 miles. 10. 2,000 miles.

C. *Translate into French*

1. The students count well. 2. How tall are you? (say, "what height have you?"). 3. I am five feet ten inches (say, "I have five feet ten inches"). 4. Marie is five feet two inches. 5. Jeanne is taller than Marie. 6. She is five feet four inches. 7. Pierre is the tallest boy in the class. 8. He is six feet. 9. How old are you? (say, "what age have you?"). 10. I am fifteen years old (say, "I have fifteen years").

D. *Translate into French*

1. One day we were walking in the woods. 2. We have three theatres and twenty-five cinemas in the town. 3. They are most interesting. 4. How old are you? I am twelve and Jeanne is fifteen. 5. She is older than Pierre. 6. We have three trees in the garden. 7. We have an apple-tree, a pear-tree, and a cherry-tree. 8. We were happy in the farm. 9. I counted the horses and dogs (repeat "the"). 10. I counted thirteen horses and five dogs.

LESSON 16

The Ordinal Numbers

1st	**premier** (*fem.* **première**)	15th	**quinzième**
2nd	**deuxième**	16th	**seizième**
3rd	**troisième**	17th	**dix-septième**
4th	**quatrième**	18th	**dix-huitième**
5th	**cinquième**	19th	**dix-neuvième**
6th	**sixième**	20th	**vingtième**
7th	**septième**	21st	**vingt et unième**
8th	**huitième**	30th	**trentième**
9th	**neuvième**	40th	**quarantième**
10th	**dixième**	50th	**cinquantième**
11th	**onzième**	60th	**soixantième**
12th	**douzième**	70th	**soixante-dixième**
13th	**treizième**	100th	**centième**
14th	**quatorzième**	1,000th	**millième**

POINT I. Note **unième**, not "premier" for 21st, etc.

POINT II. Note use of **second** if there are only two.

POINT III. Watch spelling of **cinquième** and **neuvième**.

POINT IV. Observe aspirate **h** in **le huitième**.

POINT V. Though most ordinal numbers add **-ième** to the cardinal numbers, watch **trentième,** etc.

POINT VI. Note **le onzième**.

POINT VII. As after superlatives use **de** for *in*—

le premier élève de la classe

Dates

The simplest way to translate any date is as follows—

1914. Translate as *nineteen hundred and fourteen*, omitting *and*: thus, **dix-neuf cent quatorze.**

Individual Dates

Examine the following—

On the 1st of May, **le premier mai**

Note the *three* points of difference: no *on*, no *of*, and a small letter at the name of the month.

On the 2nd of May, **le deux mai**

The four points are: no *on*, cardinal number *two*, no *of*, and a small letter at the name of the month.

Cardinal numbers are used instead of ordinals, except for the first of any month.

VOCABULARY FOR EXERCISE 16

je suis né, *I was born*
quand, *when*
la place, *the place* (*in class*)
le dernier, *the last* (*fem.* la dernière)

parce que, *because*
alors, *then*
au mois de, *in the month of*
Noël, *Christmas*

EXERCISE 16

A. *Translate into English*

1. Quand êtes-vous né? 2. Je suis né en dix-neuf cent quarante. 3. Je suis né le premier janvier, dix-neuf cent trente. 4. Jeanne est née le deux février, dix-neuf cent trente-cinq. 5. Marie est née le trois mars, dix-neuf cent quarante-cinq. 6. Pierre est né le quatre avril, dix-neuf

cent trente-neuf. 7. Yvonne et Agnès sont nées le cinq mai. Très intéressant! 8. Madeleine est née le six juin; Gaspard est né le sept juillet. 9. Tom est né le huit août; Alphonse est né le neuf septembre. 10. Alfred est né le dix octobre; Georges est né le onze novembre.

B. *Translate into English*

1. Le premier élève de la classe. 2. Des deux élèves Pierre est le second. 3. Des vingt élèves Tom est le deuxième. 4. La première place est la meilleure place. 5. Le premier jour de la semaine est dimanche. 6. Le deuxième jour de la semaine est lundi. 7. Le troisième jour de la semaine est mardi. 8. Le quatrième mois de l'année est avril. 9. Le cinquième mois de l'année est mai. 10. Le onzième mois de l'année est novembre.

C. *Translate into French*

1. The fourth day of the week is Wednesday. 2. We like Thursday, the fifth day of the week. 3. The sixth day of the week is Friday. 4. The seventh day of the week is Saturday. 5. The twelfth month of the year is December. 6. We like July. 7. Why do you not like August? 8. Because we do not have (the) snow then. 9. Christmas is in the month of December. 10. Peter was born on the twenty-fifth of February.

D. *Translate into French*

1. Why do you hate November? 2. November is a sad month. 3. I like Christmas. 4. Marie hates Monday. 5. She likes Saturday. 6. I used to like Friday. 7. Why did you like Friday? 8. I was born on Friday, the 13th of March. 9. The seventh month of the year is July. 10. October is the tenth month of the year.

LESSON 17

The Numbers (cont.)

1. Note the phrases **des centaines de livres**, *hundreds of books*; and **des milliers de livres**, *thousands of books*.

2. Kings follow the rule given for dates—

	Charles premier	*Charles the First*
but	**Charles deux**	*Charles the Second*

3. Observe that **-aine** adds vagueness to a number—
une trentaine de livres, *about thirty books*

Watch the phrase, **elle frisait à la quarantaine,** *she was coming near the forties.*

4. Time—

Il est une heure	*It is one o'clock*
Il est deux heures	*It is two o'clock*
Il est sept heures	*It is seven o'clock*
Quelle heure est-il?	*What time is it?*

5. Watch the quarters—

Il est quatre heures et quart. *It is a quarter past four.*

Il est cinq heures moins le quart. *It is a quarter to five.*

6. The word **demi** adds an **-e** *after* a feminine noun. It does *not* change *before* any noun, masculine or feminine—

une demi-heure	*a half hour*
une heure et demie	*an hour and a half*
un demi-pain	*half a loaf*
un pain et demi	*a loaf and a half*

So **deux heures et demie** is *half past two;* **onze heures et demie** is *half past eleven.*

7. Watch **midi,** *midday,* and **minuit,** *midnight,* both of which are masculine—

midi et demi	*half past midday*
minuit et demi	*half past midnight*

VOCABULARY FOR EXERCISE 17

dîner, *to dine*	tard, *late*
le concert, *the concert*	le collège, *the college*
rentrer, *to go home*	vide, *empty*
la minute, *the minute*	plein, *full*

EXERCISE 17

A. *Translate into English*

1. Quelle heure est-il? 2. Il est quatre heures. 3. A quelle heure dînez-vous? 4. Je rentre à midi et demi. 5. Jeanne dîne à huit heures.

6. Les étudiants rentraient à une heure moins le quart. 7. Le concert est à sept heures et demie. 8. Nous rentrons à dix heures et quart. 9. Soixante minutes dans une heure. 10. Vingt-quatre heures dans un jour.

B. *Insert the Word for "half" in the following Sentences*

1. Une heure et (half). 2. Un pain et (half). 3. Midi et (half). 4. Minuit et (half). 5. Une (half) heure. 6. Un (half) pain. 7. Une (half) minute. 8. Une minute et (half). 9. Trois heures et (half). 10. Onze heures et (half).

C. *Translate into French*

1. What time was it? 2. It was half past six. 3. It was late. 4. It was half past twelve (midnight). 5. A quarter past four. 6. A quarter to five. 7. Sixty minutes in an hour. 8. Ninety minutes in an hour and a half. 9. Twenty-four hours in a day. 10. Three hundred and sixty-five days in a year.

D. *Translate into French*

1. I was in Newcastle at half-past seven. 2. He was in Edinburgh at midnight. 3. We were in Liverpool at six-thirty. 4. She was in Glasgow at a quarter to eight. 5. Marie was at the station at half past one. 6. She dines at half past twelve. 7. We were at the theatre at seven-thirty. 8. We were at the college at nine. 9. The cinema was empty at six. 10. It was full at eight.

LESSON 18

Demonstrative Adjectives

MASCULINES

(consonant)	**ce livre**	*this book*
	ces livres	*these books*
(aspirate "h")	**ce héros**	*this hero*
	ces héros	*these heroes*
(mute "h")	**cet homme**	*this man*
	ces hommes	*these men*
(vowel)	**cet ami**	*this friend*
	ces amis	*these friends*

FEMININES

(consonant)	**cette lettre**	*this letter*
	ces lettres	*these letters*
(aspirate "h")	**cette haine**	*this hatred*
	ces haines	*these hatreds*
(mute "h")	**cette histoire**	*this story*
	ces histoires	*these stories*
(vowel)	**cette amie**	*this friend*
	ces amies	*these friends*

POINT I. The masculine singular takes **cet** only before mute *h* or a vowel.

POINT II. The feminine singular is always **cette**.

POINT III. The plural, both genders, is always **ces**.

POINT IV. **-ci** and **-là,** *this* and *that*, are added for contrast—

this book	**ce livre-ci**
that book	**ce livre-là**

The Past Definite (Historic) of "ER" Regular Verbs

je donnai	*I gave*
tu donnas	*thou didst give*
il donna	*he gave*
nous donnâmes	*we gave*
vous donnâtes	*you gave*
ils donnèrent	*they gave*

To learn this tense, repeat it to yourself in a deliberate manner. It is used when an action took place once or suddenly in the past. Compare the following—

Chaque jour je **donnais** de l'argent aux pauvres. *Every day I used to give some money to the poor.*

Un jour il **donna** un cadeau à la femme. *One day he gave a present to the woman.*

Past Definite of "avoir" and "être"

j'eus	*I had*	je fus	*I was*
tu eus	*thou hadst*	tu fus	*thou wert*
il eut	*he had*	il fut	*he was*
nous eûmes	*we had*	nous fûmes	*we were*
vous eûtes	*you had*	vous fûtes	*you were*
ils eurent	*they had*	ils furent	*they were*

VOCABULARY FOR EXERCISE 18

aussi, *also*
le film, *the film*
la place, *the seat*
coûter, *to cost*
cher, *dear*
coûter cher, *to cost much*

la nuit, *the night*
le soir, *the evening*
rester, *to remain*
la porte, *the door*
le dîner, *the dinner*

EXERCISE 18

A. *Translate into English*

1. Cet homme est plus riche que cette femme. 2. Ces femmes sont plus heureuses que ces hommes. 3. Ce jardin est joli. 4. Cette maison est jolie aussi. 5. Cette lettre est intéressante. 6. Ce film est amusant. 7. Ces places coûtent cher. 8. Ces livres-ci sont plus intéressants que ces livres-là. 9. J'aime ces fleurs-ci; je n'aime pas ces fleurs-là. 10. Ces roses coûtent cher mais elles sont belles.

B. *Translate into English*

1. Il préféra. 2. Elle accepta. 3. Nous refusâmes. 4. Elle prépara le dîner. 5. Elles protestèrent. 6. Il cria. 7. Vous donnâtes. 8. Il fut. 9. Elle eut. 10. Ils eurent.

C. *Translate into French*

1. One night I accepted the invitation. 2. One evening he dined late. 3. Every night they used to dine at eight. 4. Every evening they used to prefer to remain in the house. 5. One evening a man knocked at the door. 6. What time was it? 7. It was seven-thirty. 8. I went home at ten. 9. He went home at ten-thirty. 10. They knocked at the door.

D. *Translate into French*

1. These apples cost much. 2. Why do you want the apples? 3. I like (the) apples. 4. These pears are sweet. 5. They are sweeter

than those apples. 6. This garden is more beautiful than that garden.
7. This film is more interesting than that film. 8. A man was knocking
at the door. 9. This house costs much. 10. That house costs more.

LESSON 19

The Possessive Adjectives

mon père	my father	**mes** frères	my brothers
mon ami	my friend	**mes** amis	my friends
ma mère	my mother	**mes** sœurs	my sisters
mon amie	my friend (*fem.*)	**mes** amies	my friends

POINT I. Note the possessive adjective agreeing in French
with the noun it qualifies both in gender and number (*her*
brother = **son** frère).

POINT II. If a feminine noun begins with a vowel or a mute
h, the masculine form is used, to make the pronunciation easier.

But one says **ma bonne amie,** because the adjective **bonne**
starts with a consonant. Similarly one says **mon ancienne
amie,** because the adjective starts with a vowel.

The remaining forms are—

ton frère	*thy brother*	**tes** frères	*thy brothers*
ta sœur	*thy sister*	**tes** sœurs	*thy sisters*
son frère	*his brother*	**ses** frères	*his brothers*
sa sœur	*his sister*	**ses** sœurs	*his sisters*
son frère	*her brother*	**ses** frères	*her brothers*
sa sœur	*her sister*	**ses** sœurs	*her sisters*
notre frère	*our brother*	**nos** frères	*our brothers*
notre sœur	*our sister*	**nos** sœurs	*our sisters*
votre frère	*your brother*	**vos** frères	*your brothers*
votre sœur	*your sister*	**vos** sœurs	*your sisters*
leur frère	*their brother*	**leurs** frères	*their brothers*
leur sœur	*their sister*	**leurs** sœurs	*their sisters*

Note that *his sister* = **sa sœur** (sa agrees with **sœur**); *their
sister* = **leur sœur** (leur never has an **e**).

The Future Tense

This is made from the Infinitive; to make the future of **donner,** *to give,* for example, one says—

je donnerai	*I shall give*	**nous donnerons**	*we shall give*
tu donneras	*thou wilt give*	**vous donnerez**	*you will give*
il donnera	*he will give*	**ils donneront**	*they will give*
elle donnera	*she will give*	**elles donneront**	*they will give*

The endings added to **donner** represent the English *shall* or *will.*

The future of **avoir** and **être** is irregular—

j'aurai	*I shall have*	**je serai**	*I shall be*
tu auras	*thou wilt have*	**tu seras**	*thou wilt be*
il aura	*he will have*	**il sera**	*he will be*
nous aurons	*we shall have*	**nous serons**	*we shall be*
vous aurez	*you will have*	**vous serez**	*you will be*
ils auront	*they will have*	**ils seront**	*they will be*

Whenever you come to a verb with an irregular future, make a special note of it.

VOCABULARY FOR EXERCISE 19

la famille, *the family*
les parents, *relations* or *parents*
la grand'mère, *the grandmother*
demain, *tomorrow*
la nièce, *the niece*

le cousin, *the cousin*
la cousine, *the cousin* (fem.)
arriver, *to arrive*
ici, *here*

EXERCISE 19

A. *Translate into English*

1. Mes parents seront ici à sept heures et demie. 2. Ma grand'mère sera à Londres demain. 3. Mon père a deux neveux. 4. Ses neveux sont mes cousins. 5. Ma mère a deux nièces. 6. Ses nièces sont mes cousines. 7. Mon oncle demeure à Glasgow. 8. Ma tante demeure à Édimbourg. 9. Ma famille demeure à Newcastle. 10. La famille de mon oncle demeure à Liverpool.

B. *Insert in French the appropriate Possessive Adjectives*

1. (His) frère. 2. (Her) frère. 3. (Thy) mère. 4. (Our) oncle. 5 (Our) cousins. 6. (Your) nièces. 7. (Their) sœurs. 8. (Her) sœur. 9. (My) tante. 10. (His) tante.

C. *Translate into French*

1. His cousins. 2. My nephews. 3. My friend. 4. My good uncles.
5. Their brother. 6. Their sisters. 7. Our aunts. 8. Your cousins.
9. My friends. 10. Their friend.

D. *Translate into French*

1. Our cousin will arrive today. 2. Our sisters will arrive tomorrow.
3. When will you accept the invitation? 4. I shall accept the invitation
tomorrow. 5. I shall refuse. 6. He will protest. 7. He will not eat
his dinner. 8. She will not stay in London. 9. They will not live in
Newcastle. 10. You will not refuse.

LESSON 20

The Word "such"

The adjective is **tel** (*fem*. **telle**). The adverb is **si**.

POINT I. When the word *such* is followed by a noun, put
tel or **telle** for *such*—

such a man	un **tel** homme
such men	de **tels** hommes
such a woman	une **telle** femme
such women	de **telles** femmes

POINT II. When the word *such* is followed in English by an
adjective, put "*si*" for "*such*"—

such a good friend	un **si** bon ami
such good friends	de **si** bons amis
such an interesting book	un livre **si** intéressant
such interesting books	des livres **si** intéressants

Note that the position of **si** depends on the position of the
adjective.

The Word "si"

Apart from meaning *such*, **si** can mean—

1. *so*, in exclamation—

Il est **si** intelligent! *He is so clever!*

2. *so*, after a negative comparison—

Il n'est pas **si** riche que vous. *He is not so rich as you.*

3. *yes*; the normal word for *yes* is **oui**—

Vous refusez l'invitation? **Oui.** *You are refusing the invitation? Yes.*

But, after a statement which you wish to contradict, employ **si**—

Vous ne refuserez pas l'invitation? **Si!** *You will not refuse the invitation? Oh yes, I shall.*

4. *If*; this meaning of **si** should be watched closely—

Si vous travaillez, nous serons contents. *If you work we shall be happy.*

5. *Whether*. Put the same tense in French as in English—

Do you know whether he will arrive tomorrow? Savez-vous **s'**il arrivera demain?

Conditional Tense

This is made from the Infinitive. So, to make the Conditional of **donner**, *to give*, one says—

je donnerais	*I should give*
tu donnerais	*thou wouldst give*
il donnerait	*he would give*
elle donnerait	*she would give*
nous donnerions	*we should give*
vous donneriez	*you would give*
ils donneraient	*they would give*
elles donneraient	*they would give*

Conditional of **avoir** and **être** are irregular: **j'aurais,** etc., and **je serais,** etc.

POINT I. The best way for the student to master the tenses after *if* is as follows—

Do not look at the *if* clause, look at the principal clause.

(a) If the principal clause is future, the *if* clause takes PRESENT—

If only you will work, I shall be so happy. Si seulement vous **travaillez,** je serai si content.

(b) If principal clause is conditional, *if* clause takes IMPERFECT—

If only you would work, I should be so happy. Si seulement vous **travailliez,** je serais si content.

By looking at the principal clauses only, you do not allow the examiner to trap you with his *will* and *would*.

Imperative Mood

donnons!   *let us give!*
donne!   *give!* (speaking to a child)
donnez!   *give!*

VOCABULARY FOR EXERCISE 20

le football, *the football*
le tennis, *the tennis*
le golf, *the golf*
le jeu, *the game*
la partie, *the single game*
l'Américain, *the American*
l'Écossais, *the Scotsman*
dur, *hard*
dangereux, *dangerous*
actif, *active*
le temps, *the time*
ravi, *delighted*

EXERCISE 20

A. *Translate into English*

1. Elle est si intelligente! 2. Ils sont si actifs! 3. Le football est si intéressant aux Anglais! 4. Le tennis est si intéressant aux Français! 5. Le golf est si intéressant aux Américains! 6. Elle n'est pas si riche que vous. 7. Vous n'acceptez pas l'invitation? Mais si! 8. Si j'étais à votre place, je travaillerais plus dur. 9. Si j'avais votre âge, je refuserais. 10. Si vous étiez riche, seriez-vous content?

B. *Translate into French the appropriate word for "such"*

1. Un . . . homme. 2. Une . . . jolie femme. 3. Des livres . . . intéressants. 4. Des hommes . . . dangereux. 5. De . . . femmes sont dangereuses. 6. De . . . livres sont bons. 7. De . . . bons amis. 8. De . . . jolies femmes. 9. Des jeux . . . intéressants. 10. Des parties . . . amusantes.

C. *Translate into French*

1. I should refuse. 2. He would protest. 3. They would eat. 4. We should accept. 5. You would arrive. 6. They would play. 7. She would dance. 8. We should sing. 9. He would be. 10. They would have.

D. *Translate into French*

1. If they have the time, the Scotsmen will play at (**au**) golf. 2. If they had the time, the Englishmen would play at football. 3. If they arrive at six, we shall be happy. 4. If she accepted the invitation, we should be delighted. 5. If only you will work, I shall be so happy. 6. If only you would work, I should be so happy. 7. If the invitation is not here at five, I shall refuse. 8. If you play at golf, I shall be pleased. 9. Do you know if she will arrive? (*if = whether*, has same tense in French as in English). 10. Do you know if she will refuse?

LESSON 21

Spelling Changes in "ER" Regular Verbs

The following groups of verbs have a slight irregularity in part of the present tense, and all through the future and conditional.

A. Verbs ending in **-yer,** e.g. **payer,** *to pay for.*

PRESENT TENSE

je paie	*I pay*	**nous payons**	*we pay*
tu paies	*thou dost pay*	**vous payez**	*you pay*
il paie	*he pays*	**ils paient**	*they pay*

FUTURE

je paierai, etc.

CONDITIONAL

je paierais, etc.

It will be seen that when a mute **e** follows the **y, y** changes into **i.** In the present tense, it is helpful to the student to remember the letter L—

1st singular	**ie**	**Y**	
2nd ,,	**ies**	**Y**	
3rd ,,	**ie**	**ient**	3rd plural

All verbs ending in **-ayer, -oyer,** and **-uyer,** act as above—

essa**yer**	*to try*	il essa**ie**	*he tries*
nett**oyer**	*to clean*	elle netto**ie**	*she cleans*
essu**yer**	*to wipe*	elle essu**ie**	*she wipes*

B. Verbs ending in **-eter** and **-eler** take a grave accent above the **e** in the tenses and persons mentioned above—

| ach**eter** | *to buy* | il ach**è**te | *he buys* |
| g**eler** | *to freeze* | il g**è**le | *it is freezing* |

C. **Jeter,** *to throw,* and **appeler,** *to call,* double the consonant instead—

il je**tt**e *he throws*
elle appe**ll**e *she calls*

D. Verbs with a neutral **e** take a grave accent on the first **e**—
m**e**ner *to lead* il m**è**ne *he leads*

E. But those with **é** change it to **è** in present tense, 1st, 2nd, 3rd singular and 3rd plural only—
esp**é**rer *to hope* j'esp**è**re *I hope*
But: il espérera, *he will hope.*

F. Verbs ending in **-ier** will need two **i**'s in the imperfect tense, 1st and 2nd plural—

| étud**ier** | *to study* | nous étud**ii**ons | *we were studying* |
| | | vous étud**ii**ez | *you were studying* |

G. Verbs ending in **-ger** require **e** before an **a** or an **o**—

| mang**er** | *to eat* | il mang**e**ait | *he was eating* |
| | | nous mang**e**ons | *we are eating* |

H. Verbs ending in **-cer** will need a cedilla (**ç**) under the **c** before an **a** or an **o**—

| avan**cer** | *to advance* | il avan**ç**ait | *he was advancing* |
| | | nous avan**ç**ons | *we are advancing* |

VOCABULARY FOR EXERCISE 21

la balle, *the ball*   toujours, *always*
la fenêtre, *the window*

EXERCISE 21

A. *Translate into English*

1. Elle essuie la fenêtre. 2. Elle nettoie la maison. 3. Il paie toujours.
4. J'achète de jolies fleurs. 5. Elle jette la balle. 6. Il gèle aujourd'hui.
7. Il gèlera demain. 8. J'achèterai le livre demain. 9. Il appelle le
chien. 10. Il appelait son père.

B. *Translate into French*

1. I shall hope. 2. He hopes. 3. She leads. 4. We were leading.
5. We shall lead. 6. I study. 7. You were studying. 8. You will study.
9. He eats. 10. He was eating.

C. *Translate into French*

1. It is freezing. 2. I am not buying. 3. She will not buy. 4. I am
calling Jean. 5. I advance. 6. He was advancing. 7. We are advancing.
8. We are eating. 9. You were not studying. 10. I pay.

D. *Translate into French*

1. I was throwing the ball into the garden. 2. Did you throw the
ball? 3. It is freezing today. 4. Will it freeze tomorrow? 5. I always
buy good books. 6. I take such animals into the garden. 7. I always
used to eat such meals. 8. I call Marie. 9. Her mother calls Jeanne.
10. She will pay for the meals.

LESSON 22

Indefinite Adjectives

A. The following indefinite adjectives should be watched
carefully because they change their meaning according to their
positions before or after the noun—

   (i) un **certain** ami à moi   *a certain friend of mine*
      certains amis   *certain friends*

but: des nouvelles **certaines**   *sure news*

(ii) **même** le roi   even *the king* (adverb)
    le **même** roi   *the* same *king*
    le roi **même**   *the king* himself

B. The word **quel** depends for its meaning on whether it is followed by an exclamation mark or an interrogation mark—

Quel homme!	*What a man!*
Quels hommes!	*What men!*
Quelle femme?	*Which woman?*
Quelles femmes?	*Which women?*

C. **Chaque,** meaning *each*, is used only in the singular, and **plusieurs,** meaning *several*, only in the plural. The feminine form is the same as the masculine—

chaque femme	*each woman*
plusieurs fleurs	*several flowers*

D. Watch the adjective **tout**, meaning *all*. The masculine plural form is **tous**—

tout le monde	*everybody*
tous les hommes	*all men*
toute femme	*every woman*
toute la famille	*the whole family*
toutes les femmes	*all women*

Irregular "ER" Verbs

There are only two, namely, **aller,** *to go*, and **envoyer,** *to send*.

Aller is made up of three Latin verbs, meaning *to go*, hence its apparent irregularity.

Allant, the present participle, is regular, and so is **Allé,** the past participle. But, instead of saying, *I have gone*, the French use **Je SUIS allé.** Similarly other **-er** verbs which suggest going or coming take **être**, instead of **avoir**, e.g. **je suis entré,** *I have gone in*, **je suis arrivé,** *I have arrived*, **je suis tombé,** *I have fallen*.

The present tense of **aller** is irregular (all except the 1st and 2nd persons plural coming from Latin *vadere*).

je **vais**	*I go*	nous **allons**	*we go*
tu **vas**	*thou goest*	vous **allez**	*you go*
il **va**	*he goes*	ils **vont**	*they go*
elle **va**	*she goes*	elles **vont**	*they go*

j'allais, the imperfect, is regular; and likewise **j'allai,** the past definite, is regular.

Check through the endings of each tense.

The future and conditional are both irregular, being based on the Latin *ire.*

FUTURE

j'**irai**	*I shall go*	nous **irons**	*we shall go*
tu **iras**	*thou wilt go*	vous **irez**	*you will go*
il **ira**	*he will go*	ils **iront**	*they will go*
elle **ira**	*she will go*	elles **iront**	*they will go*

CONDITIONAL

j'**irais**	*I should go*	nous **irions**	*we should go*
tu **irais**	*thou wouldst go*	vous **iriez**	*you would go*
il **irait**	*he would go*	ils **iraient**	*they would go*
elle **irait**	*she would go*	elles **iraient**	*they would go*

S'en aller, *to go away,* is based on **aller,** *to go.*

Envoyer, *to send,* changes **y** to **i** in the present tense, 1st, 2nd and 3rd sing., and 3rd plur., and is irregular in the future and conditional, e.g. **j'enverrai,** *I shall send,* etc.; **j'enverrais,** *I should send,* etc.

The verb **renvoyer,** *to dismiss* or *send back,* is based on **envoyer.**

IMPERATIVE FORMS

va	*go*	**va-t'en**	*go away*
allons	*let us go*	**allons-nous-en**	*let us go away*
allez	*go*	**allez-vous-en**	*go away*
envoie	*send*	**renvoie**	*send back*
envoyons	*let us send*	**renvoyons**	*let us send back*
envoyez	*send*	**renvoyez**	*send back*

VOCABULARY FOR EXERCISE 22

la mer, *the sea*	sur, *on*
le sable, *the sand*	ramasser, *to pick up*
la chance, *the luck*	écouter, *to listen to*
le bord, *the edge, the side*	gagner, *to win*
la coquille, *the shell*	le prix, *the prize*
la carte-postale, *the postcard*	la reine, *the queen*

EXERCISE 22

A. *Translate into English*

1. Un certain ami à moi va à Paris. 2. Quelle chance! 3. Même la reine. 4. La même reine. 5. La reine même. 6. Quelle femme va au bord de la mer? 7. Ma cousine Lucie. 8. Quels étudiants travaillent dur? 9. Tous les étudiants travaillent dur. 10. Nous aimons la mer.

B. *Translate into English*

1. Chaque Anglais aime la mer. 2. Les enfants marchent sur le sable. 3. Tous les enfants au bord de la mer ramassent des coquilles. 4. Ah! les jolies coquilles! 5. Plusieurs femmes parlaient. 6. Tous les hommes écoutaient. 7. Tout le monde était content. 8. Toute la famille était dans le jardin. 9. Tous les étudiants essayaient. 10. Pourquoi? Ils désirent gagner le prix.

C. *Translate into French*

1. Each flower. 2. Several trees. 3. Even the mother will send some money. 4. The same father. 5. Which shell? 6. That shell. 7. Which prizes? 8. Those prizes. 9. All men try. 10. All men do not win the prize.

D. *Translate into French*

1. The whole family is at the seaside. 2. What luck! They send post-cards to all their friends. 3. I like the sea, but I do not like the sand. 4. Such seas are dangerous. 5. The children pick up shells on the sand. 6. They play every day. 7. Several women were going to dance. 8. I am going to Paris, you are going to London, and they are going to Newcastle. 9. I shall go to Edinburgh, if you go to Edinburgh. 10. He would go to Liverpool, if you went to Liverpool.

LESSON 23

The Personal Pronouns

Subject	Object	Indirect Object (Dative)
je parle	Jeanne **me** préfère	Jeanne **me** donne un livre
I speak	Jeanne prefers me	Jeanne gives a book to me

Similarly—

tu parles	thou dost speak	**vous** parlez	you speak
il parle	he speaks	**ils** parlent	they speak
elle parle	she speaks	**elles** parlent	they speak
nous parlons	we speak		

Jeanne **te** préfère	Jeanne prefers thee
Jeanne **le** préfère	Jeanne prefers him
Jeanne **la** préfère	Jeanne prefers her
Jeanne **nous** préfère	Jeanne prefers us
Jeanne **vous** préfère	Jeanne prefers you
Jeanne **les** préfère	Jeanne prefers them
Jeanne **les** préfère	Jeanne prefers them

Jeanne **te** donne un livre	Jeanne gives you a book
Jeanne **lui** donne un livre	Jeanne gives him a book
Jeanne **lui** donne un livre	Jeanne gives her a book
Jeanne **nous** donne un livre	Jeanne gives us a book
Jeanne **vous** donne un livre	Jeanne gives you a book
Jeanne **leur** donne un livre	Jeanne gives them a book
Jeanne **leur** donne un livre	Jeanne gives them a book

In addition, there is the pronoun **se**, *oneself, himself, herself, themselves*—

il **s'**amuse	he enjoys himself
elle **s'**amuse	she enjoys herself
ils **s'**amusent	they enjoy themselves
elles **s'**amusent	they enjoy themselves

Note that **se** can be indirect as well as direct—

il **se** parle	he speaks to himself

It can mean *to each other*, e.g.—

Ils **s'**envoient des lettres. *They send letters to each other*

Y means *there, to it, to them*; **en** means *of it, of them, from it, from them, some, any*—

Mon ami est à Paris. J'**y** vais aussi. *My friend is in Paris. I am going there also.*

J'**y** donne mon attention. *I give my attention to it* or *to them* (generally meaning things).

Compare this last with—

Je **leur** donne mon attention. *I give my attention to them* (meaning persons).

Je m'**en** vais. *I am going away* (literally *from it*).

J'ai des livres. **En** avez-vous. *I have some books. Have you any?*

Oui, j'**en** ai. *Yes, I have some.*

POINT I. The apostrophe is used before a verb beginning with a vowel or mute **h**—

Il m'aime. *He loves me.*

POINT II. Note the position of all these pronouns *before* the verb in a simple tense, *before* the auxiliary **avoir** or **être** in a compound tense—

je **leur** parle   *I speak to them*
je **leur** ai parlé   *I have spoken to them*

Similarly: Il **en** est arrivé, *He has arrived from there.*

The Regular "IR" Verbs

Just as the **-er** regular verbs have the key letters **e** and **ai**, so the **-ir** verbs have the key letters **I** and **IS**—

finir   *to finish*
finissant   *finishing* (present participle)
j'ai fini   *I have finished*

Remember that **-ir** generally represents *-ish* in English. It is, therefore, easy to make the French verb without a dictionary, e.g. *perish* = **périr**, *demolish* = **démolir**, *cherish* = **chérir**, *embellish* = **embellir**, etc.

The future is made by adding the future endings **-ai, -as, -a, -ons, -ez, -ont** to the infinitive—

Je finir**ai**, etc.

The conditional is made by adding the conditional endings **-ais, -ais, -ait, -ions, -iez, -aient,** to the infinitive—

Je finir**ais**, etc.

VOCABULARY FOR EXERCISE 23

la personne, *the person*   polir, *to polish*

EXERCISE 23

A. *Translate into English*

1. Je la déteste. 2. Elle les aime. 3. Il nous préfère. 4. Ils les ramassent. 5. Je les finirai. 6. Je m'en vais. 7. Il s'en va. 8. Ils s'amusent. 9. Ils s'envoient des lettres. 10. Chaque personne s'amuse.

B. *Translate into English*

1. Mon ami est à Paris. J'y irai aussi. 2. J'ai des fleurs. En avez-vous? 3. Oui, j'en ai. 4. Ma sœur n'en a pas. 5. Jeanne lui donne des violettes. 6. Jeanne leur donne des roses. 7. Alfred ramasse des pommes dans le jardin. 8. Jeanne y ramasse des poires. 9. Je leur ai parlé. 10. Ils ne m'ont pas parlé.

C. *Translate into French*

1. He will perish. 2. They will demolish the house. 3. The mother will cherish the children. 4. Finishing. 5. Embellishing. 6. I have finished the letter. 7. They have demolished the house. 8. She has polished the chair. 9. Polishing. 10. We have finished.

D. *Translate into French*

1. I have not spoken to them. 2. They have spoken to me. 3. If I dance, he will sing. 4. Our father is going away to Paris. 5. Are you going there? 6. No, we are not going there. 7. Each woman amuses herself. 8. Each child enjoys himself at the seaside. 9. I should finish the letter if I had the time. 10. They will finish the letters if they have the time.

LESSON 24

Order of Personal Pronouns

If a number of the personal pronouns come *before* the verb, the best way to remember which comes first is to think of their persons. A first person pronoun comes before a second, and a second before a third—

Just memorize: 1st before 2nd before 3rd—

> Il **me le** donne   *He gives me it* (1st before 3rd)
> Il **vous la** donne   *He gives you it* (2nd before 3rd)

If two 3rd persons occur, put the direct one before the indirect one—

> Il **le lui** donne   *He gives it to him* (direct before indirect)
> Il **les leur** donne   *He gives them to them*

All the above pronouns come before **y,** which comes before **en**—

> Avez-vous des poires dans votre jardin? Oui, nous **y en** avons. *Have you pears in your garden? Yes, we have* (*some there*).

> Il **les y** envoie   *He sends them to it*
> Il **leur en** donne   *He gives them some*

If the *Imperative* Mood is being used, two points have to be remembered—

1. The pronouns follow the verb unless the command is negative—

> Donnez-**le** à Jeanne.
but: Ne **le** donnez pas à Jeanne.

2. The word order then in the Imperative Affirmative is *not* "1st before 2nd before 3rd," but rather direct object before indirect—

> Donnez-**le-nous.** Donnez-**les-leur.**

Note that the vowels of **le** and **la** do not elide before **à**—

> Donnez-**le** à mon frère. Donnez-**la** à votre sœur.

Regular "IR" Verbs (cont.)

The present tense of **finir** is—

je **finis**	*I finish*	nous **finissons**	*we finish*
tu **finis**	*thou art finishing*	vous **finissez**	*you finish*
il **finit**	*he finishes*	ils **finissent**	*they finish*
elle **finit**	*she finishes*	elles **finissent**	*they finish*

Remember that the plural is taken from the present participle, **finissant** by removing **-ant.**

The Imperfect Tense of **finir** is—

je **finissais**	*I was finishing*	nous **finissions**	*we were finishing*
tu **finissais**	*thou wert finishing*	vous **finissiez**	*you were finishing*
il **finissait**	*he was finishing*	ils **finissaient**	*they were finishing*
elle **finissait**	*she was finishing*	elles **finissaient**	*they were finishing*

Remember that the Imperfect also is formed from the Present Participle **finissant** by removing **-ant.**

EXERCISE 24

A. *Translate into English*

1. Il me le donne. 2. Elle nous les envoie. 3. Ils les y envoient. 4. Elles y vont. 5. Nous le leur donnons. 6. Vous leur en parlez. 7. Il y en a. 8. Nous n'y en avons pas. 9. Ils nous l'envoient. 10. Nous le leur envoyons.

B. *Translate into English*

1. Donnez-le-nous. 2. Envoyez-le-leur. 3. Envoyez-le à mon père. 4. Ne lui en parlez pas. 5. Ne nous le donnez pas. 6. Je finis ma lettre. 7. Nous finissons nos lettres. 8. Elles finissaient à neuf heures. 9. Si je finis à cinq heures, serez-vous content? 10. Si vous finissiez à six heures et demie je serais ravi.

C. *Translate into French*

1. Give it to them. 2. Send it to us. 3. Don't speak to them of it. 4. Speak to us of it. 5. I have some flowers in my garden. Have you some there? 6. Yes, I have some there. 7. He has given us some. 8. They have refused it to them. 9. He has refused it to us. 10. I am sending them some.

D. *Translate into French*

1. I shall send some to you tomorrow. 2. Don't send us any tomorrow. 3. Send us some today. 4. He has sent us some. 5. Do not

speak to him of it. 6. Speak to them of it. 7. They are finishing the house. 8. The mothers cherish the children. 9. If I polished the chairs, would you be pleased? 10. He sent some there every day.

LESSON 25

Demonstrative Pronouns

When not referring to something mentioned before, use **ceci** for *this*, **cela** for *that*—

Henri sait **ceci**	Henri sait **cela**
Henri knows this	*Henry knows that*

But if referring to a noun previously mentioned, use **celui-ci, celle-ci** (*fem.*), for *this one*, **celui-là, celle-là** (*fem.*), for *that one*. The plural forms are **ceux-ci** (*masc.*), **celles-ci** (*fem.*), for *these ones*, and **ceux-là** (*masc.*), **celles-là** (*fem.*) for *those ones*—

Des deux chevaux, **celui-ci** est gris, **celui-là** est blanc.
Of the two horses, this one is grey, that one is white.

Des deux roses, **celle-ci** est rouge, **celle-là** est blanche.
Of the two roses, this one is red, that one is white.

The translation *the latter* may also be given to **celui-ci,** *the former* to **celui-là**—

Des deux étudiants, **celui-ci** est diligent, **celui-là** est paresseux. *Of the two students, the latter is hard-working, the former is lazy.*

If the above pronouns are followed by **de** (*of*) or **qui** (*who* or *which*), do not put in **-ci** or **-là**—

Je n'aime pas ce thé. **Celui** de votre mère est meilleur.
I do not like this tea. That of your mother (your mother's) is better.

Celui qui travaille gagnera le prix. *The one who works will win the prize.*

The pronoun **ce** is often used conversationally, instead of **il,** for *it*—

C'est vrai, instead of "il est vrai," *it is true.*
C'est un Français, instead of "il est Français," *he is French.*

Ce is usually found before a qualified noun.

Ce must be used instead of **il** with other pronouns—

    C'est nous. *It is we.*

    C'est de celui de mon frère que je parle. *It is my brother's I am speaking of.*

    C'est le mien. *It is mine.*

Ce should also be used before names of people—

    C'est Georges. *It is George.*

Note the use of **ce** before **premier,** *first,* **dernier,** *last,* and all superlatives—

    C'est la première fois. *It is the first time.*

    C'est le plus beau de tous les jardins. *It is the finest of all the gardens.*

Regular Verb "finir" (cont.)

PAST DEFINITE

je **finis**	*I finished*	nous **finîmes**	*we finished*
tu **finis**	*thou didst finish*	vous **finîtes**	*you finished*
il **finit**	*he finished*	ils **finirent**	*they finished*

VOCABULARY FOR EXERCISE 25

le bouledogue, *the bulldog*	la vache, *the cow*
l'épagneul (*m.*), *the spaniel*	la chèvre, *the goat*
le bœuf, *the ox*	voici, *here is, here are*
l'âne (*m.*), *the donkey*	voilà, *there is, there are*
l'écureuil (*m.*), *the squirrel*	tiens! *look!*
le travail, *the work*	choisir, *to choose*
bâtir, *to build*	

EXERCISE 25

A. *Translate into English*

1. Pierre sait ceci, Jean sait cela. 2. C'est vrai, il est intelligent. 3. Des deux chevaux, celui-ci est noir, celui-là est blanc. 4. Des deux vaches, celle-ci est brune, celle-là est blanche. 5. Voici deux chèvres, celle-ci est plus petite que cella-là. 6. Ces chiens-ci sont des épagneuls (**é** = *s*); ceux-là sont des bouledogues. 7. Tiens! Voilà deux écureuils dans l'arbre! Celui-ci est plus grand que celui-là. 8. Marie chante ceci; Jeanne chante cela. 9. Des deux chiens, je préfère celui-ci. Celui de mon frère est meilleur. 10. Celui qui ne travaille pas ne gagnera pas le prix.

B. *Insert the appropriate Demonstrative Pronoun in the following*

1. (The one) de mon père (speaking about horses). 2. (It) est vous.
3. (It) est celui de mon oncle (speaking of books). 4. (He) qui joue.
5. (She) qui danse. 6. (It) est intéressant. 7. (It) est amusant. 8. (It) est
Alfred. 9. (The former) est riche; (the latter) est pauvre (speaking of
men). 10. (The latter) est diligente; (the former) est paresseuse
(speaking of women).

C. *Translate into French*

1. Here is Marie! 2. It is you. 3. Of the two books, the one of my
sister is better than my brother's. 4. Of the two oxen, this one is brown,
that one is white. 5. Of the two donkeys, this one is smaller than that
one. 6. My brother's (referring to a horse). 7. My sister's (referring to
a horse). 8. My aunt's (referring to flowers). 9. My uncle's (referring
to flowers). 10. My father's (referring to a garden).

D. *Translate into French*

1. One day he finished the work. 2. One day they demolished the
house. 3. One day she chose a red rose. 4. The men were building a
house. 5. They were finishing their work. 6. Of the two houses, this
one is better than that one. 7. Jeanne has chosen this work; Marie has
chosen that. 8. He who works hard will win the prize. 9. Of all these
horses, these ones are the best. 10. It is the best garden of all.

LESSON 26

The Possessive Pronouns

Ce livre est **le mien**	*This book is mine*
Ces livres sont **les miens**	*These books are mine*
Cette lettre est **la mienne**	*This letter is mine*
Ces lettres sont **les miennes**	*These letters are mine*

Similarly—

le tien, etc.	thine
le sien, etc.	his or hers
le nôtre, etc.	ours
le vôtre, etc.	yours
le leur, etc.	theirs

Watch the changes which take place with the prepositions **à** and **de**—

> J'ai parlé à son frère; il a parlé **au mien.** *I have spoken to his (her) brother; he has spoken to mine.*
>
> J'ai parlé de son frère; il a parlé **du mien.** *I have spoken of his brother; he has spoken of mine.*

POINT I. Watch the agreement of these pronouns with the noun possessed—

> J'ai parlé au frère de Jeanne et **au sien.** *I have spoken to Jeanne's brother and to hers.*

POINT II. *A brother of mine* is translated **un de mes frères.** *A sister of ours* is translated **une de nos sœurs.**

VOCABULARY FOR EXERCISE 26

le chapeau, *the hat*	la robe, *the dress*
l'habit (*m.*), *the coat*	la manche, *the sleeve*
le soulier, *the shoe*	la chaussette, *the sock*
le sabot, *the clog*	lourd, *heavy*
le bas, *the stocking*	

EXERCISE 26

A. *Translate into English*

1. Ce chapeau-ci est le mien; ce chapeau-là est le vôtre. 2. Cet habit est le sien, cette robe est la sienne. 3. Ces souliers sont les leurs. 4. Ces sabots sont les siens. 5. Ces gants sont les nôtres. 6. Ces chaussettes sont les vôtres. 7. Jeanne est une de nos amies. 8. Pierre est un de leurs amis. 9. Henri est un de nos amis. 10. Vorace est un de nos chiens.

B. *Insert the appropriate Possessive Pronoun in the following*

1. Ce livre est (mine). 2. Ces chapeaux sont (ours). 3. Ces habits sont (theirs). 4. Ces sabots sont (his). 5. Ces bas sont (hers). 6. Ces robes sont (theirs). 7. Ces souliers sont (yours). 8. Ces gants sont (thine). 9. Il a parlé à mon frère; j'ai parlé (to his). 10. Il a parlé de mon père; j'ai parlé (of his).

C. *Translate into French*

1. She has finished the sleeves of her dress. 2. She has chosen white gloves. 3. Mine are better than hers. 4. She is a friend of ours. 5. Her father is a friend of ours also. 6. The clogs are heavier than the shoes.

7. His hat is bigger than mine. 8. Mine is smaller than his. 9. She spoke to John's brother and to ours. 10. Marie spoke of her sister and of ours.

D. *Translate into French*

1. Choosing. 2. I have chosen. 3. I was building. 4. They finished. 5. We have finished. 6. She polished. 7. She cherishes. 8. They demolish. 9. She will choose. 10. I shall build.

LESSON 27

The Interrogative Pronouns

1. When the word *who*, *whom*, or *whose* introduces a question, we generally use the word **qui**—

(Subj.)	**Qui** parle?	*Who speaks?*
(Obj.)	**Qui** aimez-vous?	*Whom do you love?*
(After a pre- position)	De **qui** parlez-vous?	*Of whom do you speak?*
	A **qui** donnez-vous?	*To whom do you give?*

A qui, followed by the verb **être,** can translate *whose*—

	A qui est ce gant?	*Whose glove is this?*
(plural)	**A qui** sont ces gants?	*Whose gloves are these?*

2. But when the word *what* introduces a question, French requires a different word for each different case—

What is falling?	**Qu'est-ce qui** tombe?	(Subj.)
What do you prefer?	**Que** préférez-vous?	(Obj.)
Of what do you speak?	De **quoi** parlez-vous?	(After a pre- position)

3. Distinguish the adjective *which* from the pronoun *which*—

Which book?	**Quel** livre?	(Adjective)
Which of the books?	**Lequel** des livres?	(Pronoun)

The pronoun can easily be remembered. It is the one *not* followed immediately by a noun in English.

Feminine examples:

Which woman?	**Quelle** femme?
Which of the women?	**Laquelle** des femmes?

Plural examples:

Which men?	**Quels** hommes?
Which of the men?	**Lesquels** des hommes?
Which women?	**Quelles** femmes?
Which of the women?	**Lesquelles** des femmes?

Look out for the usual change with **à** and **de**—

To which of the men?	**Auquel** des hommes?
Of which of the men?	**Duquel** des hommes?

Watch the verb, in order to know when to put **lequel** and when **lesquels**—

Which of the men is arriving? **Lequel** des hommes arrive?
Which of the men are arriving? **Lesquels** des hommes **arrivent?**

VOCABULARY FOR EXERCISE 27

avec, *with*	sans, *without*
pour, *for*	

EXERCISE 27

A. *Translate into English*

1. Qui chante? 2. Qui détestez-vous? 3. De qui parlez-vous?
4. A qui envoyez-vous ce chien? 5. Avec qui travaillez-vous? 6. Sans qui? 7. Pour qui bâtissez-vous? 8. Qu'est-ce qui arrive? 9. Que chantez-vous? 10. De quoi parlez-vous?

B. *Translate into English*

1. Quelle fleur? 2. Laquelle des fleurs? 3. Quels hommes arrivent?
4. Lesquels des hommes sont arrivés? 5. Quelle femme danse? 6. Laquelle des femmes dansait? 7. Desquels des hommes parlez-vous? Je parle de ceux-ci. 8. Desquelles des femmes parlez-vous? Je parle de celles-ci. 9. Auquel des hommes envoyez-vous les gants?

C. *Translate into French*

1. Who builds? 2. Whom do you prefer? 3. Of whom do you speak? 4. What do you desire? 5. With what do you work? 6. Without what? 7. Which shoe? 8. Which hats? 9. Whose cow is this? 10. Whose goats are these?

D. *Translate into French*

1. Who has arrived? 2. Whom did you prefer? 3. What did you finish? 4. Of what were you speaking? 5. With what do you work? 6. Which of the students has finished? This one. 7. Which of the boys have finished? These ones. 8. Of which boys do you speak? Of mine. 9. Of which of the boys do you speak? Of yours. 10. Of which of the women did you speak? Of this one.

LESSON 28

The Disjunctive Pronouns

moi	*I, me*	**nous**	*we, us*
toi	*thou, thee*	**vous**	*you*
lui	*he, him*	**eux**	*they, them*
elle	*she, her*	**elles**	*they, them (fem.)*
soi	*oneself*		

These pronouns have five main uses—

1. After a comparison—

Elle est plus riche que **moi**. *She is richer than I.*

2. After *any* preposition—

elle alla à **lui**   *she went to him*
avec **lui**   *with him*
sans **elle**   *without her*

3. After the pronoun **ce**—

C'est **moi**	*It is I*	C'est **nous**	*It is we*
C'est **toi**	*It is thou*	C'est **vous**	*It is you*
C'est **lui**	*It is he*	Ce sont **eux**	N.B. *It is they*
C'est **elle**	*It is she*	Ce sont **elles**	

4. For a double subject—

Vous et moi nous **allons** à Paris. *You and I are going to Paris.*

Vous et eux vous **allez** à Paris. *You and they are going to Paris.*

Lui et elle vont à Paris. *He and she are going to Paris.*

Note the verb agreement in each case.

5. For any kind of emphasis. This may be conveyed in many ways—

(*a*) In answer to a question: Qui parle? **Moi.**
(*b*) With **même** (*self*): J'ai parlé **moi-même.**
(*c*) Before a clause: C'est **moi** qui ai chanté. (Watch verb agreement.)
(*d*) With **seul,** *alone,* **seulement,** *only.* **Lui seul,** *he alone;* **moi seulement,** *only I.*

POINT I. Normally, *I spoke to him* is **Je lui ai parlé.** If the word "I" were emphasized, we could say—

> **Moi, je lui ai parlé,** or
> **C'est moi qui lui ai parlé**

POINT II. Watch double objects, direct or indirect—

Je les aime	*I love them,* but
J'aime **elle et lui**	*I love her and him*

Similarly—

Je lui donne le livre. *I give the book to him;* but

Je donne le livre à **lui** et à **elle.** *I give the book to him and her.*

Je parle à **lui,** pas à **elle.** *I speak to him, not to her.*

EXERCISE 28

A. *Translate into English*

1. C'est moi. 2. Qui a parlé? C'est lui. 3. Non, c'est elle. 4. Ce sont eux qui ont chanté. 5. Ce sont elles qui ont dansé. 6. Chaque étudiant travaille pour soi. 7. Elle est plus riche que lui. 8. Vous êtes plus intelligents qu'eux. 9. Ils allèrent à elle. 10. Elle alla à lui.

B. *Translate into English*

1. Vous et moi nous allons à Londres. 2. Eux et moi nous allons à Édimbourg. 3. Vous et lui vous allez à Glasgow. 4. Vous et elle vous allez à Paris. 5. Lui et elle vont à Newcastle. 6. Qui dansait? Moi. 7. J'ai bâti la maison moi-même. 8. Il a fini le travail lui-même. 9. Lui seul parle allemand. 10. Il avait une maison à lui seul.

C. *Translate into French*

1. I gave the house to him and to her. 2. I built the house for him, not for her. 3. She chose the gloves for them, not for us. 4. He gave

her an apple. 5. It is he who has given her an apple. 6. It is she who has spoken. 7. Who went to him? I (did). 8. Who sang? He alone. 9. Who danced? She alone. 10. I like him and her.

D. *Translate into French*

1. Going. 2. I have gone. 3. She goes away. 4. She sends. 5. I was building. 6. She chooses. 7. She chose. 8. He gave it to me alone. 9. He sent it to him, not to me. 10. She speaks to him and to us.

LESSON 29

Relative Pronouns

Subject: **Qui**—
> L'homme **qui** parle　　*The man who speaks*

Object: **Que**—
> L'homme **que** je préfère　*The man whom I prefer*

A good way to remember **qui** and **que** is as follows: If the English words *who, that, which,* are immediately followed by a verb, put **qui**—

> La femme **qui** chante　*The woman who sings*
> L'accident **qui** arrive　*The accident which happens*
> Le cheval **qui** mange　*The horse which eats*

Conversely, if the English words *whom, that, which,* are *not* immediately followed by a verb, put **que**—

> *The child whom I see*　L'enfant **que** je vois (**voir**—*to see*)
> *The accident that he sees*　L'accident **qu'**il voit
> *The horse which she sees*　Le cheval **qu'**elle voit

Of whom or *of which* is best translated by **dont**—

> *The woman of whom I speak*　La femme **dont** je parle
> *The accident of which I speak*　L'accident **dont** je parle
> *The horse of which I speak*　Le cheval **dont** je parle

So far, we have seen the same pronouns used, whether speaking of human beings, animals, or things. But where the French needs a preposition a special division must be made. After all such prepositions, use **qui** for persons, **lequel, laquelle** (*fem. sing.*), **lesquels** (*masc. plur.*), **lesquelles** (*fem. plur.*), for animals or things—

The man for whom I work	L'homme pour **qui** je travaille
The woman for whom I work	La femme pour **qui** je travialle
The horse with which I work	Le cheval avec **lequel** je travaille
The cow with which I work	La vache avec **laquelle** je travaille

POINT I. Note that the preposition **à** will combine as usual—

The horse to which I give an apple. Le cheval **auquel** je donne une pomme.

POINT II. The **lequel** forms *may* be used for persons when clearness or euphony requires it—

La tante de mon ami **laquelle** m'a parlé. *My friend's aunt, who spoke to me.*

Or, e.g.—

The gentleman with whom he works. Le monsieur avec **lequel** il travaille

sounds better than

Le monsieur avec **qui il** travaille

POINT III. **Qui** after a preposition *cannot* be used instead of **lequel** for animals and things—

The animal with which I work must be "L'animal **avec lequel** je travaille," not "avec qui."

POINT IV. **Où,** *where,* may be used for *in which*—

la salle **où** j'étudie, *the room in which I study*

VOCABULARY FOR EXERCISE 29

l'armée (*f.*), *the army*	passer, *to pass*
la balle, *the bullet*	lutter, *to fight, struggle*
l'épée (*f.*), *the sword*	remporter, *to win*
l'ennemi (*m.*), *the enemy*	essuyer, *suffer, defeat, wipe*
la bataille, *the battle*	contre, *against*
la victoire, *the victory*	fort, *strong*
la défaite, *the defeat*	faible, *weak*

EXERCISE 29

A. *Translate into English*

1. L'épée avec laquelle il tue l'ennemi. 2. La bataille dans laquelle deux mille hommes luttaient contre cinq mille hommes. 3. L'armée qui avait remporté la victoire. 4. L'ennemi qui a essuyé la défaite. 5. Le soldat qui lutte contre trois de l'ennemi. 6. L'armée qui a dix mille hommes. 7. Les soldats qui ont marché. 8. Les soldats qui ont remporté la victoire. 9. L'ennemi que le soldat a tué. 10. Les balles dont nous parlions.

B. *Insert the French Relative Pronouns in the following*

1. La balle avec (which). 2. L'armée à (which). 3. Les victoires pour (which). 4. L'homme (who) parle. 5. La femme (whom) je vois. 6. Le jardin (of which) je parle. 7. Les fleurs (of which) je parle. 8. La chèvre (to which) je donne. 9. L'homme (to whom) je donne. 10. Les soldats (to whom) je donne.

C. *Translate into French*

1. The soldier who kills. 2. The soldier whom he kills. 3. The victory which he gains. 4. The defeats of which we speak. 5. The students to whom we give. 6. The horses to which we give. 7. The goat with which I work. 8. The girl of whom I speak. 9. The gentleman with whom he works. 10. The animal with which he works.

D. *Translate into French*

1. The garden which I have chosen is beautiful. 2. The tree which you have admired is green. 3. The man against whom you have fought is strong. 4. The child with whom I have worked is weak. 5. The men of whom I speak are the soldiers. 6. Of which soldiers? Of those who have won the victory. 7. We speak of the enemy who has suffered the defeat. 8. The book that I have preferred is the one of which you were speaking. 9. The garden in which I prefer to pass my time. 10. The flowers of which you speak are beautiful.

LESSON 30

The Relative Pronoun "whose"

Use **dont** to translate *whose*—

Subject following: *The man whose son speaks.* L'homme **dont** le fils parle.

62 A GRADED FRENCH GRAMMAR

Object following: *The man whose son I admire.* L'homme
dont j'admire le fils.

Note the word order after **dont,** according to whether the
noun following *whose* is a subject or object.

If the word *whose* is preceded by a preposition, the following
change occurs—

The man to whose son I speak. L'homme **au fils de qui** je parle.

Remember: **dont** cannot be used to translate *whose,* if there
is a preposition before the word *whose.*

The Relative Pronoun "what"

I know what happens	Je sais **ce qui** arrive
I know what you prefer	Je sais **ce que** vous préférez
I know what you speak of	Je sais **ce dont** vous parlez

Similarly, *all that* is **tout ce qui, tout ce que,** or **tout ce
dont**—

I know all that happens	Je sais **tout ce qui** arrive
I know all that you prefer	Je sais **tout ce que** vous préférez
I know all that you speak of	Je sais **tout ce dont** vous parlez

The Irregular "IR" Verbs
THE "SENTIR" GROUP

sentir	*to feel*
sentant	*feeling* (Note: no **iss**)
j'ai **senti**	*I have felt*

je **sens**	*I feel*	nous **sentons**	*we feel*
tu **sens**	*thou dost feel*	vous **sentez**	*you feel*
il **sent**	*he feels*	ils **sentent**	*they feel*
je **sentis**	*I felt*	je **sentais**	*I was feeling* (because formed from present participle)
je **sentirai**	*I shall feel*	je **sentirais**	*I should feel*

The verbs which belong to this group are—

mentir	*to tell a lie*	**dormir**	*to sleep*
partir	*to go away*	**s'endormir**	*to fall asleep*
sortir	*to go out*	**se repentir de**	*to repent*
servir	*to serve*	**se servir de**	*to make use of*
se servir	*to help oneself*		

POINT I. Remember that **sortir** and **partir,** like **arriver** and **aller,** use **être** in the Perfect Tenses—

Je **suis** sorti *I have gone out*
Elle **est** partie *She has gone away*

POINT II.

I feel the pain	Je sens la douleur
I feel tired	Je **me** sens fatigué (lit. *I feel myself tired*)

EXERCISE 30

A. *Translate into English*

1. La mère dont le fils est malade. 2. Le père dont le fils parle. 3. La femme au fils de qui je parle. 4. L'actrice avec le fils de qui je travaille. 5. Je sais ce qui tombe. 6. Je sais ce que vous admirez. 7. Je sais ce dont vous parlez. 8. Nous sentons tout ce que vous sentez. 9. Je sais tout ce qui arrive. 10. Je sais tout ce dont vous parlez.

B. *Translate into English*

1. Il ment. 2. Elle est sortie. 3. Nous sommes partis. 4. Quand êtes-vous sorti? 5. Le soldat sert. 6. Servez-vous, Madame. 7. Je me sers de cette chaise. 8. Elle dormait. 9. L'enfant s'endormit. 10. Elle se repent de ce qu'elle a admiré.

C. *Translate into French*

1. I feel. 2. She feels. 3. They were feeling. 4. I am going away. 5. She has gone away. 6. He serves. 7. Help yourself! 8. She was sleeping. 9. The child is falling asleep. 10. She makes use of this pen.

D. *Translate into French*

1. I admire what he admires. 2. She detests what I detest. 3. We admire all that you admire. 4. We prefer what you speak of. 5. I detest the man who tells a lie. 6. I feel what you feel. He feels the pains also. 7. They went away at half past seven. 8. They went out at a quarter past four. 9. We admire those who serve. 10. We shall sleep. He feels tired also.

LESSON 31

Negative Pronouns

Remember all negatives must take **ne** before the verb—

Personne **n'**arrive	*Nobody arrives*	(Subject)
Je **n'**admire personne	*I admire no one*	(Object)
Rien **n'**arrive	*Nothing happens*	(Subject)
Je **n'**ai rien	*I have nothing*	(Object)
Jamais je **n'**ai admiré	*Never have I admired*	
Je **n'**ai jamais admiré	*I have never admired*	
Ni l'un ni l'autre **n'**arrivent	*Neither the one nor the other arrives*	
Je **n'**admire ni l'un ni l'autre	*I admire neither the one nor the other*	
Pas un **ne** part	*Not one goes away*	
Je **ne** préfère pas un des jardins	*I prefer none of the gardens*	

If there is no verb, there is no **ne**—

Qui est là?	*Who is there?*	**Personne!**	*Nobody.*
Qu'avez-vous?	*What have you?*	**Rien!**	*Nothing.*

The Irregular "IR" Verbs
THE "OUVRIR" GROUP

ouvrir	*to open*
ouvrant	*opening* (irregular, because no **iss**)
j'ai **ouvert**	*I have opened*

j'**ouvre**	*I open*	nous **ouvrons**	*we open*
tu **ouvres**	*thou dost open*	vous **ouvrez**	*you open*
il **ouvre**	*he opens*	ils **ouvrent**	*they open*
j'**ouvris**	*I opened*	j'**ouvrais**	*I was opening*
j'**ouvrirai**	*I shall open*	j'**ouvrirais**	*I should open*

The verbs which belong to this group are—

s'ouvrir	*to open* (of a thing)	**souffrir**	*to suffer*
découvrir	*to discover, uncover*	**couvrir**	*to cover*
offrir	*to offer*		

EXERCISE 31

A. *Translate into English*

1. Qui a découvert l'Amérique? Christophe Colomb. 2. Personne

n'était dans la maison. 3. Je n'ai parlé à personne. 4. Rien ne tombait. 5. Je n'admire rien. 6. Jamais je n'ai préféré de tels arbres. 7. Je n'ai jamais admiré de telles maisons. 8. Je ne préfère ni l'un ni l'autre. 9. Pas un n'est arrivé. 10. Pas une des femmes ne chantait.

B. *Translate into English*

1. Je n'admire pas une des fleurs. 2. Qui est là? Est-ce Marie? Personne. 3. Personne n'aime l'ennemi. 4. Elle couvre la table. 5. Nous offrons tout ce que nous avons. 6. Elle souffre. 7. Elle est souffrante (*ill*). 8. Il a découvert ce qu'ils ont dans la maison. 9. Qu'ont-ils dans la maison? Rien. 10. Nous n'aimons ni l'un ni l'autre des jardins.

C. *Translate into French*

1. She discovers. 2. He has discovered. 3. Christopher Columbus discovered America. 4. He uncovered. 5. She was suffering. 6. I have offered. 7. We offer. 8. He offered. 9. They have opened. 10. She opens the door.

D. *Translate into French*

1. The door opens (itself). 2. We have opened the door. 3. Not one has arrived. 4. Not one of the women has gone away. 5. Not one of the sisters has gone out. 6. What did you offer (to) them? 7. We have offered (to) them what we offered (to) you. 8. I know all that she has suffered. 9. I accept what you have offered. 10. I refuse what she has offered.

LESSON 32

Indefinite Pronouns

1. **L'un, l'autre,** *the one, the other*—

   L'un est riche, **l'autre** est pauvre. *The one is rich, the other is poor.*

Les uns, les autres, *some, the others*—

   Les uns sont forts, **les autres** sont faibles. *Some are strong, the others are weak.*

2. **D'autres,** *others*—

   D'autres ont refusé. *Others have refused.*

Do not confuse with **des autres,** *of the others.*

3. **On.** The indefinite word *one,* as compared with **un,** the numerical word *one—*

> **On** admire. *One admires, people admire.*

On is used also to convey the passive—

> Ici **on** parle français. *French is spoken here.*

It should be followed by **soi,** *oneself.*

> On ne travaille pas pour **soi.** *One does not work for oneself.*

For euphony, **l'on** is written in the following—

si **l'on**	*if one*	et **l'on**	*and one*
que **l'on**	*that one*	ou **l'on**	*or one*
où **l'on**	*where one*		

But this **l** is omitted generally when another **l** is near—

> si **on** les admire *if one admires them*

4. **Chacun,** *each one,* is followed by **soi,** *oneself—*

> **Chacun** pour **soi.** *Each one for himself.*

Do not confuse with the adjective **chaque,** *each;* **chaque** is generally followed by a noun—

> **chaque** femme   *each woman*

Chacun is often followed by **de—**

> **Chacun** des hommes travaille. *Each of the men is working.*

5. **Quelqu'un (Quelques-uns),** *Someone, anyone, some—*

> **Quelqu'un** est là. *Someone is there.*

Quelques-uns (quelques-unes) translates *some* when the word *of* follows with a plural noun—

> *Some of the students,* **quelques-uns** des étudiants.

Do not confuse with **un peu de** in a phrase such as **un peu de lait,** *some milk.*

Irregular "IR" Verbs

The "Venir" Group

venir	*to come*		
venant	*coming*		
je suis **venu**	*I have come*		
je **viens**	*I come*	nous **venons**	*we come*
tu **viens**	*thou dost come*	vous **venez**	*you come*
il **vient**	*he comes*	ils **viennent**	*they come*
je **vins**	*I came*	nous **vînmes**	*we came*
tu **vins**	*thou didst come*	vous **vîntes**	*you came*
il **vint**	*he came*	ils **vinrent**	*they came*
je **viendrai**	*I shall come*	je **venais**	*I was coming*
		je **viendrais**	*I should come*

The verbs which belong to this group are—

revenir	*to come back*	**tenir**	*to hold*
devenir	*to become*	**retenir**	*to retain*
convenir	*to suit* (uses **avoir**)	**contenir**	*to contain*
convenir	*to agree* (uses **être**)	**détenir**	*to detain*
se souvenir de	*to remember*		

Just as the verb *to go* and its group use **être,** so the verb *to come* and its group use **être. Tenir** and its compounds use **avoir.**

Verbs Conjugated with "être"

aller	*to go*	**arriver**	*to arrive*
sortir	*to go out*	**venir**	*to come*
partir	*to go away*	**revenir**	*to come back*
monter	*to go up*	**devenir**	*to become*
tomber	*to fall*	**convenir**	*to agree*
descendre	*to go down*	**retourner**	*to go back*
entrer	*to go in*	**naître**	*to be born*
rester	*to remain*	**mourir**	*to die*

The foregoing verbs are conjugated with **être** because in compound tenses they most often denote the achievement of a state—

Elle **est partie.** *She has gone away* or *She is away*

Rester, *to remain,* is included because it most often denotes the maintenance of a state.

EXERCISE 32

A. *Translate into English*

1. L'un est pauvre, l'autre est riche. 2. Les uns sont faibles, les autres sont forts. 3. D'autres l'ont admiré. 4. Ici on parle anglais. 5. Ici on parle allemand. 6. Si l'on admire ce qui est beau, on est heureux. 7. Si on l'admire, on est heureux. 8. Chacun travaille pour soi. 9. On déteste tout ce qui est mauvais. 10. On préfère ce que l'on admire.

B. *Translate into English*

1. On ne travaille pas pour soi. 2. On n'aime pas de telles histoires. 3. Chacun des hommes a un beau jardin. 4. J'aime quelques-unes des fleurs. 5. Quelqu'un est là. Qui est-ce? Personne. 6. Elle est venue à huit heures. 7. Elle vient tous les jours. 8. Elle viendra demain à midi et demi. 9. Ils ne viennent jamais à minuit. 10. Je viendrais demain si j'avais le temps.

C. *Translate into French*

1. He has gone. 2. I have entered. 3. She has gone out. 4. They have fallen. 5. We have arrived. 6. Thou hast come. 7. You have returned. 8. She has come back. 9. We have become rich. 10. They have gone up.

D. *Translate into French*

1. Someone is coming. 2. No one is there. 3. Who will come tomorrow? 4. No one will come. 5. My friends have become rich. 6. The soldiers have become strong. 7. He remembers his mother. 8. Each one is working for himself. 9. They never come at half past three. 10. They always (**toujours,** *after verb*) go back at ten.

LESSON 33

Indefinite Pronouns (cont.)

6. **Quelque chose,** *something.* This pronoun, and **rien,** *nothing,* always take **de** before an *adjective*—

> J'ai **quelque chose de** bon pour chacun. *I have something good for each one.*
> Je n'ai **rien de** bon. *I have nothing good.*

Before a verb infinitive, these pronouns take **à**—

> J'ai **quelque chose à** confesser. *I have something to confess.*
> Je n'ai **rien à** manger. *I have nothing to eat.*

Sometimes adjective and verb follow, each with its own preposition—

> J'ai **quelque chose de** bon **à** manger. *I have something good to eat.*

7. **Tout**, *everything*, should be distinguished from **tous** (**toutes**, *fem.*), meaning *all*—

	J'admire **tout**	*I admire everything*
but,	Je les admire **tous**	*I admire them all*
and,	Je les admire **toutes**	*I admire them* (fem.) *all*

The Words of Quantity

beaucoup	*much, many*	**plus**	*more*
trop	*too much, too many*	**moins**	*less, fewer*
assez	*enough*	**autant**	*as much, as many*
tant	*so much, so many*	**peu**	*little, few*
un peu	*a little, some*	**si peu**	*so little, so few*

A. These words take **de** before a noun—

beaucoup **d'**enfants	*many children*
beaucoup **de** thé	*much tea*
trop **de** femmes	*too many women*
trop **de** lait	*too much milk*
assez **de** sucre	*enough sugar*
autant **de** livres	*as many books*
autant **de** café	*as much coffee*
tant **de** fleurs	*so many flowers*
tant **de** limonade	*so much lemonade*
peu **d'**hommes	*few men*
peu **d'**argent	*little money*
un peu **de** crème	*a little cream*
si peu **de** soldats	*so few soldiers*
si peu **d'**eau	*so little water*

Caution: If they are followed by the words *of the* in English, these must be translated—

> **beaucoup des** hommes   *many* of the *men*
> **beaucoup du** beurre   *much* of the *butter*

or preferably beaucoup de ces hommes, beaucoup de ce beurre.

B. Before a verb infinitive, the above take **à**—

> beaucoup **à** choisir   *much to choose*
> trop **à** décider   *too much to decide*
> tant **à** nettoyer   *so much to clean*

C. They are often followed by both noun and infinitive—

> J'ai beaucoup **de** fleurs **à** arranger. *I have many flowers to arrange.*

D. Before an adjective, adverb, or each other, they take *no* preposition—

> Je suis trop fatigué   *I am too tired*
> Il est beaucoup plus riche que nous   *He is much richer than we*
> Elle est beaucoup trop fatiguée   *She is much too tired*

E. **Trop** and **assez,** if followed by an adjective, must then take **pour** before an infinitive—

> Elle est **trop fatiguée pour** travailler. *She is too tired to work.*
> Elle est **assez riche pour** acheter. *She is rich enough to buy.*

Caution: Sometimes the adjective itself governs a preposition, which must be remembered—

> Elle est trop fatiguée **de** travailler. *She is too tired of working.*

Some examinations set the following trap—

> *She is too tired of working to begin now.* Elle est trop fatiguée **de** travailler **pour** commencer maintenant.

Much and *many* may also be translated by **bien,** followed by **du, de la, des: bien des** amis, *many friends.*

The Irregular "IR" Verbs

MOURIR

mourir	*to die*		
mourant	*dying*		
il **est mort**	*he has died*		
je **meurs**	*I am dying*	nous **mourons**	*we die*
tu **meurs**	*thou art dying*	vous **mourez**	*you die*
il **meurt**	*he is dying*	ils **meurent**	*they die*
je **mourus**	*I died*	nous **mourûmes**	*we died*
tu **mourus**	*thou didst die*	vous **mourûtes**	*you died*
il **mourut**	*he died*	ils **moururent**	*they died*
		je **mourais**	*I was dying*
je **mourrai**	*I shall die*	je **mourrais**	*I should die*

VOCABULARY FOR EXERCISE 33

montrer, *to show*
raconter, *to relate, tell*
regarder, *to look at*
demander, *to ask for*
chercher, *to look for*

la faim, *the hunger*
la soif, *the thirst*
la fatigue, *the weariness*
la chose, *the thing, matter*

EXERCISE 33

A. *Translate into English*

1. Nous avons quelque chose d'intéressant à vous montrer. 2. Elle a quelque chose de nouveau à vous raconter. 3. Il n'y a rien de nouveau à regarder. 4. Il n'y a rien de bon à écouter. 5. J'ai demandé quelque chose d'amusant. 6. Il déteste tout. 7. Il les déteste tous. 8. Il les aime toutes. 9. Mon ami Charles a beaucoup à payer. 10. Il a acheté trop de livres.

B. *Translate into French*

1. Many of the men. 2. Enough women. 3. As many students. 4. As much of the money. 5. So many flowers. 6. Little money. 7. Few friends. 8. A little wine. 9. So few fathers. 10. So little money.

C. *Translate into French*

1. She is much too tired to work now. 2. They are much too tired of working to start now. 3. We are rich enough to buy the house. 4. They are strong enough to work. 5. We are dying of hunger. 6. The soldiers are dying of thirst. 7. I am looking for the book which was in the room. 8. He has paid for the flowers. 9. We have looked for our father. 10. They have listened to the woman.

D. *Translate into French*

1. He will die of weariness. 2. She would die if she worked all day.
3. Dying of hunger. 4. The soldier was dying. 5. I have asked for
some bread. 6. They have looked for many things. 7. We have paid
for the victory. 8. Jeanne has something interesting to relate to us.
9. Pierre has something new to show us. 10. Yvette has nothing new
to tell us.

LESSON 34

The Words "plus" and "moins"

When these words represent quantity, they take **de** before a
noun—

    plus de livres   *more books* (or *no more books*)
    moins d'amis   *fewer friends*

But when they suggest comparison, they take **que**—

    plus que vous   *more than you*
    moins que vous   *less than you*

CAUTION: Do not be misled by numbers. The only deciding
factor is quantity or comparison—

    Un lion mange **plus de** trois lapins. *A lion is eating more
    than three rabbits* (for its meal).

    Le lion mange **plus que** trois lapins. *The lion eats more than
    three rabbits* (*eat*).

A good way to test yourself is to repeat the first English verb.
If the sentence makes sense, put **que**; otherwise **de**—

    I ask for more than he (*asks for*) **plus que.**
    I ask for more than ten books (*ask for*) **plus de.**

Examiners are fond of the phrases *the more* and *the less*. There
are three main types—

1. Two *verbs* only:
    The more you work, the more you win. **Plus** on travaille,
    plus on gagne.

NOTE: No "le" and no "que."

2. Two *adjectives* only:

The more diligent you are, the happier you are. **Plus** diligent, **plus** on est heureux.

Note the position of the adjective.

3. Two *nouns* only:

The more friends you have, the more joy you have. **Plus** on a d'amis, **plus** on a de joie.

Sometimes, the three types are mixed by the examiners, e.g.—

The more you work (type 1) *the happier you are* (type 2). **Plus** on travaille, **plus** on est heureux.

Note the following—

Plus on est, **plus** on rit. *The more, the merrier* (**rire,** *to laugh*). **Le plus** tôt sera le mieux. *The sooner, the better.*

The Word "both"

1. When *both* is followed by *the*, a possessive adjective, or a demonstrative adjective, translate it by **deux,** and put it before the noun—

both the men	les **deux** hommes
both my friends	mes **deux** amis
both these women	ces **deux** femmes

2. But when *both* is a pronoun, translate it by **tous les deux,** or **tous deux** (*fem.* **toutes les deux** or **toutes deux**)—

We are both coming	Nous venons **tous deux**
They are both going	Ils y vont **tous les deux**

3. Similarly, to say—

We three are coming, put: Nous venons **tous les trois.**
We seven are going. Nous allons **tous les sept.**

The Irregular "IR" Verbs
THE "COURIR" GROUP

Courir, *to run*, is similar in form to **mourir,** *to die*, except in the past participle and present tense. (Observe that this verb uses **avoir**, not **être**.)

courir	*to run*		
courant	*running*		
j'ai **couru**	*I have run*		

je **cours**	*I run*	nous **courons**	*we run*
tu **cours**	*thou dost run*	vous **courez**	*you run*
il **court**	*he runs*	ils **courent**	*they run*

je **courus**	*I ran*	nous **courûmes**	*we ran*
tu **courus**	*thou didst run*	vous **courûtes**	*you ran*
il **courut**	*he ran*	ils **coururent**	*they ran*

		je **courais**	*I was running*
je **courrai**	*I shall run*	je **courrais**	*I should run*

Similarly, **accourir**, *to run up.*

EXERCISE 34

A. *Translate into English*

1. J'ai moins de livres que mon frère. 2. J'en ai moins que lui. 3. Le lion mange plus de trois lapins. 4. Le lion mange plus que trois lapins. 5. Plus je travaille, plus je gagne. 6. Moins je suis diligent, moins je suis heureux. 7. Moins on a d'argent, moins on a de joie. 8. Plus on est, plus on rit. 9. Le plus tôt sera le mieux. 10. Plus on travaille, plus on est heureux.

B. *Translate into English*

1. Les deux étudiants. 2. Ces deux garçons. 3. Mes deux amis. 4. Mes frères viennent tous deux. 5. Mes sœurs viennent toutes deux. 6. Nous allons au théâtre tous les trois. 7. Nous sommes allés au ciné tous les quatre. 8. J'ai couru leur raconter la chose. 9. Il court les regarder. 10. Elles courent les chercher.

C. *Translate into French*

1. Both the trees. 2. Both these trees. 3. Both my friends. 4. His sisters are both running. 5. Her brothers were both running. 6. We five have run to tell them the matter. 7. We three shall run to look for them. 8. You four run to look at them. 9. Both of us are going to the theatre. 10. Both of you are going to the cinema.

D. *Translate into French*

1. I have more than five books. 2. She has more of them than you.
3. A man eats more than three cats. 4. The more you try, the happier
you are. 5. The more friends you have, the more joy you have. 6.
They were running to tell us. 7. A man ran up. 8. We ran to look at
him. 9. I should run if I were strong enough (enough strong). 10. I
shall run and (to) tell them the matter.

LESSON 35

The Verb "penser," to think of

1. When **penser** is followed by an infinitive without any
preposition, it means *to intend*—

Je pense l'essayer. *I am intending to try it.*

2. When *to think of* means *to turn your thoughts to*, use **penser
à**—

Je pense à vous. *I am thinking of you.*

3. When *to think of* means *to have an opinion of*, use **penser
de**—

Que pensez-vous de lui? *What do you think of him?*

Look out for sentences such as—

(a) *What do you think of her? I never think of her.* **Que pensez-
vous d'elle? Je ne pense jamais à elle.**

(b) *What do you think of it? I never think of it.* **Qu'en pensez-
vous? Je n'y pense jamais.**

(c) *I am thinking of what you admire.* **Je pense à ce que vous
admirez.**

The Reflexive Verb

There are three main types—

1. Reflexive in English also, e.g. **s'amuser,** *to amuse oneself.*

2. Reflexive in French, not in English, e.g. **se laver,** *to wash.*

3. Expressed by a different English phrase, e.g. **se tromper,**
to be mistaken (**tromper,** *to deceive*).

POINT I.   Remember that the reflexive pronoun must conform—

je vais **m'**amuser	*I am going to amuse myself*
tu vas **t'**amuser	*thou art going to amuse thyself*
il va **s'**amuser	*he is going to amuse himself*
elle va **s'**amuser	*she is going to amuse herself*
nous allons **nous** amuser	*we are going to amuse ourselves*
vous allez **vous** amuser	*you are going to amuse yourself(-ves)*
ils vont **s'**amuser	*they are going to amuse themselves*
elles vont **s'**amuser	*they are going to amuse themselves*

This feature must be watched in all tenses—

je m'habille	*I dress*
nous nous lèverons	*we shall get up*

POINT II.   Reflexive verbs use **être** as auxiliary—

je me suis levé	*I have got up*
tu t'es levé	*thou hast got up*

POINT III.   Watch the Imperative—

Levez-vous!	*Get up!*
Ne vous levez pas!	*Don't get up!*

POINT IV.   Watch the interrogative forms of the Perfect—

Vous êtes-vous levé?	*Have you got up?*

The Irregular "IR" Verbs
THE "CUEILLIR" GROUP

cueillir	*to gather* (watch spelling **cue-**)
cueillant	*gathering*
j'ai **cueilli**	*I have gathered*

je **cueille**	*I gather*	nous **cueillons**	*we gather*
tu **cueilles**	*thou dost gather*	vous **cueillez**	*you gather*
il **cueille**	*he gathers*	ils **cueillent**	*they gather*
je **cueillis**	*I gathered*	je **cueillais**	*I was gathering*
je **cueillerai**	*I shall gather*	je **cueillerais**	*I should gather*

(Note the **e**)

Similarly, **accueillir,** *to welcome.*

VOCABULARY FOR EXERCISE 35

se coucher, *to go to bed, to*
 set (sun)
se tromper, *to be mistaken*
le soleil, *the sun*
étrange, *strange*
comment, *how*
s'enrhumer, *to catch a cold*

s'écrier, *to exclaim*
se fâcher, *to become angry*
se promener, *to take a walk*
la lune, *the moon*
puis, *then*
maintenant, *now*

EXERCISE 35

A. *Translate into English*

1. Le soleil se lève à cinq heures et se couche à neuf heures. 2. Nous nous levons à sept heures. 3. Nous nous couchons à onze heures du soir. 4. Quand vous levez-vous? 5. Comment vous appelez-vous? 6. Je m'appelle Robert. Et vous? 7. Chose étrange! Je m'appelle Robert aussi. 8. Ils se lavent et puis ils s'habillent. 9. Je me suis amusé au théâtre. 10. Vous êtes-vous amusé au concert?

B. *Translate into English*

1. Levez-vous! 2. Couchez-vous! 3. Ne vous fâchez pas! 4. Promenez-vous! 5. Ne vous amusez pas maintenant! 6. Cueillez des roses! 7. Je les cueillerai demain. 8. Nous accueillerons nos amis. 9. Elle cueillait des fleurs dans le jardin. 10. Elle s'amusait beaucoup.

C. *Translate into French*

1. I am thinking of you in Paris. 2. What do you think of the new student? 3. I never think of the new students. 4. What do you think of it? 5. I never think of it. 6. She was thinking of what you were admiring. 7. We intend to go to Liverpool. 8. I was thinking of my brother in Newcastle. 9. What do you think of Edinburgh? 10. They are thinking of both their brothers.

D. *Translate into French*

1. The moon rises at ten and sets at eight. 2. When do you get up? 3. We get up at half past six. 4. When do you go to bed? 5. We go to bed at eleven. 6. What is your name? 7. My name is Pierre. 8. "Take a walk!" she exclaimed (say "exclaimed she"). 9. He has caught a cold. 10. He has become angry, because he has been mistaken.

LESSON 36

The Agreement of the Past Participle

1. After the verb *to be*, the Past Participle agrees with the subject—

The woman is loved	La femme **est aimée**
The woman has been loved	La femme **a été aimée**

2. After the verb *to have*, the Past Participle does not usually change—

Nous **avons dîné**   *We have dined*

But, if there is a direct object in front of the verb, the Past Participle agrees with it—

Quels **cadeaux** avez-vous **achetés?** *What presents have you bought?*

Les **cadeaux** que j'ai **achetés.** *The presents which I have bought.*

Nearly every examination has this feature, and some examiners put in the following traps—

(a) *The presents which I have wanted to buy.* Les cadeaux **que j'ai désiré acheter.**

The preceding direct object is controlled by **acheter,** not by **désiré.**

(b) *Have you bought some?* **En** avez-vous **acheté?**

The Past Participle does not agree with **en.**

(c) *Have you bought them?* **Les** avez-vous **achetés?**

Look out for a preceding direct object represented by a pronoun instead of a noun.

3. The Past Participle of a reflexive verb must agree with the preceding direct object, in spite of the fact that the reflexive verbs use **être**—

Elle s'est levée	*She has got up*
Nous nous sommes couchés	*We have gone to bed*

The "RE" Regular Verbs

perdre	*to lose*		
perdant	*losing*		
j'ai **perdu**	*I have lost*		
je **perds**	*I lose*	nous **perdons**	*we lose*
tu **perds**	*thou dost lose*	vous **perdez**	*you lose*
il **perd**	*he loses*	ils **perdent**	*they lose*
je **perdis**	*I lost*	nous **perdîmes**	*we lost*
tu **perdis**	*thou didst lose*	vous **perdîtes**	*you lost*
il **perdit**	*he lost*	ils **perdirent**	*they lost*
		je **perdais**	*I was losing*
je **perdrai**	*I shall lose*	je **perdrais**	*I should lose*
perds	*lose*	**perdons**	*let us lose*
		perdez	*lose*

VOCABULARY FOR EXERCISE 36

mordre, *to bite*	attendre, *to wait for, expect*
vendre, *to sell*	entendre, *to hear*
répondre, *to answer*	fondre, *to melt*
le fermier, *the farmer*	le tonnerre, *the thunder*
la pluie, *the rain*	les éclairs (*m.*), *the lightning*
le brouillard, *the fog*	le vent, *the wind*
le bruit, *the noise*	l'Écosse (*f.*), *Scotland*
s'ennuyer, *to become bored*	la Russie, *Russia*

EXERCISE 36

A. *Translate into English*

1. Le chien a mordu le chat. 2. Le fermier a vendu la farine. 3. Quelle farine a-t-il vendue? 4. Qui avez-vous attendu? 5. Les choses que j'ai attendues ne sont pas arrivées. 6. La pluie a fondu la neige. 7. Elle s'est ennuyée au concert. 8. Nous nous sommes amusés au théâtre. 9. J'entends le tonnerre. 10. Je n'aime pas les éclairs.

B. *Translate into English*

1. Il y a beaucoup de pluie en Écosse. 2. Il y a beaucoup de neige en Russie. 3. Nous entendons le vent et la pluie. 4. La neige a couvert toutes les fleurs. 5. Il y a beaucoup de brouillard à Londres. 6. La mère a été aimée. 7. Quelles fleurs avez-vous choisies? 8. J'ai choisi les

fleurs que Jeanne a cueillies.   9. Quels cadeaux avez-vous achetés?
10. Les cadeaux que j'ai achetés sont pour ma soeur.

C. *Translate into French*

1. What books have you bought? 2. What animals has he sold?
3. What students did you wait for? 4. What noises have you heard?
5. We have heard the noise of the thunder. 6. We have become angry.
7. She has caught a cold in the rain. 8. We do not like the fogs of the
city. 9. No one likes too much wind. 10. We speak of the rain which
we have heard all night.

D. *Translate into French*

1. When did you lose the money which your father gave you?
2. That dog has bitten too many cats, and now he will die. 3. The lady
whom we expected did not come. 4. The gentleman whom we expected has gone away. 5. The apples which I had hoped to buy are all
sold. 6. They were sold yesterday. 7. These students have gone to
bed at half past ten. 8. The girls rose at a quarter past seven. 9. I lost
my dog in 1950. Of what did he die? 10. She replied that she would
accept the invitation if it came today.

LESSON 37

The Reciprocal Verbs

These are like the Reflexive verbs in form, e.g. **Elles se détestent** can mean *They hate each other* as well as *They hate
themselves.*

If there is any doubt, the French add **l'un l'autre** (*fem.* **l'une
l'autre,** *plural*, **les uns les autres,** *fem. plural*, **les unes les
autres**), e.g. **Elles se détestent l'une l'autre** can mean only
They hate each other.

It is important to note that one cannot omit the **se.**

In a phrase such as **Ils se parlent,** it is not necessary to add
l'un à l'autre, because the meaning is clear without it.

If a verb has a special preposition, it must be inserted between
l'un and **l'autre**—

    Ils se battent l'un avec l'autre. *They fight with each other*
    (from the verb **se battre avec,** *to fight with*).

Similarly—

Ils se méfient l'un de l'autre. *They mistrust each other* (from the verb **se méfier de,** *to mistrust*).

Ils se fient l'un à l'autre. *They trust each other* (from the verb **se fier à,** *to trust*).

Agreement of the Past Participle (cont.)

This remains the same as for Reflexive verbs—

Ils se sont aimés l'un l'autre. *They have loved each other.*

The Past Participle agrees with the preceding direct object **se.** Likewise—

Ils se sont méfiés l'un de l'autre

But beware of the verbs in which **se** is indirect—

Ils se sont parlé. *They have spoken to each other.*

Ils se sont envoyé des cadeaux l'un à l'autre. *They have sent some presents to each other.*

Here the direct object is **cadeaux,** and it follows the past participle.

Some examiners set the following type of sentence—

What presents have they sent to each other? **Quels cadeaux se sont-ils envoyés l'un à l'autre?**

Here **envoyés** agrees with its preceding direct object **cadeaux,** not with **se.**

The Irregular "RE" Verbs
THE "FAIRE" GROUP

faire	*to make, to do,* etc.		
faisant	*making*		
j'ai **fait**	*I have made*		
je **fais**	*I make*	nous **faisons**	*we make*
tu **fais**	*thou dost make*	vous **faites**	*you make*
il **fait**	*he makes*	ils **font**	*they make*
je **fis**	*I made*	nous **fîmes**	*we made*
tu **fis**	*thou didst make*	vous **fîtes**	*you made*
il **fit**	*he made*	ils **firent**	*they made*
		je **faisais**	*I was making*
je **ferai**	*I shall make*	je **ferais**	*I should make*

This verb is used constantly in an idiomatic sense—

j'ai fait or **rendu visite**	*I have paid a visit*
j'ai fait trois milles	*I have gone three miles*
j'ai fait une promenade	*I have gone for a walk*

But one of its most important uses is to translate the verb *to be*, in speaking of the weather—

Quel temps fait-il?	*What is the weather like?*
Il fait beau	*It is fine*
Il fait mauvais	*It is bad*
Il fait humide	*It is damp*
Il fait sec	*It is dry*
Il fait froid	*It is cold*
Il fait chaud	*It is warm*
Il fait lourd	*It is sultry* (**lourd,** adj. *heavy*)

Before a noun, the word *some* is inserted—

Il fait du vent	*It is windy*
Il fait du brouillard	*It is foggy*
Il fait du soleil	*It is sunny*
Il fait des éclairs	*There is lightning*
Il fait de la pluie	*It is raining*

VOCABULARY FOR EXERCISE 37

la nation, *the nation*	quel dommage! *what a pity!*
rendre visite à quelqu'un, *to visit someone*	

EXERCISE 37

A. *Translate into English*

1. Ces deux garçons se méfient l'un de l'autre. 2. Ces deux nations se fient l'une à l'autre. 3. Les femmes se sont envoyé des fleurs. 4. Quelles fleurs se sont-elles envoyées? 5. Les cadeaux qu'elles se sont envoyés étaient beaux. 6. Que faites-vous là? 7. Je le ferai si vous le faites. 8. Si vous le faisiez, je le ferais aussi. 9. Moi, le faire! Je ne fais jamais de telles choses. 10. Ils font ce qu'ils désirent faire.

B. *Translate into English*

1. Quel temps fait-il aujourd'hui? 2. Il fait beau. 3. S'il fait du soleil, je ferai une promenade dans les bois. 4. C'est ce que j'allais faire,

moi. 5. Allons tous les deux rendre visite à nos amis. 6. Il fait de la pluie. Quel dommage! 7. Hier il faisait du brouillard à Londres. 8. Demain il fera beau à Liverpool. 9. Aujourd'hui il fait du vent à Newcastle. 10. S'il fait trop lourd, nous n'irons pas dans les bois.

C. *Translate into French*

1. She has gone five miles. 2. There is lightning. 3. There was thunder yesterday. 4. Tomorrow it will be fine. 5. They are taking a walk. 6. If it is too dry, we shall remain in the house. 7. If it were fine, we should visit our aunt. 8. What have you done? 9. We have done what they have done. 10. One day he walked fifteen miles.

D. *Translate into French*

1. The women used to like each other. 2. But they never sent each other presents. 3. Both these men hate each other. 4. They mistrust each other. 5. The girls trust each other. 6. They have spoken to each other today. 7. The presents which they sent each other yesterday are beautiful. 8. When the weather is fine, we take a walk. 9. When the weather is bad, we stay in the house. 10. What was the weather like yesterday?

LESSON 38

The Impersonal Verbs

1. Apart from the weather impersonal verbs, made from **faire,** there are others, such as: **pleuvoir,** *to rain—*

il pleut	*it rains*
il pleuvait	*it was raining*
il a plu	*it has rained*
il plut	*it rained*
il pleuvra	*it will rain*
il pleuvrait	*it would rain*

neiger, *to snow*

il neige	*it is snowing*
il neigeait	*it was snowing*
il a neigé	*it has snowed*
il neigea	*it snowed*
il neigera	*it will snow*
il neigerait	*it would snow*

Similarly: **il bruine,** *it is drizzling*; **il gèle,** *it is freezing*; **il dégèle,** *it is thawing*; **il tonne,** *it is thundering*; **il grêle,** *it is hailing*.

2. Many verbs can be made impersonal by putting **il** in front, and keeping the verb singular, e.g. **Il arrive des accidents,** literally, *There happen accidents*, i.e. *Accidents occur.*

3. Watch the verb **y avoir,** *there to be—*

il y a	*there is, there are*
il y avait	*there was, there were*
il y a eu	*there has been, there have been*
il y eut	*there was, there were*
il y aura	*there will be*
il y aurait	*there would be*

4. Many impersonal verbs can be made by adding an adjective to **il est—**

il est possible que	*it is possible that*
il est douteux que	*it is doubtful whether*

5. Watch impersonal verbs like **il s'agit de,** *it concerns—*

Il s'agit de moi	*It concerns me*
De quoi s'agit-il?	*What is it about?*
il s'ensuit que	*it follows that*

The Irregular "RE" Verbs

THE "DIRE" GROUP

dire	*to say* or *tell*
disant	*saying*
j'ai dit	*I have said*

je **dis**	*I say*	nous **disons**	*we say*
tu **dis**	*thou dost say*	vous **dites**	*you say*
il **dit**	*he says*	ils **disent**	*they say*
je **dis**	*I said*	nous **dîmes**	*we said*
tu **dis**	*thou didst say*	vous **dîtes**	*you said*
il **dit**	*he said*	ils **dirent**	*they said*
		je **disais**	*I was saying*
je **dirai**	*I shall say*	je **dirais**	*I should say*
		disons!	*let us say!*
dis!	*say!*	**dites!**	*say!*

The most important in the group are—

redire	*to repeat*	which takes the form		**vous redites**
contredire	*to contradict*	,,	,, ,, ,,	**vous contredisez**
prédire	*to predict*	,,	,, ,, ,,	**vous prédisez**
médire de	*to slander*	,,	,, ,, ,,	**vous médisez**
maudire	*to curse*	,,	,, ,, ,,	**maudissant** and **maudissez**

VOCABULARY FOR EXERCISE 38

regretter, *to regret*   trembler, *to tremble*
le matin, *the morning*

EXERCISE 38

A. *Translate into English*

1. Il pleuvait ce matin. 2. Il pleut tous les jours. 3. Nous parlons de la pluie et du beau temps. 4. Il neigeait hier. La neige blanche couvrait les jardins. 5. Tiens! Il bruine. 6. Il arrive des accidents tous les jours. 7. Il y a un cheval dans la ferme. 8. Il y avait des animaux dans le bois. 9. Il y aura des fleurs dans le jardin. 10. Il y aurait des pommes si les enfants ne les avaient pas mangées.

B. *Translate into English*

1. De quoi s'agit-il? Vous tremblez! 2. Il s'agit de vous, mon bon ami. 3. J'entends dire que vous avez médit de moi! 4. Moi, le faire! Jamais! 5. Vous vous trompez, mon ami. 6. Je vous dis que non. 7. Ne me contredisez pas! 8. Je ne vous contredis pas. 9. C'est vous qui mentez. 10. Ah! c'est trop! La bataille va commencer.

C. *Translate into French*

1. I say what you say. 2. She says (that) yes. 3. He says (that) no. 4. What is wrong? 5. I shall say what I think. 6. Don't say that! 7. They told me when he would come. 8. He says that it will be fine tomorrow. 9. He predicts something possible. 10. Never say too much!

D. *Translate into French*

1. No one predicts what he will do. 2. I am thinking of what you say. 3. What do you say? 4. I say that it is too much. 5. I don't say that. 6. Tell me what you think of him. 7. If I told you what I thought of him, we should regret it. 8. I have heard (to say) that he is ill. 9. People say that he is stronger than his brother. 10. "I shall refuse the invitation," said she.

LESSON 39

The Impersonal Verbs (cont.)

1. The Past Participle never changes after an impersonal verb—

les neiges qu'il a fait	*the snows there have been*
les pluies qu'il y a eu	*the rains there have been*

2. Do not confuse the impersonal verb **il y a,** *there is,* with **voilà,** *there is*—

Il y a un Dieu. *There is a God* (a statement).

Voilà mon ami qui vient. *There is my friend coming* (noun pointed out).

3. The Causative Verb. The French use **faire** where the English use *have*—

I am having a house built. **Je fais bâtir** une maison, literally, *I am causing to be built a house.*

Watch the perfect tenses—

I have had a house built. **J'ai fait bâtir une maison.**

If the action applies to oneself only, the reflexive form is used—

I have had my hair cut. **Je me suis fait couper les cheveux.**
I have had a house built for myself. **Je me suis fait bâtir une maison.**

The Past Participle remains invariable after causative verbs—

La maison que j'ai fait bâtir. *The house that I have had built.*

4. Remember that **il y a** is often used in a time sense—

Combien de temps **y a-t-il** que vous **étudiez** le français? *How long have you been studying French?*

Il y a six mois que je l'étudie. *I have been studying it for six months.*

Note the tense in French.

5. The impersonal verb **falloir,** *it is necessary,* is often used, instead of **il est nécessaire**—

Il faut travailler	*It is necessary to work*
Il me faut travailler	*It is necessary for me to work,* i.e. *I must work*
il fallait	*it was necessary*
Il a fallu refuser	*It has been necessary to refuse*
Il fallut accepter	*It was necessary to accept*
Il faudra se résigner	*It will be necessary to resign oneself*
Il faudrait résister	*It would be necessary to resist*

The Irregular "RE" Verbs

THE "PRENDRE" GROUP

à tout prendre	*all things considered*	
prenant son temps	*taking one's time*	
Il a **pris** son parti	*He has made his decision*	

je **prends**	*I take*	nous **prenons**	*we take*
tu **prends**	*thou dost take*	vous **prenez**	*you take*
il **prend**	*he takes*	ils **prennent**	*they take*
je **pris**	*I took*	nous **prîmes**	*we took*
tu **pris**	*thou didst take*	vous **prîtes**	*you took*
il **prit**	*he took*	ils **prirent**	*they took*
		je **prenais**	*I was taking*
je **prendrai**	*I shall take*	je **prendrais**	*I should take*

The most important of this group are—

apprendre	*to learn*	**méprendre**	*to mistake*
comprendre	*to understand*	**reprendre**	*to take again,* or *reprove*
entreprendre	*to undertake*	**surprendre**	*to surprise*

VOCABULARY FOR EXERCISE 39

bloquer, *to block*   ruiner, *to ruin*
facile, *easy*

EXERCISE 39

A. *Translate into English*

1. Les neiges qu'il a fait ont bloqué le village. 2. Il y a des hommes qui mentent. 3. Voilà notre ami Charles! 4. Je me fais bâtir une maison.

5. Elle s'est fait faire une robe. 6. La robe qu'elle s'est fait faire est belle.
7. Je me suis fait couper les cheveux. 8. Combien de temps y a-t-il que
vous demeurez à Liverpool? 9. Il y a dix mois que je demeure dans
cette ville. 10. Il faut travailler si l'on désire gagner quelque chose.

B. *Translate into English*

1. Il a fallu revenir. 2. Il fallait refuser. 3. Il me fallut accepter.
4. Il leur faudra protester. 5. A tout prendre. 6. Elle a pris son parti.
7. Je prends tout cela. 8. Ils prennent ce qu'ils désirent. 9. Je fus
surpris. 10. J'ai appris trop tard.

C. *Translate into French*

1. I understand. 2. I never have undertaken such things. 3. She is
surprised. 4. It is necessary to fight. 5. He must learn. 6. It is necessary
for us to understand. 7. How long will it be necessary to work? 8. I
have made my decision. 9. She will make up her mind tomorrow (will
make her decision). 10. The more I learn, the easier the work becomes.

D. *Translate into French*

1. Our soldiers have surprised the enemy. 2. I have mistaken the
matter. 3. He undertook too much work. 4. I understand what he
says. 5. Did you understand all she said? 6. It is necessary for me to
learn all that. 7. There are some women who are beautiful. 8. There is
our friend Yvonne! 9. The rains that there have been will ruin the
farmers. 10. We have been living in Edinburgh for three months.

LESSON 40

The Word "to take"

Prendre is used for taking an object up.

It uses **à** to express *from*, also **dans** and **sur**, according to
where the object is when taken—

Il **prend** la lettre **à** la femme, **sur** la table, **dans** sa poche.
*He takes the letter from the woman, from the table, from his
pocket.*

The verbs that mean to take to a place are: **porter**, *to take
a thing*; **mener**, *to take a person or animal*—

Portez la lettre à la femme   *Take the letter to the woman*
Menez votre ami à la ville   *Take your friend to town*

Apporter is *to bring a thing*; **amener**, *to bring a person or animal*—

Apportez du thé	*Bring some tea*
Amenez votre ami	*Bring your friend*

Emporter is *to take away a thing*; **emmener**, *to take away a person or animal*—

Emportez cette lettre	*Take away this letter*
Emmenez cet homme	*Take this man away*

Thus, in tabular form—

	Thing	Person or Animal
to take to	**porter à**	**mener à**
to bring	**apporter**	**amener**
to take away	**emporter**	**emmener**

Watch the double **p** and double **m** in these verbs. If one were transporting a person bodily, **porter,** etc., could be used.

The Question Words

Note the word order after these words—

Pourquoi	*why*	e.g. **Pourquoi votre frère travaille-t-il?** *Why is your brother working?*
Quand	*when*	e.g. **Quand votre mère est-elle partie?** *When did your mother leave?*
Comment	*how*	e.g. **Comment s'appelle votre ami?** *What is your friend's name?*
Où	*where*	e.g. **Où se trouve votre père?** *Where is your father?*
Qui	*who*	e.g. **Qui est-il?** *Who is he?*
Qui	*whom*	e.g. **Qui préférez-vous?** *Whom do you prefer?*
Qu'est-ce qui	*what*	e.g. **Qu'est-ce qui tombe?** *What is falling?*
Que (object)	*what*	e.g. **Que dites-vous?** *What do you say?*

The Irregular "RE" Verbs

THE "METTRE" GROUP

mettre	*to put*		
mettant	*putting*		
j'ai **mis**	*I have put*		
je **mets**	*I put*	nous **mettons**	*we put*
tu **mets**	*thou dost put*	vous **mettez**	*you put*
il **met**	*he puts*	ils **mettent**	*they put*
je **mis**	*I put*	nous **mîmes**	*we put*
tu **mis**	*thou didst put*	vous **mîtes**	*you put*
il **mit**	*he put*	ils **mirent**	*they put*
		je **mettais**	*I was putting*
je **mettrai**	*I shall put*	je **mettrais**	*I should put*

The most important verbs of this group are—

promettre	*to promise*	**soumettre**	*to submit*
permettre	*to permit*	**remettre**	*to remit* or *post-*
commettre un	*to commit a*		*pone*
crime	*crime*	**démettre**	*to dismiss*
omettre	*to omit*	**transmettre**	*to transmit*

Mettre itself can mean *to take time* to do a thing. It must then be followed by **à**—

Il **mit** trois heures **à** le faire. *He took three hours to do it.*

VOCABULARY FOR EXERCISE 40

le délai, *the delay*
le violon, *the violin*
le village, *the village*
la musique, *the music*

la radio, *the radio*
classique, *classic, classical*
fatal, *fatal*

EXERCISE 40

A. *Translate into English*

1. Il mit la lettre à la poste. 2. Il porta la lettre à la poste. 3. Il mena le cheval à la ferme. 4. Elle amena une amie au concert. 5. On a emmené l'homme qui faisait du bruit. 6. Apportez votre violon, et nous aurons de la musique. 7. Quelle musique préférez-vous, le jazz ou la musique classique? 8. Pourquoi le demandez-vous? 9. J'écoute avec plaisir la radio. 10. J'ai pris mon parti. J'étudie la musique.

B. *Translate into English*

1. Qui a donné le lait au chat? Ce n'est pas moi, monsieur. 2. Qu'avez-vous omis? 3. Celui qui commet un crime paie ce qu'il a fait. 4. Où se trouve votre mère? Elle m'a promis des roses. 5. Quand vous les a-t-elle promises? 6. Vous n'allez pas au théâtre ce soir? 7. Mon père ne le permet pas. C'est dommage! 8. Ne remettez jamais ce qu'il vous faut étudier. 9. Pourquoi pas? Le délai est fatal. 10. Elle mit deux heures à nettoyer la chambre.

C. *Translate into French*

1. Take the horse to the village. 2. I have taken my friend to the seaside. 3. She will take her friend to the concert. 4. Take away that letter. 5. She took four hours and a quarter to study it. 6. Where did you put my pen? 7. When did you take it? 8. To whom did you take it? 9. To whom did you promise an apple? 10. Do not omit anything.

D. *Translate into French*

1. If I had the time I should take my friend to the concert. 2. How do you transmit it? 3. What did you say when he spoke to you? 4. Why were you surprised? 5. Where did you put your new shoes? 6. What is your name? I am called Jacques. 7. How long have you been promising me that? 8. If you take that horse away, you will pay for it. 9. Permit me! No, I do not permit that. 10. That old gentleman took five hours to do the work.

LESSON 41

The Word "to be"

1. We have seen that not only **être** but also **faire** can mean *to be*, speaking of the weather; **avoir** means *to be* when speaking of a person in the following instances—

raison (*f.*) e.g.	**J'ai raison**	*I am right*
tort (*m.*)	**J'ai tort**	*I am wrong*
froid (*m.*)	**Il a froid**	*He is cold*
chaud (*m.*)	**Elle a chaud**	*She is warm* (note no **e**)
soif (*f.*)	**Nous avons soif**	*We are thirsty*
faim (*f.*)	**Vous avez faim**	*You are hungry*
honte (*f.*)	**Ils ont honte**	*They are ashamed*

peur (*f.*)	**Elles ont peur**	*They are afraid*
besoin (*m.*)	**Tu as besoin de ces choses**	*Thou art needing these things*
âge (*m.*)	**Quel âge a-t-il? Il a dix ans**	*How old is he? He is ten*
taille (*f.*)	**Quelle taille a-t-il? Il a six pieds**	*How tall is he? He is six feet*

So,   *it is cold* (meaning an object)   il **est** froid
      it is cold (meaning the weather)   il **fait** froid
      he is cold (meaning a person)   il **a** froid

2. **Se trouver**, *to find oneself*, can mean *to be*, referring to the situation of a person or an object—

> Le village **se trouve** à trois milles de la ville. *The village is situated three miles from the town.*
> Il **se trouve** dans le jardin. *He is in the garden.*

3. **Aller**, *to go*, and **se porter**, *to feel*, can mean *to be*, referring to health (see Lesson 42)—

> Comment **allez-**vous? Je **me porte** à merveille. *How are you? I am wonderfully well.*

POINT I. To say, *This summer has been very warm*, put **Il a fait très chaud cet été.**

POINT II. Watch the illness phrases, for particular parts of the body—

> **J'ai mal à la gorge**   *I have a sore throat*
> **J'ai froid aux doigts**   *I have cold fingers*

The Word "wrong"

1. *What is wrong?* **Qu'y a-t-il?**
2. *What is wrong with you?* **Qu'avez-vous?**
Note the use of **avoir** with the *person*.
3. *I took the wrong train.* **Je me suis trompé de train.**
4. *I took the wrong gloves.* **Je me suis trompé de gants.**
5. Distinguish carefully—

> I *am wrong*   **j'ai tort**
> it *is wrong*   **il n'est pas juste**

The Word "for"

1. With future time, **pour** is generally used—

J'irai à Paris **pour** trois mois. *I shall go to Paris for three months.*

Watch for concealment under an apparent past tense—

I was to go to Paris for three months (but did not go). **Il me fallait aller à Paris pour trois mois.**

2. With completely past time use **pendant** or omit altogether—

J'étais à Paris **pendant** trois mois l'année dernière. *I was in Paris for three months last year.*

3. If the time is continued into the present, use **depuis** and a present tense—

Je travaille ici **depuis** trois heures. *I have been working here for three hours.*

The form with **il y** a may be used instead—

Il y a trois heures que je travaille ici

But remember that **il y a** may also mean *ago*. The **que** will help the student to distinguish the two forms.

The Irregular "RE" Verbs

The "Connaître" Group

Connaître, *to know a person or geographical place,* and *to be acquainted with.*

connaissant	*knowing*		
j'ai **connu**	*I have known*		
je **connais**	*I know*	nous **connaissons**	*we know*
tu **connais**	*thou dost know*	vous **connaissez**	*you know*
il **connaît**	*he knows*	ils **connaissent**	*they know*
je **connus**	*I knew*	nous **connûmes**	*we knew*
tu **connus**	*thou didst know*	vous **connûtes**	*you knew*
il **connut**	*he knew*	ils **connurent**	*they knew*
		je **connaissais**	*I used to know*
je **connaîtrai**	*I shall know*	je **connaîtrais**	*I should know*

The most important verbs of this group are—

reconnaître, *to recognize*; **méconnaître,** *to ignore a person.*

ignorer means *not to know a thing or a person*—

    J'ignore cet homme   *I do not know this man*
    J'ignore ce que vous dites *I do not know what you say*

To ignore (*a thing*) is **passer sous silence**; *to ignore* (*a person*) is **méconnaître**—

    Elle **passe sous silence** ce qu'il dit. *She ignores what he says.*

    Elle **méconnaît** son amie. She *slights* her friend.

VOCABULARY FOR EXERCISE 41

l'été (*m.*), *the summer*   boire, *to drink*

EXERCISE 41

A. *Translate into English*

1. Qu'avez-vous? J'ai mal aux mains. 2. Quelle taille avez-vous? J'ai six pieds deux pouces. 3. Quel âge avez-vous? J'ai vingt ans. 4. Il a froid, lui; il désire manger quelque chose. 5. Elle a soif, elle; elle désire quelque chose à boire. 6. Elles avaient peur des animaux à la ferme. 7. J'ai honte de ce que j'ai fait. 8. Il dit que j'ai tort. Que dites-vous? 9. Moi, je dis que vous avez raison. 10. Mon ami avait besoin de mon livre.

B. *Translate into English*

1. Je connais l'homme dont vous parlez. 2. Ma mère ne le connaît pas. 3. Mon père dit qu'il le reconnaît. 4. Celui qui méconnaît ses amis les perdra. 5. En été il fait chaud en Angleterre et nous avons chaud. 6. J'irai à Liverpool pour deux mois. 7. Il y a dix mois j'étais à Newcastle pendant trois semaines. 8. Il y a dix mois que je travaille ici. 9. Il n'a jamais connu Londres. 10. Si je connaissais cette femme je la reconnaîtrais.

C. *Translate into French*

1. One never knows oneself. 2. I recognized your mother at the concert. 3. I do not know that man. 4. She has been studying French for three months. 5. She has a sore throat. 6. Marie has a sore finger. 7. This summer has been warm. 8. The farm is five miles from the town. 9. The iron is cold. 10. It is freezing today. We are cold.

D. *Translate into French*

1. If the weather is cold, I shall catch a chill. 2. If the weather is warm, we shall go the seaside. 3. The farm is situated three miles from the station. 4. We have cold hands. Let us go into the house. 5. I was ashamed of my old book. 6. Were you afraid of the cat? 7. I say you are right (remember **que** = *that*). 8. If we were hungry, we should look for something to eat. 9. There was nothing to drink in the house and they were thirsty. 10. I want what you are needing (remember *that of which*).

LESSON 42

The Word "to be" (cont.)

When inquiring about a person's health, use **aller**, to go, or **se porter**—

> **Comment allez-vous?**
> **Comment vous portez-vous?** } *How are you?*
> **Je vais très bien, merci**
> **Je me porte très bien, merci** } *I am very well, thanks*

The Concealed Tenses

Watch the following words closely—

aussitôt que	*as soon as*	**quand**	*when*
dès que	*as soon as*	**lorsque**	*when*

1. If they are used to denote a habitual action, they take the present tense if the principal clause is present—

> *When I go to London, I always enjoy myself.* **Quand je vais à Londres, je m'amuse toujours.**

2. With habitual action, they take the imperfect, if the principal clause is past—

> *When I went to London, I always used to enjoy myself.* **Quand j'allais à Londres, je m'amusais toujours.**

3. With a single action, they take the future, if the principal clause is future—

> **Quand j'irai à Londres, je m'amuserai.** *When I go to London, I shall enjoy myself.*

4. After reported speech in the past, they take the conditional (if, in direct speech, the main clause would be future)—

Elle dit que lorsqu'elle irait à Londres, elle s'amuserait. *She said that when she went to London she would enjoy herself.*

5. These conjunctions also bring out the big difference between the pluperfect, **j'avais fait,** *I had done,* and the past anterior, **j'eus fait,** *I had done.*

With habitual action, use the pluperfect—

Every day, when I had done my work, she used to enter. **Tous les jours, quand j'avais fait mon travail, elle entrait.**

With a single action, use the past anterior—

One day, when I had done my work, she entered. **Un jour, quand j'eus fait mon travail, elle entra.**

POINT I. Watch for the verbs which take **être** as auxiliary—

One day, when I had entered the house, he spoke. **Un jour, quand je fus entré dans la maison, il parla.**

Every day as soon as I had entered the house, he used to speak. **Tous les jours, aussitôt que j'étais entré dans la maison, il parlait.**

POINT II. If there is no comma after the time noun, it is usual to put **que** for *when* after the word *one*; and to put **où** for *when,* after the word *the*—

One day when he came	**Un jour qu'il vint**
The day when he came	**Le jour où il vint**

Similarly, one says **au moment où,** *at the moment when,* and **juste où,** *just when.*

The Irregular "RE" Verbs
THE "ÉCRIRE" GROUP

écrire	*to write*		
écrivant	*writing*		
j'ai **écrit**	*I have written*		
j'**écris**	*I write*	nous **écrivons**	*we write*
tu **écris**	*thou art writing*	vous **écrivez**	*you write*
il **écrit**	*he writes*	ils **écrivent**	*they write*

j'écrivis	*I wrote*	nous **écrivîmes**	*we wrote*
tu **écrivis**	*thou didst write*	vous **écrivîtes**	*you wrote*
il **écrivit**	*he wrote*	ils **écrivirent**	*they wrote*
		j'écrivais	*I was writing*
j'**écrirai**	*I shall write*	j'écrirais	*I should write*
		écrivons	*let us write*
écris	*write*	**écrivez**	*write*

VOCABULARY FOR EXERCISE 42

l'encre (*f.*), *the ink*
le télégramme, *the telegram*
la poitrine, *the chest, breast*
le médecin, *the doctor*

faire venir, *to send for* (literally *to cause to come*)
bientôt, *soon*
le match de football, *the football match*

EXERCISE 42

A. *Translate into English*

1. Comment vous portez-vous, mon ami? 2. Je me porte très bien, merci. 3. Et vous, monsieur? Assez bien, merci. 4. Et comment va votre frère? Il y a trois semaines qu'il ne me fait visite. 5. Il se porte mal. Il a mal à la poitrine. 6. Il s'est enrhumé le jour où il est allé au match de football. 7. C'est dommage. Avez-vous fait venir le médecin? 8. Oui, il dit que mon frère est très malade. 9. J'espère qu'il ira mieux bientôt. 10. Nous le mènerons au bord de la mer, s'il fait beau.

B. *Translate into English*

1. Aussitôt que j'eus fait mon travail ce jour-là, il sortit. 2. Tous les jours aussitôt que j'avais fait mon travail il sortait. 3. Quand je lui écrirai, je lui dirai les nouvelles. 4. Quand je vais à Édimbourg, je m'amuse toujours. 5. Un soir que j'arrivai tard, il me dit la nouvelle. 6. Qu'avez-vous écrit? J'ai écrit une longue lettre à ma mère. 7. Quelles lettres avez-vous écrites? J'en ai écrit trois. 8. Ils se sont écrit des lettres. 9. Quand je n'avais pas d'argent, j'écrivais un télégramme à mes parents. 10. J'écrivais toujours: "J'ai besoin d'argent. Envoyez-le-moi, s'il vous plaît."

C. *Translate into French*

1. When he writes to his father, he always asks for some money. 2. When he writes to his mother, he will ask for some money. 3. When I was ill, my friends used to write to me. 4. Some of my friends were at the seaside. 5. They used to send me some postcards which they had written. 6. As soon as I wrote the telegram, I sent it to my sister.

7. I hope that she will send me what I want. 8. How are you? 9. I am very well, thank you. 10. How about you? (*say*, and you?). I have a sore hand.

D. *Translate into French*

1. Write to me every day. 2. She says that she will write every day. 3. She says that she will write when she has the time. 4. They said that they would write when they had the time. 5. I need ink. Have you some? 6. I have no ink. 7. I was wanting to write a letter. 8. Have you told the news to your mother? 9. Let us write well. If we write badly, we shall regret it. 10. As soon as she comes, tell her what they say.

LESSON 43

Verbs used with Dependent Infinitives

There are five main groups—

GROUP I. Those that take *no* preposition before an infinitive. The most important are—

aller	*to go*	e.g. **Allez chercher** le médecin. *Go and fetch the doctor.*
venir	*to come*	**Venez cueillir** des fleurs. *Come and gather flowers.*
courir	*to run*	**Courez acheter** le livre. *Run and buy the book.*
faire	*to make*	Il **fit bâtir** une maison. *He had a house built.*
laisser	*to let*	Il **laisse partir** ses amis. *He lets his friends depart.*
préférer	*to prefer*	Il **préfère jouer.** *He prefers to play.*
oser	*to dare*	Il **ose parler.** *He dares to speak.*
sembler	*to seem*	Il **semble être** vrai. *It seems to be true.*
désirer	*to desire*	Il **désire étudier.** *He desires to study.*

pouvoir	*to be able*	**pouvoir patiner,**	*to be able to skate.*
savoir	*to know how*	**savoir patiner,**	*to know how to skate.*
vouloir	*to wish*	**vouloir répéter,**	*to want to repeat.*
devoir	*to have to*	**devoir refuser,**	*to have to refuse.*
aimer mieux	*to prefer*	Il **aime mieux accepter.**	*He prefers to accept.*
espérer	*to hope*	Il **espère réussir.**	*He hopes to succeed.*

The Irregular "RE" Verbs

CROIRE

croire	*to believe*		
croyant	*believing*		
j'ai **cru**	*I have believed*		
je **crois**	*I believe*	nous **croyons**	*we believe*
tu **crois**	*thou art believing*	vous **croyez**	*you believe*
il **croit**	*he believes*	ils **croient**	*they believe*
je **crus**	*I believed*	nous **crûmes**	*we believed*
tu **crus**	*thou didst believe*	vous **crûtes**	*you believed*
il **crut**	*he believed*	ils **crurent**	*they believed*
		je **croyais**	*I was believing*
je **croirai**	*I shall believe*	je **croirais**	*I should believe*
		croyons	*let us believe*
crois	*believe*	**croyez**	*believe*

To believe in is usually **croire à**—

  Elle **croit aux** revenants. *She believes in ghosts.*
  Les paysans **croient aux** esprits malins. *The peasants believe in evil spirits.*

However, **croire en** is used with **Dieu**—

  Nous **croyons** tous **en** Dieu. *We all believe in God.*

The Word "so"

1. After the verbs **espérer,** *to hope,* **croire,** *to believe,* **penser,** *to think,* **dire,** *to say,* **savoir,** *to know,* the word *so* is translated by **le**—

Je l'espère	*I hope so*
Je le crois	*I believe so*

One may also say, **J'espère que oui.**

2. After negative comparisons and exclamations, use **si**—

Elle est **si** gentille!	*She is so kind!*
Elle n'est pas **si** riche que nous	*She is not so rich as we*

3. After a rhetorical question, use **donc**—

Vous ne venez **donc** pas? *So you are not coming?*

4. When *so* means *thus,* or is followed by a comma, use **ainsi**—

So, having done my work **Ainsi,** ayant fait mon travail

EXERCISE 43

A. *Translate into English*

1. Je vais chercher le médecin, parce que ma soeur est malade. 2. Venez cueillir des roses dans le jardin! 3. Courez acheter des pommes. 4. Elle s'est fait bâtir une nouvelle maison. 5. Il a laissé tomber sa montre. 6. Je préférais patiner quand j'étais jeune. 7. Je n'osais leur parler. 8. Il semble être vrai. 9. Désirez-vous rendre visite à Paris? 10. J'aime mieux rester à Liverpool.

B. *Translate into English*

1. Tout le monde croit en Dieu. 2. Quelques paysans croient aux esprits malins. 3. Je connais une femme qui croit aux revenants. 4. A-t-elle honte de ce qu'elle a dit? Je l'espère. 5. Avez-vous tort? Je ne le pense pas. 6. A-t-elle raison? Je ne le crois pas. 7. Dites-vous qu'elle est riche? Je le dis. 8. Vous ne parlez donc pas? 9. Vous n'acceptez donc pas? 10. Elle est si intelligente!

C. *Translate into French*

1. We believe in God. 2. They used to believe in ghosts. 3. Do you think so? 4. I believe so. 5. Do you say so? 6. I hope so. 7. So,

having finished my work, I entered the ⸱
to the cinema. 9. She is not so happy

D. *Translate into French*

1. Go and tell the news to yo⸱
3. It seems to be cold weather to⸱
the boys play. 6. Come and sing with ⸱
her brothers. 8. I believe that it was snow⸱
weather today? 10. I hope so, because we hop⸱

LESSON 44

Verbs which require a Preposition before an Infinitive

GROUP II. The classic nine verbs which take **à** before a person and **de** before an infinitive. These are best learned in three sections.

dire	*to tell*	e.g.	**Je dis à mon ami de venir.**
commander	*to command*		**Je commande aux soldats de venir.**
ordonner	*to order*		**J'ordonne aux étudiants de travailler.**
permettre	*to permit*		**Elle permit à son amie de partir.**
promettre	*to promise*		**Elle promit à son amie de partir.**
persuader	*to persuade*		**Elle persuada à son amie de partir.**
demander	*to ask*		**Il demanda à son fils de le faire.**
conseiller	*to advise*		**Il conseilla à son fils de le faire.**
défendre	*to forbid*		**Il défendit à son fils de le faire.**

The Irregular "RE" Verbs

The "Croître" Group

...e	*to grow*		
...sant	*growing*		
...crû	*he has grown*		
...crois	*I grow*	nous **croissons**	*we grow*
...u **crois**	*thou dost grow*	vous **croissez**	*you grow*
il **croît**	*he grows*	ils **croissent**	*they grow*
je **crûs**	*I grew*	nous **crûmes**	*we grew*
tu **crûs**	*thou didst grow*	vous **crûtes**	*you grew*
il **crût**	*he grew*	ils **crûrent**	*they grew*
		je **croissais**	*I was growing*
je **croîtrai**	*I shall grow*	je **croîtrais**	*I should grow*

Croître is the general word *to grow*. But, if referring to a *person* growing, use **grandir**—

> Elle **grandit** vite. *She is growing quickly.*

For plants, one often uses **pousser**—

> Les fleurs **poussent** vite. *The flowers are growing fast.*

For the transitive verb *to grow*, use **cultiver**—

> Le fermier **cultive** le blé. *The farmer grows wheat.*

When *grow* means *become*, use **devenir**—

> *He is growing lazy.* Il **devient** paresseux.

Note the following—

> *He is growing lazier and lazier.* **Il devient de plus en plus paresseux.**

With parts of the body, use the word *the*, not the possessive adjective. Watch the following—

> *He has lost his life.* Il a perdu **la** vie.
> *His hands are cold.* Il a froid **aux** mains.

It is clear that the life and the hands could only belong to the subject *he* and not to any other person.

But some verbs can refer to other people as well as to ourselves, e.g. *He has cut his hand.* This could mean *his own hand* or *some other man's hand.* If, therefore, the French wrote **il a**

coupé la main, it would not be clear to whose hand we were referring.

To distinguish the two types, we have the following—

(a) *He has cut his hand (his own hand).* **Il s'est coupé la main.**
(b) *He has cut his hand (another's hand).* **Il lui a coupé la main.**

VOCABULARY FOR EXERCISE 44

l'église (*f.*), *the church*
le clocher, *the belfry*
le cimetière, *the churchyard*
tranquille, *quiet*
la sonnette, *bell (little)*
la tête, *the head*

assister à, *to be present at, to attend*
la cloche, *the bell (church)*
sonner, *to ring*
massif, *massive*
la lune, *the moon*

EXERCISE 44

A. *Translate into English*

1. Il y a beaucoup d'églises dans cette ville. 2. Le cimetière de l'église est tranquille. 3. Écoutez les cloches qui commencent. 4. Les cloches se trouvent dans le clocher. 5. J'entends sonner les cloches massives. 6. Le cheval faisait sonner sa sonnette. 7. J'ai promis à mon père d'assister au concert. 8. J'ai persuadé à mon ami de m'accompagner au théâtre. 9. Elle dit à son frère d'apporter toutes les pommes. 10. Le général ordonna aux soldats d'avancer.

B. *Translate into English*

1. Notre mère nous permit d'aller au cinéma. 2. Mon cousin demanda à son père de lui donner une montre. 3. Mon oncle me conseilla de travailler. 4. Sa mère lui défendit d'aller au théâtre. 5. La lune croissait. 6. Les enfants grandissaient vite. 7. Mes roses poussent vite quand il fait beau. 8. Cet étudiant devient de plus en plus diligent. 9. Elle a perdu la tête. 10. Elle s'est coupé la main.

C. *Translate into French*

1. He told his friends to buy some roses. 2. The general ordered his soldiers to advance. 3. We listened to the bells ringing. 4. We asked his mother to accept the invitation. 5. She advised her son to refuse the money. 6. The farmer grows wheat. 7. The wheat is growing fast. 8. The children are growing quickly. 9. Jeanne grows lazy. 10. Marie is becoming more and more jealous.

D. *Translate into French*

1. The churchyard is quiet. 2. We prefer to hear the sweet voices of the children. 3. We like to hear the bells ringing. 4. He persuaded his cousin to attend the concert. 5. She promised her mother to work. 6. But she is becoming lazier and lazier. 7. Did you tell him to write to you? 8. He asked us to write the letters. 9. Marie promised to do what her mother asked her to do. 10. Wheat is grown in France.

LESSON 45

Verbs which take a Preposition "à" before an Infinitive

GROUP III. (*a*) All verbs suggesting keenness to do an action—

aimer	*to like*	**J'aime à patiner.** *I like to skate.*
encourager	*to encourage*	**Je les encourage à étudier.** *I encourage them to study.*
inviter	*to invite*	**Je les invite à venir.** *I invite them to come.*
apprendre	*to learn or teach*	**J'apprends à écrire.** *I learn to write.*
enseigner	*to teach*	**Je leur enseigne à écrire.** *I teach them to write.*
chercher	*to seek*	**Je cherche à découvrir le trésor.** *I seek to find the treasure.*

(*b*) All verbs of beginning, e.g. **commencer,** *to begin—*

Je **commence à** comprendre. *I begin to understand.*

(*c*) All verbs of succeeding, e.g. **réussir,** *to succeed—*

Je **réussis à** obtenir le prix. *I succeed in obtaining the prize.*

(*d*) All verbs of forcing, if two different people are involved, e.g. **forcer,** *to force—*

Je **force mes enfants à** étudier. *I force my children to study.*

The Irregular "RE" Verbs
LIRE

lire	*to read*		
lisant	*reading*		
j'ai **lu**	*I have read*		
je **lis**	*I read*	nous **lisons**	*we read*
tu **lis**	*thou art reading*	vous **lisez**	*you read*
il **lit**	*he reads*	ils **lisent**	*they read*
je **lus**	*I read*	nous **lûmes**	*we read*
tu **lus**	*thou didst read*	vous **lûtes**	*you read*
il **lut**	*he read*	ils **lurent**	*they read*
		je **lisais**	*I was reading*
je **lirai**	*I shall read*	je **lirais**	*I should read*
		lisons!	*let us read!*
lis!	*read!*	**lisez!**	*read!*

Sizes and Dimensions

These can be translated by **avoir** or **être**—

Quelle est la hauteur de ce mur? *What is the height of this wall?*

Ce mur est haut de dix pieds.
Ce mur a dix pieds de haut. } *This wall is ten feet high.*

Quelle est la largeur de cette chambre? *What is the width of this room?*

Cette chambre est large de quinze pieds.
Cette chambre a quinze pieds de large. } *This room is fifteen feet wide.*

Quelle est la longueur de ce pont? *What is the length of this bridge?*

Ce pont est long de cent mètres.
Ce pont a cent mètres de long. } *This bridge is a hundred metres long.*

Quelle est la profondeur de ce puits? *What is the depth of this well?*

Ce puits est profond de cinquante mètres.
Ce puits a cinquante mètres de profond.
This well is fifty metres deep.

Quelle est l'épaisseur de ce mur? *What is the thickness of this wall?*

Ce mur est épais de vingt centimètres.
Ce mur a vingt centimètres d'épais.
This wall is twenty centimetres thick.

In each case the nouns **longueur, profondeur, épaisseur,** etc., could be used instead of the adjectives after **de.**

POINT I. Instead of *What is the height*, etc., English might say *How high*, etc. The French remains the same.

POINT II. If two measurements are involved, they are generally joined by **sur** to translate *by*—

Ce mur a vingt pieds de long **sur** dix pieds de haut. *This wall is twenty feet long by ten feet high.*

VOCABULARY FOR EXERCISE 45

l'Espagne (*f.*), *Spain*   sérieux, *serious*
espagnol, *Spanish*

EXERCISE 45

A. *Translate into English*

1. Il faut encourager les étudiants à travailler. 2. Mes étudiants aiment à faire leur travail. 3. Notre mère a invité nos cousins à nous rendre visite. 4. Ils apprennent à parler français et allemand. 5. Ma sœur apprend à parler espagnol. 6. Elle espère aller en Espagne. 7. Pourquoi n'apprenez-vous pas aussi à parler espagnol? 8. Moi, j'ai assez à faire si j'apprends à parler français. 9. Mon père dit que j'ai raison, mais ma sœur dit que j'ai tort. 10. Le professeur enseigne aux étudiants à penser.

B. *Translate into English*

1. Il cherchait à découvrir ce que je disais. 2. Il commençait à neiger quand nous retournions. 3. Ma soeur a réussi à obtenir le premier prix de français. 4. Son père le forçait à travailler. 5. Ils n'aimaient pas à travailler. 6. Ils préféraient jouer au football et au tennis. 7. Si j'avais votre âge, je ne perdrais pas mon temps à lire de telles choses. 8. Toutes les grandes personnes disent la même chose. 9. Je crois qu'ils ont raison. 10. Moi, je lis des livres sérieux.

C. *Translate into French*

1. I have read that book. 2. They are always reading. 3. "I shall read tomorrow," says the lazy student. 4. Tomorrow never comes. 5. If I had the time, I should read. 6. How high is this house? 7. This house is twenty feet high. 8. How deep is the well? 9. The well is thirty feet deep. 10. How wide is the room?

D. *Translate into French*

1. That bridge is fifty feet long. 2. How thick is the wall? 3. The wall is two feet thick. 4. That house is thirty metres long by twenty-five metres high. 5. Where did you read the news? 6. If we read every day, we learn to understand better. 7. We read the news of the battle. 8. If we read of the heroes of those days, we seek to become heroes. 9. They encourage us to be better. 10. Marie has invited her friends to come to her house.

LESSON 46

Verbs which require Prepositions before an Infinitive

GROUP IV. The following verbs take **de**—

(*a*) All verbs suggesting emotions—

regretter	to regret	**Je regrette de dire.** *I regret to say.*
avoir honte	to be ashamed	**J'ai honte de refuser.** *I am ashamed to refuse.*
avoir peur	to be afraid	**J'ai peur de dire.** *I am afraid to say.*
être heureux	to be happy	**Je suis heureux de noter.** *I am happy to note.*

(b) All verbs suggesting trying—

tâcher
tenter } *to try*
essayer

e.g. **J'essaie de faire de mon mieux.** *I try to do my best.*

(c) All verbs of stopping—

cesser   *to stop*   e.g. **Il cesse de pleuvoir.** *It stops raining.*

empêcher   *to stop someone else doing a thing*   **Empêchez-le de parler.** *Stop him from speaking.*

When reflexive, this verb means *to help (prevent oneself from)*

e.g. **Je ne pouvais m'empêcher de rire.** *I could not help laughing.*

Watch **s'arrêter**, *to stop*, which takes **pour** for *in order to*,

e.g. **Elle s'arrêta pour regarder les bijoux.** *She stopped to look at the jewels.*

But,   **Elle cessa de regarder les bijoux.** *She stopped looking at the jewels.*

(d) All verbs of hurrying—

se dépêcher
se presser }
s'empresser

Il se dépêcha de finir. *He hastened to finish.*

Elle s'empressa de lui parler. *She hurried to speak to him.*

(e) All verbs of offering, refusing, requesting and deserving—

offrir   *to offer*   **J'offre de les accompagner.** *I offer to accompany them.*

refuser   *to refuse*   **Je refuse de les admettre.** *I refuse to admit them.*

prier   *to request*   **Je vous prie de m'excuser.** *I request you to excuse me.*

mériter   *to deserve*   **Il mérite de réussir.** *He deserves to succeed.*

The Irregular "RE" Verbs

THE "CRAINDRE" GROUP

The best way to learn this group is to know the basic endings: **-indre, -ignant, -int, -ins, -ignis.**

Cra- added before these endings gives the verb **craindre.** Similarly, **pla-** gives **plaindre,** *to pity*; **jo-** gives **joindre,** *to join*; **pe-** gives **peindre,** *to paint.*

craindre	*to fear*		
craignant	*fearing*		
j'ai **craint**	*I have feared*		
je **crains**	*I fear*	nous **craignons**	*we fear*
tu **crains**	*thou dost fear*	vous **craignez**	*you fear*
il **craint**	*he fears*	ils **craignent**	*they fear*
je **craignis**	*I feared*	nous **craignîmes**	*we feared*
tu **craignis**	*thou didst fear*	vous **craignîtes**	*you feared*
il **craignit**	*he feared*	ils **craignirent**	*they feared*
		je **craignais**	*I was fearing*
je **craindrai**	*I shall fear*	je **craindrais**	*I should fear*
		craignons!	*let us fear!*
crains!	*fear!*	**craignez!**	*fear!*

VOCABULARY FOR EXERCISE 46

la dame, *the lady*
l'exercice (*m.*), *the exercise*
la page, *the page*
le secret, *the secret*

le visiteur, *the visitor*
révéler, *to reveal*
se plaindre, *to complain*

EXERCISE 46

A. *Translate into English*

1. Je suis content d'entendre dire que vous avez gagné le premier prix. 2. Je regrettais d'être venu si tard. 3. Elle avait honte de révéler ce qu'elle avait fait. 4. Ayant commis un crime il avait peur de revenir en Écosse. 5. J'étais heureux de les entendre chanter. 6. Elle détestait écouter la radio. 7. Ils tâchaient de faire de leur mieux. 8. Il a cessé de neiger. Allons faire un homme de neige. 9. Il s'empressa de révéler le secret. 10. Je ne pouvais m'empêcher de rire.

B. *Translate into English*

1. Il s'arrêta pour regarder le train. 2. Il cessa de regarder le train. 3. Dépêchez-vous de finir votre travail. Nous allons jouer au tennis. 4. Il s'empressa de ramasser le gant que la dame avait laissé tomber. 5. Marie a offert de faire mes exercices pour moi. 6. J'ai refusé de lui permettre de faire une telle chose. 7. Elle a prié les visiteurs d'entrer dans le jardin. 8. Je crains d'admettre ce que j'ai fait. 9. Pourquoi le craignez-vous? 10. Si l'on craint, on n'aime pas.

C. *Translate into French*

1. He joins the two pages. 2. I fear to say. 3. He pities us. 4. We pity him. 5. She likes to paint. 6. She has feared to reveal the secret. 7. I am happy to say. 8. I regret to say. 9. She is ashamed to say. 10. Try to tell us what you have done.

D. *Translate into French*

1. Never fear, and do not complain of the work. 2. I am afraid to refuse. 3. It has stopped raining. Let us go out. 4. The girls were trying to listen to the radio. 5. But the baby was yelling. 6. So they did not succeed in hearing the music. 7. I offered to take the baby to my house. 8. But they refused to accept what I offered. 9. We begged the child to stop crying, but he refused to do so. 10. I am happy to say that he is sleeping now.

LESSON 47

Verbs which take a Preposition before an Infinitive

GROUP IV (cont.). (*f*) All verbs of forcing generally take **de** if there is no other person involved—

Je fus **obligé de** parler. *I was obliged to speak.*

GROUP V. Some verbs take **de** or **à** with widely different meanings—

venir de	*to have just*
venir à	*to happen to*
tenir de	*to take after*
tenir à	*to be anxious to, or to insist on*
jouer de	*to play a musical instrument*

jouer à   *to play a game*
convenir de   *to agree*
convenir à   *to suit*, e.g.—

Je **viens de** compléter mon travail. *I have just completed my work.*

Je **venais de** compléter mon travail. *I had just completed my work.*

Il **vint à** tomber. *He happened to fall.*

Je **tiens de** mon père. *I take after my father.*

Je **tiens à** le faire. *I insist on doing it, or I am anxious to do it.*

Il **convient d'**accepter. *He agrees to accept.*

Il **convient à** mon frère. *It suits my brother.*

Observe that **convenir de** takes **être**, **convenir à** takes **avoir** in the perfect tense.

GROUP VI. The word *by* is translated by **par** and the infinitive with all verbs of beginning, continuing, and ending—

commencer *to begin*   Elle **commença par** jouer. *She began by playing.*

continuer *to continue* Elle **continua par** chanter. *She continued by singing.*

finir   *to finish*   Elle **finit par** réciter. *She finally recited* (literally, *She finished by reciting*).

Do not confuse the above with—

> **commencer à**   *to begin to*
> **continuer à**   *to continue to*
> **finir de**   *to finish doing an action*

Most other verbs express the word *by* by means of **en** and the present participle, e.g.—

Elle répondit **en** levant le bras. *She replied by lifting her arm.*

The Word "since" as a Conjunction

If *since* denotes reason, put **puisque**—

since you refuse to come   **puisque** vous refusez de venir

If *since* denotes time put **depuis que**—

Since she has gone away, the house is different. **Depuis qu'**elle est partie, la maison est différente.

The conjunction **depuis que** can often be replaced by the preposition **depuis** if a noun follows—

since she has gone away, **depuis** son départ (*literally, since her departure*).

The Irregular "RE" Verbs

VIVRE

vivre	*to live*		
vivant	*living* (often used as a masculine noun: de son **vivant,** *in his lifetime*; du **vivant** du roi, *in the king's lifetime*)		
j'ai **vécu**	*I have lived*		
je **vis**	*I live*	nous **vivons**	*we live*
tu **vis**	*thou art living*	vous **vivez**	*you live*
il **vit**	*he lives*	ils **vivent**	*they live*
je **vécus**	*I lived*	nous **vécûmes**	*we lived*
tu **vécus**	*thou didst live*	vous **vécûtes**	*you lived*
il **vécut**	*he lived*	ils **vécurent**	*they lived*
		je **vivais**	*I was living*
je **vivrai**	*I shall live*	je **vivrais**	*I should live*

Note the conjunction **tant que,** *as long as*, often seen in this connexion with the future tense—

tant que je vivrai   *as long as I live*

Note the conjunction **quand même,** *even if*, often used in this connexion with the conditional tense—

Quand même je vivrais cent ans, je ne les aimerais pas. *Even if I were to live a hundred years, I should not like them.*

Sometimes the **quand même** is omitted, and the word **que** put between the two clauses. Watch for this to occur in examinations—

Je vivrais cent ans **que** je ne les aimerais pas. *Even if I lived a hundred years, I should not like them.*

Distinguish

	vivre, *to live*	e.g. Il **vit** de choux. *He lives on cabbages.*
from	**demeurer,** *to dwell*	e.g. Il **demeure** à Glasgow. *He lives in Glasgow.*
and	**habiter,** *to live in*	e.g. Il **habite** une grande maison. *He lives in a big house.*

VOCABULARY FOR EXERCISE 47

l'ancêtre (*m.* or *f.*), *the ancestor*   la condition, *the condition*
la chanson, *the song*

EXERCISE 47

A. *Translate into English*

1. Quand le fils de Napoléon naquit, on crut d'abord qu'il ne vivait pas. 2. Mais une dame dit: "Il vit, Madame." 3. Du vivant de nos ancêtres, on croyait aux esprits malins. 4. Mon ami est allé demeurer à Édimbourg. 5. Elle habite une petite maison au bord de la mer. 6. Elle vit de poisson. 7. Tant que je vivrai, je penserai à ce que vous avez fait pour moi. 8. Quand même elle vivrait cent ans, elle n'apprendrait pas à parler allemand. 9. Je fus obligé de faire de mon mieux. 10. Elle vivrait quatre-vingts ans qu'elle n'apprendrait pas à jouer au tennis.

B. *Translate into English*

1. Je viens d'entendre des nouvelles intéressantes. 2. Elle venait de refuser l'invitation. 3. Il vint à tomber. 4. Mon cousin tient de son père. 5. Elle tient à faire de son mieux. 6. Nous jouions au football. 7. Elle jouait du piano et sa soeur jouait du violon. 8. Je conviens d'accepter les conditions. 9. Ce chapeau convient à votre soeur. 10. Si nous allions au théâtre? J'en conviens.

C. *Translate into French*

1. In our lifetime. 2. He lives on bread. 3. My brother lives in Newcastle. 4. He lives in a large house. 5. As long as I live, I shall regret it. 6. Since you went away, we have not been happy. 7. Since you insist on going to the cinema, we shall not try to stop you. 8. Even if he lived a hundred years he would not be rich. 9. She replied by lifting her hand. 10. He began by playing the piano.

D. *Translate into French*

1. She began to sing a song. 2. She continued by playing the violin. 3. He continued to read. 4. He ended by refusing to do what he promised us to do. 5. He stopped speaking. 6. He stopped to look at the shoes. 7. My brother was compelled to pay the money. 8. I have just refused to speak to them. 9. I had just arrived when she entered the house. 10. How about going to the concert? We agree.

LESSON 48

The Adverbs

The ending **-ment** corresponds to the English ending *-ly*; **-ment** is added to adjectives, according to their endings.

GROUP I. Adjectives that end in a vowel add **-ment** to the masculine singular—

facile, *easy*; **facilement,** *easily*.

GROUP II. Adjectives that end in a consonant generally add **-ment** to the feminine singular—

heureux, *happy*; **heureusement,** *happily*

GROUP III. Adjectives that end in **-nt** change the last two letters into **-mment**—

bruyant, *noisy*; **bruyamment,** *noisily*.
prudent, *prudent*; **prudemment,** *prudently*.

There are so many exceptions to these rules, however, that it is just as well for the student to remember the following phrase, **d'une manière.** Whenever in doubt add the feminine form of the adjective to this phrase, e.g. *coarsely,* **d'une manière grossière.** Similarly **d'une façon** is used.

Adverbs of Time

après-demain	*the day after tomorrow*	**demain**	*tomorrow*
aujourd'hui	*today*	**hier**	*yesterday*
avant-hier	*the day before yesterday*	**à l'avenir**	*in the future*
par le passé	*in the past*	**désormais**	*from now on*
jusqu'ici	*up to now*	**maintenant**	*now*
jamais	*ever* or *never*		

The following examples show the use of **jamais,** with or without a negative—

Avez-vous **jamais** joué?	*Have you ever played?*
N'avez-vous **jamais** joué?	*Have you never played?*

Watch the word **bientôt,** *soon.* When modified by another adverb, it becomes **tôt**—

trop tôt	*too soon*	**si tôt**	*so soon*
très tôt	*very soon*	**plus tôt**	*sooner*

Do not confuse **plus tôt,** *sooner,* with **plutôt,** *rather.*

Aussitôt, *immediately,* should be distinguished from **aussitôt que,** *as soon as.*

Watch the following—

tôt ou tard	*sooner or later*
à bientôt	*see you soon*
le plus tôt sera le mieux	*the sooner, the better*

aussitôt dit, aussitôt fait	
aussitôt dit que fait	*no sooner said than done*
sitôt dit, sitôt fait	
sitôt dit que fait	

The Irregular "RE" Verbs

Naître

naître	*to be born*
naissant	*being born* (cf. **le jour naissant,** *the dawning day*)
je **suis né**	*I was born*
j'**étais né**	*I had been born* } Watch the meanings of these two

je **nais**	*I am born*	nous **naissons**	*we are born*
tu **nais**	*thou art born*	vous **naissez**	*you are born*
il **naît**	*he is born*	ils **naissent**	*they are born*

je **naquis**	*I was born*	nous **naquîmes**	*we were born*
tu **naquis**	*thou wert born*	vous **naquîtes**	*you were born*
il **naquit**	*he was born*	ils **naquirent**	*they were born*

		je **naissais**	*I was being born*
je **naîtrai**	*I shall be born*	je **naîtrais**	*I should be born*

VOCABULARY FOR EXERCISE 48

se disputer, *to dispute*
blâmer, *to blame*
poli, *polite*
italien, *Italian*

ridicule, *ridiculous*
courageusement, *bravely*
tranquillement, *quietly*
stupidement, *foolishly*

EXERCISE 48

A. *Translate into English*

1. Elle a choisi prudemment. 2. Ils se disputaient bruyamment. 3. Elle a vécu heureusement. 4. Elle a parlé d'une façon ridicule. 5. Cet homme n'est pas poli, il a parlé d'une façon grossière à ces femmes. 6. Après-demain la nouvelle de la bataille arrivera. 7. Demain soir je rendrai visite à ma tante. 8. A l'avenir je ne me fierai pas à de tels hommes. 9. Je serai plus prudent à l'avenir que par le passé. 10. Avez-vous jamais étudié l'italien?

B. *Translate into English*

1. Désormais je refuserai de payer. 2. Je n'ai jamais dit cela. 3. Jusqu'ici tout va bien. 4. Maintenant ils désirent vivre tranquillement. 5. Les blâmez-vous? Pas moi! Jamais! 6. Tôt ou tard tout le monde sera satisfait. 7. Elle est venue trop tôt. 8. Le plus tôt sera le mieux. 9. Sont-elles parties si tôt? 10. Aussitôt dit, aussitôt fait.

C. *Translate into French*

1. "See you soon," said my friend. 2. I was born in Liverpool. 3. When were you born? 4. I was born in 1940. 5. I shall come soon. 6. Come at once. 7. The sooner, the better. 8. Yesterday I won, today I have lost. 9. The day before yesterday it was warm. 10. Today it is cold.

D. *Translate into French*

1. She was living happily in London. 2. They spoke foolishly. 3. The boys were playing noisily. 4. Soon, we shall hear the news. 5. My brother will arrive tomorrow. 6. Today it is necessary to think of the future. 7. From now on they will live happily. 8. Up to now they have tried bravely. 9. Sooner or later he will tell what he has done. 10. He will never admit it. Do you think so?

LESSON 49

Adverbs of Time (cont.)

Watch the use of **la fois** for numerical time—

une fois	*once*
dix fois	*ten times*
il y avait une fois	*there was once*
plusieurs fois	*several times*
la prochaine fois	*the next time*
la dernière fois	*the last time*
une fois pour toutes	*once and for all*
chaque fois	*each time*
toutes les fois que	*whenever*
à la fois	*at the same time*
	(in the sense of *both*)

Examples—

Il était **à la fois** riche et intelligent. *He was both rich and intelligent.*

Note the compounds of **fois**—

quelquefois	*sometimes*
autrefois	*formerly*
parfois	*at times*
toutefois	*nevertheless*

When the time is not numerical, use **temps**—

de temps en temps	*from time to time*
tout le temps	*all the time* (Do not confuse with **toutefois,** meaning *nevertheless*)
en même temps	*at the same time*—

Il lisait un livre; **en même temps** elle écoutait la radio. *He was reading a book; at the same time she was listening to the radio.*

autres temps, autres mœurs *other times, other manners*

Distinguish carefully—

toujours	*always*
rarement	*seldom*
souvent	*often*

Remember that **longtemps** means *long* in speaking of time, whereas **long** means *long* in speaking of distance—

Il y a **longtemps** que je ne vous ai vu. *I have not seen you for a long time.*

Watch the words **tard** and **en retard** for *late*. In speaking of the time of the day, use **tard**—

| Il est **tard** | It is late |
| Il se fait **tard** | It is becoming late |

But in speaking of a person with the verb **être**, use **en retard**—

Elle est **en retard**   *She is late*

With any other verb than **être** one generally uses **tard**—

Elle travaille **tard**   *She works late*

But if the meaning is *behind time*, one may equally well use **en retard**—

Il arrive **en retard**   *or*   Il arrive **tard**

Distinguish carefully—

| **aujourd'hui en huit** | *a week from today* |
| **il y a huit jours aujourd'hui** | *a week ago today* |

The Irregular "RE" Verbs

BATTRE

battre	*to beat*
battant	*beating*
j'ai **battu**	*I have beaten*

je **bats**	*I beat*	nous **battons**	*we beat*
tu **bats**	*thou art beating*	vous **battez**	*you beat*
il **bat**	*he beats*	ils **battent**	*they beat*

je **battis**	*I beat*	nous **battîmes**	*we beat*
tu **battis**	*thou didst beat*	vous **battîtes**	*you beat*
il **battit**	*he beat*	ils **battirent**	*they beat*

		je **battais**	*I was beating*
je **battrai**	*I shall beat*	je **battrais**	*I should beat*
		battons	*let us beat*
bats	*beat*	**battez**	*beat*

The most important of this group are **débattre,** *to debate* and
se débattre, *to wriggle or struggle*—

Les serpents **se débattent.** *The snakes writhe.*

Les hommes **se débattaient** dans l'eau. *The men were
floundering in the water.*

also,

combattre, *to fight.*
abattre, *to fell a tree* and **s'abattre,** *to alight (of a bird).*
rabattre, *to reduce the price, beat down, pull down (a hat) over
the face.*

VOCABULARY FOR EXERCISE 49

la fortune, *the fortune*
le prince, *the prince*
la princesse, *the princess*
l'aviateur (*m.*), *aviator*

le record, *the record (in sport)*
le (paquebot) transatlantique,
  the transatlantic liner

EXERCISE 49

A. *Translate into English*

1. Le transatlantique anglais a battu le record. 2. Les serpents se
débattaient dans le puits. 3. Les hommes se débattaient dans l'eau.
4. L'oiseau s'abattit sur un arbre. 5. Il avait le chapeau rabattu. 6. Je
vous dis une fois pour toutes. 7. Ce n'est pas la première fois. 8. Il y
avait une fois un prince qui aimait une princesse. 9. Il était à la fois
aviateur et acteur. 10. Je pense quelquefois aux soldats qui ont combattu
courageusement.

B. *Translate into English*

1. Autrefois il avait une fortune; maintenant il n'a rien. 2. Elle
était à Paris tout le temps. 3. De temps en temps nous nous arrêtions
pour écouter. 4. Sa tante qui a toujours demeuré à Londres est riche.
5. Il lui a souvent fait visite. 6. On admire rarement de telles choses.
7. Cette fois j'accepte; la prochaine fois je refuserai. 8. Elle cueillait
des roses dans le jardin; en même temps il écrivait une lettre. 9. Il y a
longtemps que nous ne leur avons parlé. 10. Il se fait tard. Il faut se
dépêcher.

C. *Translate into French*

1. I was beating the other students. 2. A week from today we shall
hear the news. 3. A week ago today we finished our work. 4. It is

late. It is necessary to hurry. 5. It is the last time. 6. They are late.
7. She is working late. 8. At times she thinks of her brothers. 9. Sometimes we fear to say what we think. 10. She tried three times.

D. *Translate into French*

1. The students were debating. 2. The general fought the enemy.
3. The soldiers fought bravely. 4. They deserved to succeed. 5. A
week from today we shall be in London. 6. Several times we have been
in Edinburgh. 7. We were once in Liverpool. 8. Next time we shall
go to Newcastle. 9. Each time he tries to write, she listens to the radio.
10. He seldom goes out.

LESSON 50

Adverbs of Place

The following are the principal adverbs of place—

ici	*here*
là	*there*
çà et là	*here and there*
par ici	*this way*
par là	*that way*
ici-bas	*here below, in this world*
là-bas	*over there* or *down there*
là-haut	*upstairs* or *up there*
en haut	*upstairs* (e.g. **Où est-il? Il est en haut.** *Where is he? He is upstairs.*)
en bas	*downstairs*

Do not confuse with the phrase *to look up*—

Il leva les yeux
Il leva le front } *He looked up*
Il leva la tête

Il baissa les yeux
Il baissa le front } *He looked down*
Il baissa la tête

Watch the *where* group—

où	*where*
partout	*everywhere*
nulle part	*nowhere* (e.g. **Je ne les ai trouvés nulle part.** *I have not found them anywhere.*)
quelque part	*somewhere*
ailleurs	*elsewhere*

Do not confuse **ailleurs** with **d'ailleurs,** *besides*.

Note the addition of **où** in the following—

là où il y a un nid	*(there) where there is a nest*
partout où il va	*everywhere he goes*

Watch the spelling of—

Tout droit, *straight on,* and do not confuse with **à droite,** *to the right;* **à gauche,** *to the left.*

Note that the irregular verbs **frire,** *to fry,* **cuire,** *to cook,* and **bouillir,** *to boil,* are often seen after **faire** if a person is the subject—

elle **fait cuire** la viande	*she cooks the meat*
elle **fait bouillir** l'eau	*she boils the water*

Otherwise, **faire** is not used—

La viande **cuit**	*The meat is cooking*
L'eau **bout**	*The water is boiling*

The Irregular "RE" Verbs
BOIRE

boire	*to drink*		
buvant	*drinking*		
j'ai **bu**	*I have drunk*		
je **bois**	*I drink*	nous **buvons**	*we drink*
tu **bois**	*thou art drinking*	vous **buvez**	*you drink*
il **boit**	*he drinks*	ils **boivent**	*they drink*
je **bus**	*I drank*	nous **bûmes**	*we drank*
tu **bus**	*thou didst drink*	vous **bûtes**	*you drank*
il **but**	*he drank*	ils **burent**	*they drank*

9—(F.130)

		je **buvais**	I was drinking
je **boirai**	I shall drink	je **boirais**	I should drink
		buvons!	let us drink!
bois!	drink!	**buvez!**	drink!

The Word "country"

La patrie, the homeland, is often used in patriotic language—

Le drapeau et **la patrie**   The flag and the homeland

Le pays, the country, is used in an ordinary sense—

L'Écosse est un beau **pays**   Scotland is a beautiful country
L'Angleterre est un **pays** riche   England is a rich country

La campagne is used for the rural part of a country as distinct from the town—

Elle demeure à la **campagne**; moi, je demeure en ville.
She lives in the country; I stay in town.

La contrée and **la région** denote district.

VOCABULARY FOR EXERCISE 50

le trésor, *the treasure*	la rue, *the street*
le verre, *the glass*	l'Allemagne (*f.*), *Germany*
la cathédrale, *the cathedral*	la santé, *the health*
la rivière, *the river*	

EXERCISE 50

A. *Translate into English*

1. Pardon, monsieur, où est la cathédrale? 2. C'est la troisième rue à gauche. 3. Allez tout droit et vous arriverez à la cathédrale. 4. Par ici, madame. Le concert va commencer. 5. Est-il en haut ou en bas? 6. Elle leva les yeux. 7. Il baissa la tête. 8. Partout où l'on va, on trouve de belles choses. 9. Là où il y a un vieil arbre se trouve un trésor. 10. Elle fait cuire les pommes de terre.

B. *Translate into English*

1. Il buvait de la limonade. 2. Nous aimons à boire le vin. 3. Il a bu trois verres de lait. 4. Ils boivent à la santé du héros. 5. La patrie a besoin de nous. 6. La France est un pays charmant. 7. L'Allemagne est un pays intéressant. 8. Mon ami préfère la ville à la campagne. 9. Elle fait bouillir l'eau. 10. La viande est assez cuite maintenant.

C. *Translate into French*

1. Excuse me, sir, where is the station? 2. It is the first street to the right. 3. Here and there one finds flowers. 4. Down there was the farm. 5. She looked up when he entered. 6. We shall drink to the health of the hero. 7. In England people drink tea. 8. In France people drink coffee or chocolate. 9. I drink only the water of the river. 10. He looked down.

D. *Translate into French*

1. The country needs you. 2. England is a fine country. 3. The soldiers fight for their homeland. 4. Spain is the country that he loves. 5. Marie does not like the country. 6. There are too many trees. 7. She prefers the town, where there are plenty of shops. 8. Go straight on, and you will come to the farm. 9. Three miles to the right. 10. He drank all the lemonade.

LESSON 51

Adverbs (concluded)

The word *quite* may generally be translated by **tout à fait**—

Elle est **tout à fait** contente   *She is quite happy*

But the word **tout** may also be used in this sense.
It will remain **tout** before all adjectives except those which are feminine and begin with a consonant or aspirate **h**—

Elle est **toute** contente	*She is quite happy*
Elles sont **toutes** contentes	*They are quite happy*
Elle est **toute** honteuse	*She is quite ashamed*
Elles sont **toutes** honteuses	*They are quite ashamed*

But Elle est **tout** étonnée   *She is quite astonished*

Elles sont **tout** étonnées   *They are quite astonished*

because **étonnée** begins with a vowel.

Distinguish carefully—

Ils sont **tout** confus	*They are quite confused*
and Ils sont **tous** confus	*They are all confused*

Some adjectives are used as adverbs, and, as such, they remain invariable—

Elles paient **cher**	*They pay dear*
Les fleurs sentent **bon**	*The flowers smell sweet*
La neige tombe **dru**	*The snow falls fast*

The Regular "OIR" Verbs

The best way to learn these verbs is to know the endings—

-cevoir	Then add	**re** for **recevoir**	*to receive*
-cevant		**per** for **percevoir**	*to collect (as of taxes)*
-çu		**aper** for **apercevoir**	*to perceive (with the eye)*
-çois		**dé** for **décevoir**	*to deceive*
-çus		**con** for **concevoir**	*to conceive*

Also **s'apercevoir de,** *to perceive mentally, sense, become aware of.*

recevoir	*to receive*		
recevant	*receiving*		
j'ai **reçu**	*I have received*		
je **reçois**	*I receive*	nous **recevons**	*we receive*
tu **reçois**	*thou art receiving*	vous **recevez**	*you receive*
il **reçoit**	*he receives*	ils **reçoivent**	*they receive*
je **reçus**	*I received*	nous **reçûmes**	*we received*
tu **reçus**	*thou didst receive*	vous **reçûtes**	*you received*
il **reçut**	*he received*	ils **reçurent**	*they received*
		je **recevais**	*I was receiving*
je **recevrai**	*I shall receive*	je **recevrais**	*I should receive*
		recevons!	*let us receive!*
reçois!	*receive!*	**recevez!**	*receive!*

The phrase *it is*, when followed by an adjective, takes **de** before an infinitive—

Il est difficile de faire cela	*It is difficult to do that*
Il est prudent de refuser	*It is prudent to refuse*

But in conversational passages, one often finds **c'est** used instead of **il est,** and generally **à** instead of **de**—

C'est facile à lire	*It's easy to read*

VOCABULARY FOR EXERCISE 51

le danger, *the danger*   mystérieux, *mysterious*
la télévision, *the television*   satisfait, *satisfied*
désert, *deserted*

EXERCISE 51

A. *Translate into English*

1. Elles étaient tout à fait surprises. 2. Il était tout étonné de les entendre. 3. Elle était tout étonnée de les entendre. 4. Elle était toute confuse. 5. Mes cousines étaient toutes confuses, quand leur mère les trouva. 6. Elles regardaient la télévision et elles avaient tant de travail à faire. 7. Elles paieront cher ce qu'elles ont fait. 8. Les roses sentent bon. 9. Elles sentent plus bon que les autres. 10. La neige tombait dru quand nous arrivions à la gare. Quelle nuit!

B. *Translate into English*

1. J'ai reçu quelque chose de bon. 2. Le pauvre petit ne reçoit jamais rien. 3. S'ils reçoivent ce que leur père leur a promis, ils seront tout heureux. 4. Si elle recevait une nouvelle robe, elle serait toute contente. 5. Tant que je recevrai de tels cadeaux, je serai content de travailler dur. 6. Elle perçut quelque chose de mystérieux quand elle entra dans la maison déserte à minuit. 7. J'aperçois que vous avez fini de travailler. 8. Je ne conçois pas pourquoi il fait de telles choses. 9. Elle a déçu ses meilleures amies. 10. Celui qui reçoit un tel prix le mérite bien.

C. *Translate into French*

1. I have received. 2. They were deceiving their friends. 3. I perceive the bridge down there. 4. She perceived her error. 5. We sense the danger. 6. She is quite happy. 7. The farmers were quite satisfied. 8. They are all happy. 9. These flowers cost dear. 10. I have paid dear.

D. *Translate into French*

1. They used to receive their friends every day. 2. She perceived a bird in the tree. 3. She sensed something mysterious in the old house. 4. Even if I received your letter today it would be too late. 5. It is easy to talk. 6. It is difficult to do. 7. It is possible to do better. 8. It is dangerous to trust those men. 9. She received a present from her father. 10. Let us receive him now.

LESSON 52

The Prepositions

All of these, except **en,** are followed by the infinitive. Apart from their normal meanings, the prepositions can have different meanings according to the context.

The Preposition "à"

à normally means *to* or *at*—

à la poste	*to (at) the post-office*
à Newcastle	*at (to) Newcastle*

But **à** can also mean *in* instead of **dans,** the normal word for *in*; **à** denotes vagueness—

> **au** jardin   *in the garden (somewhere)*

With the *take* group of verbs **à** means *from*—

Je les ai pris **au** facteur   *I have taken them from the postman*

Speaking of a wall, etc., **à** means *on*—

Le tableau était suspendu **au** mur.   *The picture was hanging on the wall.*

Sur means *on the top of*—

> **sur** le parapet   *on the parapet*

Note **au haut du mur**   *on the top of the wall*

à can mean *by* in speaking of hiring a vehicle—

> prendre un taxi **à** l'heure   *to take a taxi by the hour*

à is used after adjectives denoting readiness, fitness, or inclination—

Elle est **prête à** partir. *She is ready to leave.*
Elle est **propre à** faire cela. *She is fit to do that.*
Elle est **encline à** devenir paresseuse. *She is inclined to become lazy.*

à is often used in a compound preposition, e.g. **au lieu de,**
instead of; **à l'insu de,** *unknown to*; **à cause de,** *on account of*;
à l'abri de, *in the shelter of, protected from*; **à raison de,** *at the
rate of*; **à côté de,** *beside*—

> **au lieu de lire**   *instead of reading*
> Il a fumé des cigarettes **à l'insu de** son père. *He has smoked
>   cigarettes, unknown to his father.*
> **à cause de** la pluie, *on account of the rain*
> Elle était **à l'abri du** vieux pommier. *She was in the shade
>   of the old apple tree.*
> Elle est **à l'abri du** danger. *She is safe from the danger.*
> **à raison de** vingt francs par jour, *at the rate of twenty francs
>   per day.*
> **à côté de** la rivière, *beside the river.*

à often occurs before an infinitive starting a sentence, with
the same meaning as in English—

> **à** vous entendre, on croirait, *to hear you, one would think.*

The Irregular "OIR" Verb
Voir

voir	*to see*		
voyant	*seeing* (often used as an adjective to mean *showy*, e.g.		
	la cravate **voyante,** *the loud tie*)		
j'ai **vu**	*I have seen*		
je **vois**	*I see*	nous **voyons**	*we see*
tu **vois**	*thou art seeing*	vous **voyez**	*you see*
il **voit**	*he sees*	ils **voient**	*they see*
je **vis**	*I saw*	nous **vîmes**	*we saw*
tu **vis**	*thou didst see*	vous **vîtes**	*you saw*
il **vit**	*he saw*	ils **virent**	*they saw*
		je **voyais**	*I used to see*
je **verrai**	*I shall see*	je **verrais**	*I should see*
		voyons!	*let us see!*
vois!	*see!*	**voyez!**	*see!*

VOCABULARY FOR EXERCISE 52

l'auto (*f.*), *the motor-car*   le bouquin, *the old book*
l'automobile (*f.*), *the motor-car*   le millionnaire, *the millionaire*

EXERCISE 52

A. *Translate into English*

1. J'ai pris la lettre à la poste. 2. J'ai acheté l'auto à mon ami. 3. Le miroir était suspendu au mur. 4. Sur le parapet, il y avait de vieux livres, qu'on appelle des "bouquins". 5. Au haut du mur on voyait un chat blanc. 6. Le millionnaire américain a pris le taxi à la journée. 7. Nous sommes prêts à vous aider. 8. Mon père était enclin à penser que je ne travaillais pas. 9. Au lieu de me croire, il écoutait ce que disait mon professeur. 10. A l'insu de sa mère, elle fit visite à la vieille femme.

B. *Translate into English*

1. A cause du tonnerre nous sommes restés à la maison. 2. Elles étaient à l'abri de la maison. 3. Elle était à l'abri du danger. 4. Il gagne à raison de mille francs par jour. 5. A côté du pont je vis des animaux. 6. A vous voir danser, on dirait que vous étiez heureux. 7. Je suis tout à fait heureux. 8. Cette cravate est trop voyante. 9. Une fois il vit un serpent à côté de la maison. 10. Mon fils a fait cela à mon insu.

C. *Translate into French*

1. I see what you wish to say. 2. Even if I saw such a thing, I should not believe it. 3. When I see him, I shall tell him what you have done. 4. Let us see! 5. I used to see them every day. 6. They seldom see us now. 7. If I saw him, I should know him. 8. To see you dancing, one would think you were pleased. 9. Do not believe all you see. 10. I have never seen such a thing.

D. *Translate into French*

1. The coat was hanging on the wall. 2. I am ready to believe what I see. 3. If he saw your work, you would not receive a prize. 4. I did it unknown to my father. 5. When he sees it, he will not be pleased with you (*say*, of you). 6. On account of the rain, I went away sooner. 7. Sooner or later she will see what you have done. 8. Beside the garden was an old tree. 9. Instead of blaming the boy, he was happy to see his work. 10. I am inclined to think that you do not see the danger.

LESSON 53

The Preposition "de"

de normally means *of*—

    un kilo **de** beurre   *a kilo of butter* (2 *lb.* 2 *oz.*)

But it is commonly used also to translate *in* in the following phrases: **d'une manière**, *in a manner*; **d'une façon**, *in a fashion*; **d'un ton**, *in a tone*; **d'une voix**, *in a voice*; **de nos jours**, *in our time*.

In the phrase **d'un pas**, **de** means *at*—

            d'un pas rapide   *at a rapid pace*

de can mean *from* in time phrases—

        de jour en jour   *from day to day*
        d'heure en heure   *from hour to hour*

Do not confuse this with the expression—

    vivre **au jour le jour**   *to live from hand to mouth*

Both **de** and **à** can translate *with*—

1. **de** can mean *with*—

    La boîte était remplie **de** pommes. *The box was filled with apples.*

Observe that the word for *some* is omitted—

    La table était couverte **de** papier. *The table was covered with paper.*

    La gare fourmillait **de** gens. *The station was swarming with people* (**la fourmi**, *the ant*).

    La rivière était obstruée **de** pierres. *The river was obstructed with stones.*

    Il nous a comblés **de** bienfaits. *He has overwhelmed us with kindnesses.*

If you see the word *the* in English after *with*, remember to use the contracted forms—

    La boîte était remplie **des** pommes. *The box was filled with the apples.*

    La table était couverte **du** papier. *The table was covered with the paper.*

2. **à** means *with* when you are describing a person's features or clothing—

l'homme **à** la balafre	*the man with the scar*
la jeune fille **aux** yeux bleus	*the girl with the blue eyes*
l'homme **aux** cheveux roux	*the man with the red hair*
le vieillard **aux** dents cariées	*the old man with the bad teeth*
l'homme **au** long habit noir	*the man with the long black coat*

CAUTION. If the descriptive phrase follows a verb, leave the word *with* untranslated—

> *The girl entered with her head lowered.* **La jeune fille entra, la tête baissée.**

The Irregular "OIR" Verbs

DEVOIR

devoir	*to owe*
devant	*owing*
j'ai **dû**	*I have owed*

je **dois**	*I owe*	nous **devons**	*we owe*
tu **dois**	*thou dost owe*	vous **devez**	*you owe*
il **doit**	*he owes*	ils **doivent**	*they owe*
je **dus**	*I owed*	nous **dûmes**	*we owed*
tu **dus**	*thou didst owe*	vous **dûtes**	*you owed*
il **dut**	*he owed*	ils **durent**	*they owed*
		je **devais**	*I was owing*
je **devrai**	*I shall owe*	je **devrais**	*I should owe*
		devons!	*let us owe!*
dois!	*owe!*	**devez!**	*owe!*

Devoir also means *to be supposed to*, or *to have to*. The following are examples of this use—

je dois chanter	*I am to sing, I have to sing, I must sing*
je devais chanter	*I was to sing, I had to sing*
je devrais chanter	*I ought to sing*

To understand the perfect tenses easily, just remember that **dû** = *had to*.

So, if you are asked for *I have had to work*, break the sentence into the parts—

I have | had to | work
J'ai   dû   travailler
I had had to play is: *I had | had to | play*
J'avais   dû   jouer
I should have had to try is: *I should have | had to | try*
J'aurais   dû   tâcher

This is the way to tackle a sentence like *I ought to have done.*
First change it into: *I should have | had to | do.* Then break
it up into: **J'aurais | dû | faire.**

If you apply this rule, you can never go wrong with sentences
like *I ought to have gone* = *I should have had to go* = **J'aurais dû
aller.**

Remember that **J'ai dû parler** can mean *I must have spoken*
as well as *I have had to speak*, and **dois-je?**—*am I to?* conveys the
English *shall I?*—

Dois-je le faire maintenant? *Shall I do it now?*

VOCABULARY FOR EXERCISE 53

le dentiste, *the dentist*	la forêt, *the forest*
l'étranger (*m.*), *stranger, foreigner*	amical, *friendly*
l'étrangère (*f.*), *stranger, foreigner*	insolent, *insolent*
la bouche, *the mouth*	exactement, *exactly*
la pipe, *the pipe*	plaisanter, *to joke*

EXERCISE 53

A. *Translate into English*

1. Le neveu a parlé d'un ton grossier à son oncle. 2. Elle a parlé d'une manière amicale à son cousin. 3. Les soldats ont traversé la ville d'un pas rapide. 4. D'heure en heure on se disait, "Maintenant ils seront à Carcassonne." 5. Cette pauvre femme n'avait pas beaucoup d'argent; elle vivait au jour le jour. 6. La fôret était remplie d'oiseaux qui chantaient. 7. La table était couverte de livres. 8. La gare fourmillait de voyageurs. 9. La rivière était obstruée de cailloux. 10. Notre mère nous a comblés de bienfaits.

B. *Translate into English*

1. La boîte était remplie des poires que votre mère a achetées. 2. Hier j'ai vu le soldat à la balafre. 3. La femme aux yeux bleus et aux cheveux

bruns nous a rendu visite. 4. Le garçon aux dents cariées a fait visite au dentiste. 5. L'homme au long habit noir entra dans la chambre. 6. Notre cousin sortit de la maison, la pipe à la bouche. 7. Je dois quinze francs à mon père. 8. Quand les recevra-t-il? 9. Qui sait? De nos jours il est difficile de dire exactement quand il les recevra. 10. Vous plaisantez. Oui, ne prenez pas au sérieux tout ce que je dis.

C. *Translate into French*

1. I am to sing at the concert. 2. I was to play at tennis today, but it is raining. 3. I have had to write to London. 4. She had had to refuse the invitation on account of her son. 5. He ought to have accepted the money. 6. She ought to have come to see them. 7. They ought to work. 8. They ought to have worked. 9. I owe twenty francs to my cousin. 10. I have had to pay all that I owed.

D. *Translate into French*

1. The station was swarming with people, who were going to the seaside. 2. The gardens were covered with snow. 3. The girl with the brown eyes is the cleverest in the class. 4. The man with the white teeth is our cousin. 5. The gentleman with the blue tie has been in America. 6. He speaks in a friendly manner. 7. The stranger (é = s) spoke in an insolent tone. 8. The soldiers were marching at a rapid pace. 9. I was supposed to write to my cousin yesterday. 10. I ought to have done so.

LESSON 54

The Other Prepositions

Sans. Normal meaning is *without*—

> Il le dit **sans** penser à ce qu'il disait. *He said it without thinking of what he was saying.*

But **sans** can translate *but for*—

> **Sans** sa mère il serait mort. *But for his mother he would have died.*

Watch for the English form *had it not been for*, still translated by **sans**—

> **Sans** son ami il serait tombé. *Had it not been for his friend, he would have fallen.*

Remember that *to go without,* or *to do without* is **se passer de**—
   Il **se passa de** son souper. *He went without his supper.*

Observe that *or* is translated by **ni** after **sans**—
   sans feu **ni** lieu   *without hearth or home*

Pour. Normally meaning *for* or *in order to*—
   Elle le fit **pour** sa mère. *She did it for her mother.*

This can never be confused with the conjunction **car,** meaning *for,* if one thinks of the following: **pour** = *for the sake of, on behalf of;* **car** = *since, because*—
   Elle les acheta, **car** sa mère lui avait demandé de le faire.
   She bought them, for her mother had asked her to do so.

Remember that verbs of movement do not usually take **pour** before an infinitive—
   Allez chercher mes pantoufles. *Go and fetch my slippers.*
But Elle s'arrêta **pour** regarder les bijoux. *She stopped to look at the jewels.*

Avec. Normally means *with,* in the sense of *in company with*—
   Elle alla **avec** nous. *She went with us.*

In the phrase **avec cela, avec** means *for all that*—
   Avec cela, elle avait la gaieté de son âge. *For all that, she had the liveliness of her years.*

At the end of a phrase, **avec** can mean *as well*—
   Il vendit la maison et le jardin **avec.** *He sold the house and the garden as well.*

The Irregular "OIR" Verbs

Savoir

savoir	*to know*		
sachant	*knowing* (remember **savant** is a noun, meaning *scholar,* or an adjective, meaning *scholarly*)		
j'ai **su**	*I have known* (sometimes j'ai **su** is translated *I have heard* or *I have learnt*)		
je **sais**	*I know*	nous **savons**	*we know*
tu **sais**	*thou dost know*	vous **savez**	*you know*
il **sait**	*he knows*	ils **savent**	*they know*

je **sus**	*I knew*	nous **sûmes**	*we knew*
tu **sus**	*thou didst know*	vous **sûtes**	*you knew*
il **sut**	*he knew*	ils **surent**	*they knew*
		je **savais**	*I used to know*
je **saurai**	*I shall know*	je **saurais**	*I should know*
		sachons!	*let us know!*
sache!	*know!*	**sachez!**	*know!*

Remember that the verb *to know*, when followed by a *noun* clause, must be translated by **savoir**—

Do you know who she is?	**Savez-vous** qui elle est?
Do you know where she is?	**Savez-vous** où elle est?
Do you know if she is rich?	**Savez-vous** si elle est riche?
I know that she is rich.	**Je sais** qu'elle est riche.
I know that she is in Paris.	**Je sais** qu'elle est à Paris.

Compare with the verb *to know*, translated by **connaître**, when followed by an *adjective* clause—

Do you know Margot Brown, who knows you? **Connaissez-vous** Margot Brown, qui vous connaît?

VOCABULARY FOR EXERCISE 54

l'Allemand (*m.*), *the German*
l'article (*m.*), *the article*
le tabac, *the tobacco*
le lieu, *the place*

EXERCISE 54

A. *Translate into English*

1. Mon ami l'a dit sans penser à ce qu'il disait. 2. Sans son père, il serait mort dans la mer. 3. Je devrais me passer de mon tabac cette semaine. 4. Le pauvre enfant est sans feu ni foyer. 5. Les petits ont dû se passer de leur souper. 6. Elle a acheté le cadeau pour sa mère. 7. Elle a acheté les articles, car sa mère lui avait demandé de les acheter. 8. Faites venir le médecin, car Charles est malade. 9. Oui, je l'enverrai chercher sans délai. 10. La femme s'arrêta pour regarder les jolis bijoux.

B. *Translate into English*

1. Mon père est allé avec nous au match de football. 2. Ma mère a vendu la maison et le jardin avec. 3. Avec cela, Jeanne a la gaieté de son âge. 4. Je sais ce qui arrive. 5. Mon oncle sait ce que vous faites.

6. Mon père sait ce dont vous avez besoin. 7. Savez-vous qui il est?
8. Connaissez-vous Pierre Lemaire? 9. Je sais que vous le connaissez.
10. Je connais Marie Lenoir qui sait que vous êtes un de mes amis.

C. *Translate into French*

1. Do you know where she is? 2. Do you know why she works?
3. Do you know when she will come? 4. My cousin knows that you
know him. 5. My sister knows a German. 6. I have had to know this
book. 7. Did you know that she has refused to come? 8. I did not
know that. 9. She did it unknown to her father. 10. Now he knows
what she has done.

D. *Translate into French*

1. Had it not been for you, I should have died. 2. But for this money
we should be very poor. 3. I have had to do without the cigarettes.
4. The poor children have had to go without their supper. 5. In order
to win, one must work. 6. In order to succeed, one must try all the
time. 7. She stopped to look at the water. 8. He sold the house and the
car as well. 9. Knowing that it was late, he went home. 10. Soon we
shall know what you have done.

LESSON 55

The Other Prepositions (cont.)

Par. Normally means *by*. But the translation is often *out of*
when an abstract noun follows—

> Elle lui donna de l'argent **par** pitié. *She gave him some money
> out of pity.*

Observe that, instead of **par,** many verbs take **de** to translate
by—

> Il était suivi **de** trois hommes. *He was followed by three men.*
> La maison était entourée **d'**une haie. *The house was sur-
> rounded by a hedge.*

Some verbs take **par** for a literal statement, **de** for a figurative
statement—

> Il fut frappé **par** le tableau. *He was struck by the picture.*
> Il était frappé **de** la beauté du tableau. *He was struck by the
> beauty of the picture.*

Chez. Normally means *at the house of*—

Il demeure **chez** nous. *He is staying with us (at our house).*

It is also used for shops—

Je vais **chez** le boucher. *I am going to the butcher's.*

But **chez** translates *in* for figurative statement—

On devrait encourager la diligence **chez** les enfants. *One should encourage diligence in children.*

Chez can mean *among*—

Chez les Français cela ne se fait pas. *Among the French that is not done.*

Chez also indicates *with*—

Chez nous la vigne ne croît pas. *In our country the vine does not grow.*

Devant means *before*, speaking of place—

Elle est assise **devant** nous. *She is sitting in front of us.*

Avant means *before*, speaking of time—

Elle est arrivée **avant** nous. *She arrived before we did.*

Note that **avant** must take **de** before an infinitive—

Avant de parler il but un verre d'eau. *Before speaking he drank a glass of water.*

Après means *after*—

après la guerre   *after the war*

It is often used figuratively—

et après?   *and what next?*

Remember that **après** is the only preposition to take a perfect infinitive instead of the present infinitive—

after speaking   **après avoir parlé**

Watch for the verbs that take **être**—

after going   **après être allé**

Similarly, watch reflexive verbs—

After going to bed, I fell asleep. **Après m'être couché,** je m'endormis.

The Irregular "OIR" Verbs
Pouvoir

pouvoir	*to be able*		
pouvant	*being able*		
j'ai **pu**	*I have been able*		

je **peux**	*I am able*	nous **pouvons**	*we are able*
tu **peux**	*thou art able*	vous **pouvez**	*you are able*
il **peut**	*he is able*	ils **peuvent**	*they are able*

In question form, one says **puis-je?** for *am I able?*

je **pus**	*I was able*	nous **pûmes**	*we were able*
tu **pus**	*thou wert able*	vous **pûtes**	*you were able*
il **put**	*he was able*	ils **purent**	*they were able*
		je **pouvais**	*I was able*
je **pourrai**	*I shall be able*	je **pourrais**	*I should be able, I could*

Remember that **pu** means *been able*. Hence *I shall have been able,* **j'aurai pu,** etc.

If you have the sentence *I could have played,* mentally translate into *I should have | been able | to play*; you then have **j'aurais | pu | jouer.**

Observe that **pouvoir** denotes physical capacity; **savoir** denotes mental ability—

> Le célèbre pianiste polonais **sait** jouer aussi du violon. *The famous Polish pianist can also play the violin.*
> Il s'est blessé le doigt; il ne **peut** pas jouer ce soir. *He has hurt his finger; he cannot play tonight.*

VOCABULARY FOR EXERCISE 55

l'artiste (*m.*), *the artist*
l'oranger (*m.*), *the orange-tree*
le boulanger, *the baker*
le capitaine, *the captain*

l'industrie (*f.*), *the skill, ingenuity*
l'offre (*f.*), *the offer*
la scène, *the scene*
adieu, *good-bye*

EXERCISE 55

A. *Translate into English*

1. Elle lui prêta l'argent par pitié. 2. Le capitaine était suivi de ses soldats. 3. Le jardin était entouré d'un mur. 4. L'artiste était frappé

10—(F.130)

de la beauté de la scène. 5. Notre tante demeure chez nous. 6. Je vais chez le boulanger car nous avons besoin de pain. 7. On devrait encourager l'industrie chez les enfants. 8. Chez les Anglais cela ne se fait pas. 9. Chez nous l'oranger ne croît pas. 10. Elle est assise devant sa mère.

B. *Translate into English*

1. Elle est arrivée au concert avant sa mère. 2. Avant de partir elle dit adieu à sa famille. 3. Après la guerre on dit qu'il y aura des maisons. 4. Après avoir bâti les maisons ils firent des jardins. 5. Après être sortis, ils virent un accident. 6. Après nous être couchés nous nous endormîmes. 7. Puis-je vous offrir une cigarette? 8. Je ne fume pas. Je ne peux pas accepter votre offre. 9. Auriez-vous pu courir aussi vite que votre frère? 10. Mon ami sait jouer du violon, mais il ne peut pas jouer ce soir.

C. *Translate into French*

1. We were able to write the letters. 2. I have been able to work. 3. Could you do it? 4. I could have gone. 5. She could have come. 6. They could have refused. 7. Not being able to accept. 8. They can read French books. 9. But they cannot read tonight. 10. They have sore eyes.

D. *Translate into French*

1. She lent him the money out of pity. 2. Marie was followed by her friends. 3. The garden was surrounded by a hedge. 4. I was struck by the tree. 5. I was struck by the beauty of the tree. 6. She went to the baker's. 7. We arrived at the theatre before our father. 8. After going out they went to the cinema. 9. After getting up they dressed. 10. Before going away they said good-bye.

LESSON 56

The Prepositions (concluded)

Watch **dans** and **en** in a time sense.

Dans means at the end of a given time, **en** means within a given time—

> Quand part le train de Liverpool? **Dans** une heure. *When does the Liverpool train leave? In an hour.*
> Le train va de Glasgow à Liverpool **en** sept heures. *The train goes from Glasgow to Liverpool in seven hours.*

For the sake of euphony, you will often find **en** used instead of **dans** when the next word is **des**—

> **en** des circonstances   *in some circumstances*

The word **sur** usually means *on the top of*—

> **sur** le mur   *on the wall*

Do not confuse with an object hanging on a wall, which is **à**—

> Le tableau était suspendu **au** mur. *The picture was hanging on the wall.*

Observe the meaning *out of* for **sur** with numbers—

> un **sur** dix   *one out of ten*

When accompanied by **quoi, sur** indicates *whereupon*—

> **sur** quoi il partit   *whereupon he left*

Sur is often used instead of **de** to translate *in* before the word **ton**—

> Il me parla **sur** un ton de mépris. *He spoke to me in a scornful tone.*

Vers and **envers** both mean *towards*.
Vers is used for a direction, **envers** for an emotion—

> Il se dirigea **vers** le bois. *He made towards the wood.*
> Elle est cruelle **envers** nous. *She is cruel to us.*

Sometimes **pour** is used instead of **envers,** especially when speaking of animals—

> Elle est bonne **pour** les animaux. *She is kind to animals.*

The word *in* with respect to seasons and years is translated **en**—

en 1914	*in 1914*
en hiver	*in winter*
en été	*in summer*
en automne	*in autumn*

But: **au** printemps   *in spring*

If a particular season of a year is mentioned, use **dans l'**—

> **dans l'**automne de 1914

The word *in* before geographical places should receive special attention—

1. Before a city, put **à**—

à Londres   *in London*

Watch the few cities which take the definite article—

au Caire   *in Cairo*
au Havre   *in Havre*

2. Before a country, first decide the gender of the country as follows: Most countries ending in **-e** are feminine. They take **en** for *in*—

en France   *in France*

Most countries not ending in **-e** are masculine. They take **au** for *in*—

au Canada   *in Canada*

3. Before an English or Scottish shire, it is usual to put **dans le**—

dans le Lanarkshire

4. Before plural countries, put **aux** for *in*—

aux États-Unis   *in the U.S.A.*
aux Indes   *in India*

The Irregular "OIR" Verbs
VOULOIR

vouloir   *to wish*
voulant   *wishing*
j'ai **voulu**   *I have wanted to*

je **veux**	*I want*	nous **voulons**	*we want*
tu **veux**	*thou dost want*	vous **voulez**	*you want*
il **veut**	*he wants*	ils **veulent**	*they want*
ie **voulus**	*I wanted*	nous **voulûmes**	*we wanted*
tu **voulus**	*thou didst want*	vous **voulûtes**	*you wanted*
il **voulut**	*he wanted*	ils **voulurent**	*they wanted*
		je **voulais**	*I was wanting*
je **voudrai**	*I shall want to*	je **voudrais**	*I should like to*
veuille!	*wish!*	**veuillez!**	*wish!*

Note that **veuillez** translates *please* or *be good enough to*—
Veuillez coudre cet habit. *Please sew this coat.*

Observe that the English expression *I wish I had a car* is translated **Je voudrais avoir une auto.**

Je veux often denotes determination—
Je veux le faire! *I will do it!*

VOCABULARY FOR EXERCISE 56

le Brésil, *Brazil*
le Chili, *Chile*
l'Égypte (*f.*), *Egypt*
le dédain, *the disdain*
le poète, *the poet*
la chaumière, *the cottage*
la larme, *the tear (in the eye)*
la motocyclette, *the motor-cycle*

le champ, *the field*
accroupi, *crouching*
européen, *European*
tourner, *to turn* (Eng.
   transitive)
se tourner, *to turn* (Eng.
   intransitive)

EXERCISE 56

A. *Translate into English*

1. Quand part le train d'Édimbourg? Dans deux heures. 2. Le train
va de Newcastle à Édimbourg en moins de trois heures. 3. En de telles
circonstances je devrais refuser l'offre. 4. Le chat était accroupi sur le
mur. 5. Le miroir était suspendu au mur. 6. Trois sur cinq des soldats
furent tués. 7. Son père lui dit de travailler dans la maison; sur quoi
elle sortit sans rien dire. 8. Elle nous parla sur un ton de dédain. 9. Elle
se tourna vers moi, les yeux remplis de larmes. 10. Elle est cruelle
envers les enfants mais elle est bonne pour les chats. Quelle femme
étrange!

B. *Translate into English*

1. En 1939 la guerre commença. 2. Dans l'automne de 1939 les
nations européennes étaient en guerre. 3. En hiver les champs sont
couverts de neige. 4. En été les champs sont couverts de fleurs. 5. Les
poètes disent que les champs sont tapissés de fleurs (**le tapis** = *the carpet*).
6. Notre père a été à Paris, à Rome, et au Caire. 7. Il a été en France,
en Italie, et en Égypte. 8. Notre oncle demeure au Canada. 9. Après
la guerre beaucoup de Polonais allèrent au Brésil et au Chili. 10. Quelques-uns de nos amis sont allés aux États-Unis.

C. *Translate into French*

1. Wishing to see them he went to their house. 2. I wanted to go to India when I was young. 3. I wish I had a car. 4. She is determined to buy a car. 5. They want to see you. 6. I have wanted to work, but I have not been able to work. 7. Kindly write. 8. Please read. 9. Please accept. 10. Please listen.

D. *Translate into French*

1. In two hours we shall be in London. 2. In such circumstances I should accept the offer. 3. He directed his steps towards the old cottage. 4. My sister lives in Wiltshire. 5. We live in Dover. 6. The train goes from Newcastle to Exeter in ten hours. 7. In summer we want to play in the garden. 8. In winter we prefer to play in the house. 9. I wish I had a motor-cycle. 10. My father does not wish to buy it.

LESSON 57

The Conjunctions

et	*and*	**car**	*for*
ou	*or*	**ni**	*neither*
mais	*but*		

Et is often used figuratively—

et vous?   *and how about you?*

Watch its use with the disjunctive pronouns—

et moi aussi	*so am I*	**et** nous aussi	*so are we*
et toi aussi	*so art thou*	**et** vous aussi	*so are you*
et lui aussi	*so is he*	**et** eux aussi	*so are they*
et elle aussi	*so is she*	**et** elles aussi	*so are they*

l'un et l'autre translates *both*, whereas **l'un ou l'autre** translates *either*.

mais is often used for emphasis—

mais oui   *yes, indeed*
mais non   *why, no*

ni l'un ni l'autre translates neither, and prefers the plural to follow. Note the use of **ni** with the disjunctive pronouns—

ni moi non plus   *neither am I*, etc.

The Verbs "sit" and "stand"

SIT

If movement is meant, use the reflexive verb, **s'asseoir**—

I should like to sit down. Je voudrais **m'asseoir.**

s'asseyant	*sitting down*
je me suis **assis**	*I have sat down*
je m'**assieds**	*I sit down*
je m'**assis**	*I sat down*
asseyez-vous!	*sit down!*

The full conjugation of this verb may be seen in the Verb Table. If no verb movement is meant use **être assis**—

She was sitting on the chair. Elle **était assise** sur la chaise.

Note also: **Elle restait assise à tricoter.** *She sat knitting.*

STAND

1. The normal verb is **se tenir**—
   Elle **se tenait** à la porte. *She was standing at the door.*

2. **Debout** is added for emphasis—
   Tenez-vous debout! *Stand up!*

3. **Être debout** is used for contrasts—
   Moi, j'**étais debout**, lui, il **était assis**. *I was standing, he was sitting.*

Other past participles are sometimes translated by present participles as in the case of **assis**—

Elle était agenouillée. *She was kneeling.*
Elle était accoudée. *She was leaning.*
Le tableau était suspendu. *The picture was hanging.*
Le lion était accroupi. *The lion was crouching.*

The Subjunctive Mood

To form the present subjunctive of a regular verb, remove **-ant** from the present participle, and add the endings—

-e	**-ions**
-es	**-iez**
-e	**-ent**

For example,

donnant gives	**que je donne**	*let me give*
	qu'il donne	*let him give*
finissant gives	**que je finisse**	*let me finish*
vendant gives	**que je vende**	*let me sell*

A number of verbs form their present subjunctive irregularly. The following are the most important—

1. **aller**, *to go*, **que j'aille**, *let me go*; plural, **que nous allions, que vous alliez, qu'ils aillent.**

2. **être**, *to be*, **que je sois, que tu sois, qu'il soit**; plural, **que nous soyons, que vous soyez, qu'ils soient.**

3. **avoir**, *to have*, **que j'aie, que tu aies, qu'il ait**; plural, **que nous ayons, que vous ayez, qu'ils aient.**

4. **venir**, *to come*, **que je vienne**, etc.; plural, **que nous venions, que vous veniez, qu'ils viennent.**

5. **tenir**, *to hold*, **que je tienne**, etc.; plural, **que nous tenions**, etc.

6. **faire**, *to make*, **que je fasse**, etc.; plural, **que nous fassions**, etc.

7. **boire**, *to drink*, **que je boive**, etc.; plural, **que nous buvions, que vous buviez, qu'ils boivent.**

8. **prendre**, *to take*, **que je prenne**, etc.; plural, **que nous prenions, que vous preniez, qu'ils prennent.**

9. **recevoir**, *to receive*, **que je reçoive**, etc.; plural, **que nous recevions, que vous receviez, qu'ils reçoivent.**

10. **devoir**, *to owe*, **que je doive**, etc.

11. **pouvoir**, *to be able*, **que je puisse**, etc.; plural, **que nous puissions, que vous puissiez, qu'ils puissent.**

12. **vouloir**, *to wish*, **que je veuille**, etc.; plural, **que nous voulions, que vous vouliez, qu'ils veuillent.**

13. **mourir**, *to die*, **que je meure**, etc.; plural, **que nous mourions, que vous mouriez, qu'ils meurent.**

14. **falloir**, *to be necessary*, **qu'il faille.**

15. **valoir**, *to be worth*, **qu'il vaille.**

The Irregular "OIR" Verbs
VALOIR

valoir	*to be worth*		
valant	*being worth*		
il **a valu**	*it has been worth*	il **valait**	*it was worth*
il **vaut**	*it is worth*	il **vaudra**	*it will be worth*
il **valut**	*it was worth*	il **vaudrait**	*it would be worth*

The irregular verb **falloir**, *to be necessary*, follows the same pattern.

Watch idiomatic uses of **valoir**—

Il vaut la peine de travailler. *It is worth while working.*
Il vaudrait mieux essayer. *It would be better to try.*

But, if a person is mentioned, use **faire** instead of **valoir**—
Elle **ferait mieux** d'essayer. *She would be better to try.*

The impersonal verb **falloir** has two possible constructions with a person. *It is necessary for me to work* may be translated—
Il me faut travailler, or **Il faut que je travaille** (Subjunctive)

If no person is mentioned, the infinitive alone is used—
It is necessary to work. **Il faut travailler.**

VOCABULARY FOR EXERCISE 57

la corde, *the rope, cord*	câbler, *to cable, send a cable*
calme (*adj.*), *calm*	téléphoner, *to telephone*

EXERCISE 57

A. *Translate into English*

1. Elle va au ciné, et nous aussi. 2. Elles ne vont pas au concert, ni nous non plus. 3. Asseyez-vous, mon ami! 4. Elle était assise dans le jardin. 5. Il faut que je donne cet argent à mon père. 6. Il faut que je finisse mon travail. 7. Qu'il ait de la patience! 8. Qu'il soit calme! 9. Qu'ils aillent en Allemagne, s'ils veulent le faire! 10. Qu'il boive un verre de lait chaque soir!

B. *Translate into English*

1. Il faut que je fasse tout ce que j'ai promis de faire. 2. Il faut que je vienne les voir. 3. Qu'il tienne la corde! 4. Qu'ils prennent l'argent!

5. Il est nécessaire qu'elles reçoivent de l'argent. 6. Il faut que tout le monde meure! 7. Il vaut la peine de faire un effort. 8. Il vaudrait mieux téléphoner. 9. Elle ferait mieux de câbler. 10. Je ferais mieux d'écrire à ma tante.

C. *Translate into French*

1. And so are we. 2. And so are you. 3. Neither are they. 4. Neither am I. 5. I should like to sit down. 6. She was sitting in the house. 7. It is necessary to try. 8. It is necessary for me to try. 9. It is worth while writing to such people. 10. She would be better to do so.

D. *Translate into French*

1. Let me give. 2. Let him finish. 3. Let her have. 4. Let them hold. 5. Let him come. 6. He must go. 7. She must do it. 8. It would be better to play. 9. She would be better to sing. 10. It is worth while working.

LESSON 58

The Conjunctions (cont.)

Most conjunctions take the indicative—

    comme, *as*: **comme** il a raison, *as he is right.*
    puisque, *since*: **puisque** vous refusez, *since you refuse.*
    parce que, *because*: **parce qu'**elle a tort, *because she is wrong.*
    après que, *after*: **après qu'**il eut fini, *after he had finished.*
    de sorte que, *so that*: **de sorte qu'**elle devint riche, *so that she became rich.*
    pendant que, tandis que, *while*: **pendant qu'**elle écrivait, il fumait, *while she was writing, he was smoking.*

    tandis que generally denotes a contrast—

    Elle était riche, **tandis que** sa sœur était pauvre. *She was rich, whereas her sister was poor.*

The Past Subjunctive

To form the past subjunctive of any verb, remove the last letter from the first person singular past definite and add the following endings—

–sse	–ssions
–sses	–ssiez
–ᶜt	–ssent

Therefore, if you want the past subjunctive of **donner,** remove the last letter from the past definite, and you are left with **donna.** Add the endings, and you get—

que je donnasse	que nous donnassions
que tu donnasses	que vous donnassiez
qu'il donnât	qu'ils donnassent

Similarly, for **finir, que je finisse, que tu finisses, qu'il finît,** etc.

No matter how irregular the verb may be, the process is always the same, e.g. **boire,** past definite, **je bus,** past subjunctive, **que je busse,** etc.

There is only one verb, **haïr,** which has a slight irregularity in the third person singular—

qu'il **haït.** The circumflex is not added.

The Uses of the Subjunctive

A. In a Principal Clause

Generally to express a wish, prayer or command—

Vive la reine! *Long live the queen!*
Dieu vous bénisse! *God bless you!*
Puissiez-vous réussir! *May you succeed!*
A Dieu ne plaise qu'il vienne! *God forbid that he come!*
Qu'il travaille! *Let him work!*

B. In a Noun Clause

Generally after all verbs denoting a wish, emotion, doubt, or command, but watch two essential points—

1. There must be two different groups involved—

Je désire **qu'elle travaille.** *I want her to work.*

If it is *I wish to work,* say **Je désire travailler,** because only one person is concerned.

2. The clauses must be joined by **que**—

> Je suis heureux **qu'**il vienne. *I am happy that he is coming.*
> (Two groups concerned in an emotion.)

But—

> Je suis heureux **quand** il vient. *I am happy when he comes.*
> (Clauses not joined by **que,** i.e. adverbial.)

Doubt clauses can be difficult to spot. Easy enough is **Je doute qu'il vienne,** *I doubt whether he is coming.* But when certain verbs which normally take the indicative are made negative or interrogative, they express doubt, and hence require the subjunctive.

These verbs are: verbs of certainty (**être sûr,** etc.); **penser,** *to think*; **croire,** *to believe*; **espérer,** *to hope*; **dire,** *to say*; **savoir,** *to know*; **supposer,** *to suppose*; **compter,** *to expect*

Take as an example the verb **être sûr,** *to be sure*—

> **Je suis sûr qu'il est riche,** *I am sure that he is rich.*

(Indicative, because no doubt in the speaker's mind.)

But, **Êtes-vous sûr qu'il soit riche?** *Are you sure that he is rich?*
(Subjunctive, because the speaker does not know whether the person asked will say "yes" or "no.")

> **Je ne suis pas sûr qu'il soit riche,** *I am not sure that he is rich.*

(Subjunctive, because the speaker himself is doubtful.)

If the verb is both negative and interrogative, put the indicative—

> N'êtes-vous pas sûr qu'il **est** riche? *Are you not sure that he is rich?*

This is because the sentence is another way of making the statement of fact, **Vous êtes sûr qu'il est riche, n'est-ce pas?**

VOCABULARY FOR EXERCISE 58

l'examen (*m.*), *the examination*
le sport, *the sport*
à temps, *in time* (*soon enough*)
stupide, *stupid*

émigrer, *to emigrate*
marier, *to marry*
oublier, *to forget*

EXERCISE 58

A. *Translate into English*

1. Comme vous avez assez de temps, allez jouer dans le jardin.
2. Puisque vous désirez savoir ce que j'ai fait, je vous le dirai. 3. Parce qu'elle a refusé de se marier avec lui, il a émigré. 4. Après que le concert fut terminé, tout le monde alla chez soi. 5. Elle travailla pendant trente ans, de sorte que son fils était riche. 6. Plût au ciel qu'il vînt à temps! 7. A Dieu ne plaise qu'elle se marie avec un tel homme! 8. Puissiez-vous réussir aux examens! 9. Pendant que nous travaillions, elle jouait. 10. Elle était intelligente, tandis que son frère était un peu stupide.

B. *Translate into English*

1. Je désire réussir aux sports. 2. Je désire que vous réussissiez aux sports. 3. Je commande que les soldats reçoivent du vin. 4. Je regrette que vous ne travailliez pas. 5. Elle doute qu'il vienne. 6. Elle doute s'il viendra. 7. Je le regrette, quand vous ne travaillez pas. 8. Je suis sûr qu'elle a émigré. 9. Êtes-vous sûr qu'elle soit allée en Amérique? 10. Je ne suis pas sûr qu'elle soit allée aux États-Unis.

C. *Translate into French*

1. I think that she will come. 2. Do you think that she will come? 3. I do not think that she will come. 4. Don't you think that she will go to Canada? 5. I do not say that he is lying. 6. I believe he is wrong. 7. Do you believe he is wrong? 8. Are you sure you are right? 9. I do not believe that you are afraid. 10. Are you not sure that she is lying?

D. *Translate into French*

1. I want my students to work hard. 2. Some of the students want to work hard. 3. They regret that the lesson is difficult. 4. They wished it were easier. 5. Do you think it is easy? 6. I am sure that it is difficult. 7. Since we have worked hard, we have little to do tomorrow. 8. My uncle emigrated, because he thought he could earn more money in Canada. 9. Do you think he is right? 10. After he had gone out, he saw that he had forgotten his gloves.

LESSON 59

The Conjunctions and the Subjunctive Mood (cont.)

C. In Adverb Clauses

Some conjunctions are followed by the subjunctive. These conjunctions usually introduce adverbial clauses—

1. The time conjunctions: **jusqu'à ce que, en attendant que,** *until,* **avant que,** *before*—

> Continuez **jusqu'à ce qu'il vienne.** *Continue until he comes.*

Note that the verb **attendre,** *to wait,* cuts *until* down to **que**—

> **Attendez qu'elle arrive.** *Wait till she arrives.*
>
> Écrivez-lui **avant qu'il parte** pour les Indes. *Write to him before he departs for India.*

2. The concession conjunctions: **bien que, quoique,** *although*—

> **Bien qu'elle travaille** toute la nuit, elle ne finira pas le travail. *Although she works all night, she will not finish the job.*

3. The condition conjunctions: **en cas que,** *in case,* **pourvu que,** *provided that,* **à moins que,** *unless*—

> Faites-le **en cas qu'elle vienne.** *Do it in case she comes.*
>
> **pourvu qu'elle arrive** à temps, *provided she arrives in time.*
>
> **à moins qu'elle le fasse,** *unless she does it.*

In many passages, **à moins que** is seen along with a **ne** before the verb.

4. The purpose conjunctions: **de manière que, de sorte que, pour que, afin que,** *in order that*—

> La mère travaille dur, **afin que** son fils **soit** riche. *The mother is working hard, in order that her son may be rich.*

Do not confuse with clauses of result, which take the indicative.

5. The negation conjunction **pas,** *not*—

> **pas que je sache**   *not that I know*

The Word "que"

1. Normally means *that*—

   Je sais **que** vous avez raison. *I know that you are right.*

2. Followed by **de** means *what a!* or *how many!*—

   Que de bruit pour rien! *What a to-do about nothing!*
   Que de jours! *How many days!*

3. Followed by the subjunctive, denotes *whether*—

   Qu'elle **soit** riche ou non, il va l'épouser. *Whether she is rich or not, he is going to marry her.*

4. **Que** with an adjective usually means *how*—

   Qu'il est **intelligent**! *How clever he is!*

5. But remember that **que** plus the subjunctive is used also for commands—

   Qu'ils travaillent! *Let them work!*

6. Along with **ne, que** means *only*—

   Je **n'**ai **que** dix francs. *I have only ten francs.*

VOCABULARY FOR EXERCISE 59

le pardessus, *the overcoat*	la perle, *the pearl*
le pleur, *the tear* (in the eye)	charmant, *charming*
l'affaire (*f.*), *the matter*	épouser, *to marry*

EXERCISE 59

A. *Translate into English*

1. En attendant qu'elle vienne, entrons dans le jardin. 2. Travaillez jusqu'à ce que vous ayez fini. 3. Elle le fera avant que son père revienne. 4. Attendez que Julie et Charles viennent. 5. Quoiqu'elle ait fait de son mieux, elle n'a pas réussi. 6. En cas que la pluie vienne, mettons nos pardessus. 7. Pourvu qu'elle soit diligente, elle gagnera le prix. 8. A moins qu'il ne fasse beau, nous n'irons pas au match. 9. Le père travaille dur, afin que son fils soit riche. 10. Est-elle dans le jardin? Pas que je sache.

B. *Translate into English*

1. Ce n'est que cela? Que de pleurs pour rien! 2. Si vous étiez à sa place, vous ne parleriez pas ainsi. 3. Je ne dis pas qu'elle ait raison.

4. Qu'elle est charmante, votre sœur! 5. Elle m'a dit qu'elle me prêterait ses perles. 6. Avant que vous alliez au bal, elle vous les prêtera. 7. Ah! les jolis bijoux! Qu'ils sont beaux! 8. Pensez-vous qu'elle revienne avant minuit? 9. Je suis sûr qu'elle reviendra après minuit. 10. Je crois qu'elle rendra les bijoux demain.

C. *Translate into French*

1. Not that I say. 2. How lazy he is! 3. Whether she is poor or not, he is going to marry her. 4. How many days became days of joy on account of his brother! 5. What a fuss over nothing! 6. Do you think I am right? 7. Let them try! 8. Whether she comes or not, we are going to the concert. 9. I have only twenty francs. 10. Were she to die, she would not tell him she needs money.

D. *Translate into French*

1. Until I see your brother, I cannot speak of the matter. 2. Would to heaven he would come! 3. Do you think he will return soon? 4. I am not sure when he will return. 5. Ah! here he is! How are you? 6. I regret that you cannot see me tonight. 7. Provided you come before noon, I shall see you tomorrow. 8. Unless it is bad weather, I shall be with you at ten. 9. In the event of my coming late (in case I come late) please wait. 10. I shall wait till you arrive.

LESSON 60

The Subjunctive Mood (concluded)

D. IN ADJECTIVE CLAUSES

1. A clause dependent on a superlative requires the subjunctive—

C'est l'homme **le plus intelligent que j'aie** jamais vu. *He is the most intelligent man I have ever seen.*

But if the clause merely describes the noun, use the indicative—

L'homme le plus intelligent de la ville, qui **avait** gagné le prix, assistait au concert. *The most intelligent man in the town, who had won the prize, was present at the concert.*

The following words very often count as superlatives—

premier   *first*   e.g. le **premier** qui **ait** vu, *the first who has seen.*

dernier   *last*   le **dernier** qui **soit** venu, *the last who has come.*

seul   *only*   le **seul** que j'**aie** vu, *the only one I have seen.*

rare   *few*   les **rares** paresseux qui **aient** réussi, *the few idle who have succeeded.*

2. The so-called indefinite antecedent—

I am looking for a man who can find him. Je cherche **un homme qui puisse** le trouver.

Just compare with—

I am looking for the man who found him. Je cherche **l'homme qui l'a** trouvé.

3. A clause restricting a negative statement requires the subjunctive—

There was no one in the room whom I knew. Il n'y avait personne dans la chambre que je **connusse.**

The original statement, *There was no one in the room,* until restricted in meaning by the clause, *whom I knew,* leads one to believe the room was empty.

The Interjections

French is particularly rich in these.

Not content with describing an action, the author will often add an interjection to help one see the mental picture—

Le coup partit—**pif! paf!** *The shot sped—ping!*

Le chien aboya—**ouah! ouah!** *The dog barked—woof!*

Le coq chanta—**cocorico!** *The cock crowed—cock-a-doodle-doo!*

Il frappa à la porte—**toc! toc!** *He rapped at the door.*

Il faisait un fracas—**pan! boum!** *He was making a din.*

Sometimes these sounds are made into nouns—

le **frou-frou** de sa robe, *the rustle of her dress.*
le **glou-glou** de la rivière, *the gurgle of the stream.*
le **stri-stri** des cigales, *the chirp of the cicadas.*

Others are straightforward, as in English—

to enforce silence	—**chut!**	*silence! hush!*
to give warning	—**gare!**	*look out!*
to express disgust	—**ouais!**	*ugh!*
to express sorrow	—**hélas!**	*alas!*
to show surprise	—**comment!**	*what!*
	—**quoi donc!**	*what's that!*
	—**vraiment!**	*really!*
to draw attention	—**tiens!**	*here!*
to show agreement	—**bien entendu!**	*of course!*

VOCABULARY FOR EXERCISE 60

le quai, *the quay, platform*
le vacarme, *the din, hubbub*
japonais, *Japanese*

chinois, *Chinese*
intéresser, *to interest*
vraiment, *really, truly*

EXERCISE 60

A. *Translate into English*

1. C'est la plus belle fleur que j'aie jamais vue. 2. C'est la première fois qu'il ait refusé. 3. C'est la dernière fois que nous lui ayons parlé. 4. C'est la seule femme qui ait battu le record. 5. C'est un des rares Japonais qui aient réussi aux États-Unis. 6. Je cherche un homme qui sache parler chinois. 7. Voilà l'homme qui parle chinois. 8. Il n'y avait rien sur le quai qui m'intéressât. 9. Il n'y a aucun homme qui sache cela. 10. Il n'y avait personne dans le théâtre que je connusse.

B. *Translate into English*

1. Le coq chanta. 2. Il frappa à la porte. Toc! Toc! 3. Il faisait un vacarme. 4. Le frou-frou de sa robe. 5. Le glou-glou de l'eau. 6. Le stri-stri de la cigale. 7. Chut! Il nous entendra. 8. Ouais! Vous me surprenez. 9. Hélas! Tout est perdu. 10. Comment! Vous avez perdu votre motocyclette!

C. *Translate into French*

1. Here! Take this! 2. What! You refuse! 3. Look out! 4. Really! This is too much! 5. Never! 6. This is the finest day I have

ever seen. 7. He is one of the few students who have succeeded in three months. 8. This is the first time I have ever seen such a thing. 9. This is the only woman he has ever loved. 10. This is the only time he has told a lie.

D. *Translate into French*

1. There was no one in the room whom I knew. 2. The cleverest girl in the class, who is English, received the prize. 3. The teachers say she is the cleverest girl they have ever seen. 4. Really! I am surprised to hear that. 5. Why do you say that? 6. I am sure I am better than she. 7. You are joking! 8. No, I play tennis better than she. 9. Of course! Some sports are very important. 10. The stronger one is, the longer one can continue to fight.

VERB TABLE

Regular Verbs

jouer	*to play*	**jouant**	*playing*
je jouerai	*I shall play*	**je jouais**	*I was playing*
je jouerais	*I should play*		or *I played*
		que je joue	*that I may play*

j'ai joué	*I have played*	**je joue**	*I am playing*
j'avais joué	*I had played*		or *I play*

je jouai	*I played*	
que je jouasse	*that I might play*	

polir	*to polish*	**polissant**	*polishing*
je polirai	*I shall polish*	**je polissais**	*I was polishing*
je polirais	*I should polish*		or *I polished*
		que je polisse	*that I may polish*

j'ai poli	*I have polished*	**je polis**	*I am polishing*
j'avais poli	*I had polished*		or *I polish*

je polis	*I polished*	
que je polisse	*that I might polish*	

perdre	*to lose*	**perdant**	*losing*
je perdrai	*I shall lose*	**je perdais**	*I was losing*
je perdrais	*I should lose*		or *I lost*
		que je perde	*that I may lose*

j'ai perdu	*I have lost*	**je perds**	*I am losing*
j'avais perdu	*I have lost*		or *I lose*

je perdis	*I lost*	
que je perdisse	*that I might lose*	

recevoir	*to receive*	**recevant**	*receiving*
je recevrai	*I shall receive*	**je recevais**	*I was receiving*
je recevrais	*I should receive*		or *I received*
		que je reçoive	*that I may receive*

j'ai reçu	*I have received*	**je reçois**	*I receive*
j'avais reçu	*I have received*		

je reçus	*I received*	
que je reçusse	*that I might receive*	

Infinitive	Present Participle	Past Participle	Present
			IRREGULAI
aller	allant	allé	vais, allons vas, allez va, vont
envoyer	envoyant	envoyé	envoie, envoyons envoies, envoyez envoie, envoient
			IRREGULAI
acquérir	acquérant	acquis	acquiers, acquérons acquiers, acquérez acquiert, acquièrent
courir	courant	couru	cours, courons cours, courez court, courent
cueillir	cueillant	cueilli	cueille, cueillons cueilles, cueillez cueille, cueillent
dormir	dormant	dormi	dors, dormons dors, dormez dort, dorment
fuir	fuyant	fui	fuis, fuyons fuis, fuyez fuit, fuient
mourir	mourant	mort	meurs, mourons meurs, mourez meurt, meurent

Past ˈistoric	Future	Subjunctive Present	English
ᴇR" Vᴇʀʙs			
.lai	irai	aille, allions ailles, alliez aille, aillent	to go
ᴉvoyai	enverrai	envoie, envoyions envoies, envoyiez envoie, envoient	to send
ᴵR" Vᴇʀʙs			
cquis	acquerrai	acquière, acquérions acquières, acquériez acquière, acquièrent	to acquire
ᴏurus	courrai	coure, courions coures, couriez coure, courent	to run
ᴉeillis	cueillerai	cueille, cueillions cueilles, cueilliez cueille, cueillent	to gather
ᴏrmis	dormirai	dorme, dormions dormes, dormiez dorme, dorment	to sleep
ᴉis	fuirai	fuie, fuyions fuies, fuyiez fuie, fuient	to flee
ᴉourus	mourrai	meure, mourions meures, mouriez meure, meurent	to die

Infinitive	Present Participle	Past Participle	Present
ouvrir	ouvrant	ouvert	ouvre, ouvrons ouvres, ouvrez ouvre, ouvrent
sentir	sentant	senti	sens, sentons sens, sentez sent, sentent
servir	servant	servi	sers, servons sers, servez sert, servent
sortir	sortant	sorti	sors, sortons sors, sortez sort, sortent
tenir	tenant	tenu	tiens, tenons tiens, tenez tient, tiennent
vêtir	vêtant	vêtu	vêts, vêtons vêts, vêtez vêt, vêtent

IRREGULA

asseoir	asseyant	assis	assieds, asseyons assieds, asseyez assied, asseyent
avoir	ayant	eu	ai, avons as, avez a, ont
falloir	——	fallu	il faut
pleuvoir	pleuvant	plu	il pleut

Past Historic	Future	Subjunctive Present	English
uvris	ouvrirai	ouvre, ouvrions ouvres, ouvriez ouvre, ouvrent	to open
ntis	sentirai	sente, sentions sentes, sentiez sente, sentent	to feel, smell
rvis	servirai	serve, servions serves, serviez serve, servent	to serve
ortis	sortirai	sorte, sortions sortes, sortiez sorte, sortent	to go out
ns	tiendrai	tienne, tenions tiennes, teniez tienne, tiennent	to hold
êtis	vêtirai	vête, vêtions vêtes, vêtiez vête, vêtent	to clothe

"OIR" Verbs

Past Historic	Future	Subjunctive Present	English
ssis	assiérai or asseoirai or asseyerai	asseye, asseyions asseyes, asseyiez asseye, asseyent	to seat
us	aurai	aie, ayons aies, ayez ait, aient	to have
fallut	il faudra	qu'il faille	to be necessary
plut	il pleuvra	qu'il pleuve	to rain

Infinitive	Present Participle	Past Participle	Present
pouvoir	pouvant	pu	puis, pouvons peux, pouvez peut, peuvent
savoir	sachant	su	sais, savons sais, savez sait, savent
valoir	valant	valu	vaux, valons vaux, valez vaut, valent
voir	voyant	vu	vois, voyons vois, voyez voit, voient
vouloir	voulant	voulu	veux, voulons veux, voulez veut, veulent

IRREGULA

battre	battant	battu	bats, battons bats, battez bat, battent
boire	buvant	bu	bois, buvons bois, buvez boit, boivent
coudre	cousant	cousu	couds, cousons couds, cousez coud, cousent
croire	croyant	cru	crois, croyons crois, croyez croit, croient
conduire	conduisant	conduit	conduis, conduisons conduis, conduisez conduit, conduisent

Past Historic	Future	Subjunctive Present	English
...us	pourrai	puisse, puissions puisses, puissiez puisse, puissent	to be able
...s	saurai	sache, sachions saches, sachiez sache, sachent	to know
...lus	vaudrai	vaille, valions vailles, valiez vaille, vaillent	to be worth
...s	verrai	voie, voyions voies, voyiez voie, voient	to see
...oulus	voudrai	veuille, voulions veuilles, vouliez veuille, veuillent	to be willing

...RE" Verbs

Past Historic	Future	Subjunctive Present	English
...attis	battrai	batte, battions battes, battiez batte, battent	to beat
...us	boirai	boive, buvions boives, buviez boive, boivent	to drink
...ousis	coudrai	couse, cousions couses, cousiez couse, cousent	to sew
...rus	croirai	croie, croyions croies, croyiez croie, croient	to believe
...onduisis	conduirai	conduise, conduisions conduises, conduisiez conduise, conduisent	to lead

Infinitive	Present Participle	Past Participle	Present
croître	croissant	crû	croîs, croissons croîs, croissez croît, croissent
dire	disant	dit	dis, disons dis, dites dit, disent
écrire	écrivant	écrit	écris, écrivons écris, écrivez écrit, écrivent
être	étant	été	suis, sommes es, êtes est, sont
faire	faisant	fait	fais, faisons fais, faites fait, font
joindre	joignant	joint	joins, joignons joins, joignez joint, joignent
lire	lisant	lu	lis, lisons lis, lisez lit, lisent
mettre	mettant	mis	mets, mettons mets, mettez met, mettent
naître	naissant	né	nais, naissons nais, naissez naît, naissent

Past Historic	Future	Subjunctive Present	English
ûs	croîtrai	croisse, croissions croisses, croissiez croisse, croissent	to grow
is	dirai	dise, disions dises, disiez dise, disent	to say
crivis	écrirai	écrive, écrivions écrives, écriviez écrive, écrivent	to write
us	serai	sois, soyons sois, soyez soit, soient	to be
s	ferai	fasse, fassions fasses, fassiez fasse, fassent	to make, to do
oignis	joindrai	joigne, joignions joignes, joigniez joigne, joignent	to join
us	lirai	lise, lisions lises, lisiez lise, lisent	to read
nis	mettrai	mette, mettions mettes, mettiez mette, mettent	to put
aquis	naîtrai	naisse, naissions naisses, naissiez naisse, naissent	to be born

Infinitive	Present Participle	Past Participle	Present
paraître	paraissant	paru	parais, paraissons parais, paraissez paraît, paraissent
plaire	plaisant	plu	plais, plaisons plais, plaisez plaît, plaisent
prendre	prenant	pris	prends, prenons prends, prenez prend, prennent
rire (de)	riant	ri	ris, rions ris, riez rit, rient
rompre	rompant	rompu	romps, rompons romps, rompez rompt, rompent
suffire (à)	suffisant	suffi	suffis, suffisons suffis, suffisez suffit, suffisent
suivre	suivant	suivi	suis, suivons suis, suivez suit, suivent
vaincre	vainquant	vaincu	vaincs, vainquons vaincs, vainquez vainc, vainquent
vivre (de)	vivant	vécu	vis, vivons vis, vivez vit, vivent

Past Historic	Future	Subjunctive Present	English
arus	paraîtrai	paraisse, paraissions paraisses, paraissiez paraisse, paraissent	to appear
lus	plairai	plaise, plaisions plaises, plaisiez plaise, plaisent	to please
ris	prendrai	prenne, prenions prennes, preniez prenne, prennent	to take
is	rirai	rie, riions ries, riiez rie, rient	to laugh (at)
ompis	romprai	rompe, rompions rompes, rompiez rompe, rompent	to break
uffis	suffirai	suffise, suffisions suffises, suffisiez suffise, suffisent	to suffice
uivis	suivrai	suive, suivions suives, suiviez suive, suivent	to follow
ainquis	vaincrai	vainque, vainquions vainques, vainquiez vainque, vainquent	to conquer
écus	vivrai	vive, vivions vives, viviez vive, vivent	to live (on or upon)

PART II

LESSON 61

The Definite Article and the Indefinite Article

A. The word *the* occurs in French but not in English in the following conditions—

1. Before a name qualified by an adjective—

Poor Marie is ill. **La** pauvre Marie est malade.

2. Before a title if speaking about a person, but not if speaking to him—

Le professeur A. vient ce soir. *Professor A. is coming tonight.*
but: Bonjour, Professeur. *Good morning, Professor.*

One can, of course, say—

Bonjour, Monsieur **le** Professeur.

3. Before countries, whether masculine or feminine—

la France	*France*
le Canada	*Canada*

Remember most countries ending in **-e** are feminine, most countries not ending in **-e** are masculine.

4. Time nouns qualified by an adjective following the noun—

l'année dernière	*last year*
la semaine prochaine	*next week*

This rule does not apply to adjectives coming before the noun—

chaque année	*each year*
cette année	*this year*
plusieurs mois	*several months*

B. The word *the* occurs in English, but not in French, when nouns are in apposition, unless the second noun is qualified—

Frédéric, fils du berger. *Frederick, the son of the shepherd.*
Frédéric, **le** jeune fils du berger. *Frederick, the shepherd's young son.*

With the word **of,** the definite article is omitted, if the phrase is adjectival—

les vins de France   French wines

But, if the emphasis is on the second noun, put the definite article—

les vins de **la** France comparés à ceux de **l'**Italie, *the wines of France compared with those of Italy.*

The indefinite article is omitted in French in speaking of a man's profession, religion, or nationality—

Il est boulanger	*He is a baker*
Il est catholique	*He is a Catholic*
Il est Français	*He is a Frenchman*

One may say, instead, **c'est un boulanger,** etc., using **c'est** instead of **il est.**

If there is an adjective, the **c'est** form and the word **un** are preferred—

C'est un bon boulanger. *He is a good baker.*

C. When a noun is used in a general sense, French has the definite article—

Flowers are beautiful. **Les** fleurs sont belles.

But if the sense is not general, put the word *some—*

I am buying flowers. J'achète **des** fleurs.

Similarly with metals—

Gold is precious. **L'**or est précieux.

But, *I have gold.* J'ai **de l'**or

Similarly with abstract nouns—

Il admire **le** courage. *He admires courage.*

But, Il combattit avec courage. *He fought with courage.*

Revise **avoir** and **être,** and check the idioms from each verb as follows—

1. | | |
    |---|---|
    | J'ai faim | *I am hungry* |
    | J'ai soif | *I am thirsty* |
    | J'ai peur de dire | *I am afraid to say* |
    | J'ai honte de dire | *I am ashamed to say* |
    | J'ai raison de parler | *I am right to speak* |
    | J'ai tort de refuser | *I am wrong to refuse* |
    | J'ai froid | *I am cold* |
    | J'ai chaud | *I am warm* |
    | J'ai envie de partir | *I am eager to go* |
    | J'ai besoin de vous | *I need you* |
    | Le concert a lieu | *The concert takes place* |
    | J'ai beaucoup de choses à faire | *I have many things to do* |
    | Ayez patience | *Be patient* |
    | Ayez pitié de lui | *Have pity on him* |
    | Elle a beau prier | *It is no use her begging* |

2. | | |
    |---|---|
    | Il est tard | *It is late* |
    | Elle est en retard | *She is late* |
    | Où êtes-vous? | *Where are you?* |
    | Où en êtes-vous? | *Where are you in the book? (Where did you leave off?)* |
    | Elle en était pour sa peine | *She had all her trouble for nothing* |

VOCABULARY FOR EXERCISE 61

l'Australie (*f.*), *Australia*
l'Italie (*f.*), *Italy*
le Danemark, *Denmark*
l'avocat (*m.*), *the lawyer*

le pharmacien, *the chemist*
protestant, *Protestant*
excellent, *excellent*

EXERCISE 61

A. *Translate into English*

1. La pauvre Anne est malade.   2. Le docteur Douche vient d'arriver.
3. Bonjour, Docteur!   4. Nous aimons l'Angleterre et la France.
5. Elle va demeurer en France.   6. Le Canada est un beau pays.   7.
L'année dernière il est allé au Danemark.   8. L'année prochaine il ira en

Australie. 9. Cette semaine nous restons chez nous. 10. Charles, fils du boulanger, est le premier de la classe.

B. *Translate into English*

1. Les vins de France sont excellents. 2. Il aime les vins de l'Allemagne mieux que ceux de l'Italie. 3. Mon frère est pharmacien, mon cousin est avocat. 4. Marie est catholique, Jean est protestant et Lazare est juif. 5. Yvonne est Française, Trudi est Allemande, et Alice est Anglaise. 6. Nous avons soif, donnez-nous de la limonade à boire. 7. Elles ont faim, donnez-leur de la viande à manger. 8. J'ai peur de dire qu'elle a tort. 9. Elle a honte de dire ce qu'elle a fait. 10. Ouf! Nous avons chaud dans cette chambre.

C. *Translate into French*

1. I am eager to see Spain. 2. She needs us. 3. The concert will take place at seven. 4. We have many letters to write. 5. Be patient. We are working hard. 6. Have pity on us. 7. Try as she would, she could not succeed. 8. It is late. 9. We are late. 10. Where are we in the book?

D. *Translate into French*

1. We had all our trouble for nothing. 2. We were ashamed to tell her the truth. 3. My friend is a Spaniard. 4. My brother is a chemist. 5. This student is a Catholic, that one is a Protestant. 6. He is a good doctor. 7. Jeanne, the daughter of the baker. 8. England is a rich country. 9. Poor Alphonse has lost his money. 10. Captain Tonnerre is coming tonight.

LESSON 62

The word *some* is the same as *of the* before a noun—

J'ai **des** amis	*I have some friends*
J'ai **du** tabac	*I have some tobacco*
J'ai **de la** confiture	*I have some jam*

But, if the statement is negative, put **de** for *some*—

Je n'ai pas **d'**amis	*I have no friends*
Je n'ai pas **de** tabac	*I have no tobacco*
Je n'ai pas **de** confiture	*I have no jam*

If an adjective precedes the noun, put **de** for *some*—
>   **de** beaux jardins   *some fine gardens*

If the adjective follows the noun *in French*, put *of the*—
>   **des** livres français   *some French books*

Watch the special cases—
1. If the phrase is negative *and* interrogative, put *of the*—
   N'avez-vous pas **des** amis?   *Have you not any friends?*

2. If the noun is made up of two words, put **des**—
   des jeunes filles   *some girls* (**jeune fille** counts as a *noun*)
   des choux-fleurs   *some cauliflowers*

3. After the phrase **ce n'est pas** use *of the* for *some*—
   Ce n'est pas du tabac qu'il me faut, **c'est de l'**argent.
   It's not tobacco I need, it's money.

Of the in English must not be confused with *some*. Compare
the two examples—

some *fine friends*	**de** beaux amis
ten of the *fine friends*	dix **des** beaux amis

Revise the Regular "ER" Verbs

Watch the ten types as follows—

appeler	*to call*	**il appelle**
jeter	*to throw*	**il jette**
geler	*to freeze*	**il gèle**
acheter	*to buy*	**il achète**
mener	*to lead*	**il mène**
espérer	*to hope*	**il espère**
essayer	*to try*	**il essaie**
nettoyer	*to clean*	**il nettoie**
essuyer	*to wipe*	**il essuie**
créer	*to create*	**il crée**

And the three types—

étudier	*to study*	**nous étudions**	*we are studying*
manger	*to eat*	**il mangeait**	*he was eating*
avancer	*to advance*	**il avançait**	*he was advancing*

VOCABULARY FOR EXERCISE 62

le troupeau, *the flock, herd*
le poulet, *the chicken*
le tableau noir, *the blackboard*
la bibliothèque, *the library*
la compagne, *the companion*
le compagnon, *the companion*
la falaise, *the cliff*
la sympathie, *the sympathy*

fidèle, *faithful*
salé, *salted, salty*
brouter, *to browse, graze*
casser, *to break*
détruire, *to destroy*
irriter, *to irritate*
rôtir, *to roast*

EXERCISE 62

A. *Translate into English*

1. J'ai des amis aux États-Unis. 2. Elle n'a pas de cigarettes. 3. Nous avons de beaux tableaux dans la bibliothèque. 4. Nos amis écossais arrivent à Liverpool ce soir. 5. N'a-t-elle pas de fidèles compagnes? 6. Ce sont des jeunes filles diligentes. 7. Le fermier lui a offert des choux-fleurs. 8. Ce n'est pas de la sympathie qu'il me faut, c'est de l'argent. 9. Cinq des meilleurs jardins étaient ruinés par la pluie. 10. Il a déjà fait du soleil aujourd'hui.

B. *Translate into English*

1. Il appelle le chien. 2. Comment vous appelez-vous? 3. Je m'appelle Théophile. Vraiment? 4. Les garçons jettent des pierres. 5. Ils espèrent casser les fenêtres de la chaumière. 6. Ils préfèrent détruire ce qui est beau. 7. Il gèle ce matin. J'espère qu'il dégèlera bientôt. 8. Elle achète des fleurs pour sa mère. 9. Si j'avais de l'argent, j'achèterais des fleurs pour elle. 10. Elle mène ses troupeaux brouter les herbes salées de la falaise.

C. *Translate into French*

1. I should prefer to work. 2. I used to prefer to play. 3. She is trying hard. 4. She is cleaning the house. 5. He is wiping the blackboard. 6. The man pays. 7. The flowers which are created by God. 8. We used to study a great deal. 9. He was eating a roast chicken. 10. She was irritating her friends.

D. *Translate into French*

1. We have some good friends in Scotland. 2. Have you not some cousins in France? 3. Three of the best students have left. 4. What is your name? 5. My name is Robert. 6. My sister's name is Julie. 7. I hope you prefer to work today. 8. When it is freezing, I prefer to remain in bed. 9. The woman buys, and the daughter pays. 10. Every day he used to eat an apple.

LESSON 63

Adjectives

1. Remember that adjectives agree with their nouns in gender and number—

les jolies femmes   *the pretty women*

But if you have an adjective of colour, accompanied by the words *light* or *dark*, leave the adjectives in the masculine singular—

des cheveux châtain clair   *light-brown hair*
une robe bleu foncé   *a dark-blue dress*

2. Note the position of adjectives generally behind the noun which they qualify—

le livre intéressant   *the interesting book*

3. Watch the adjectives which change their meaning according to their position, and which can even become adverbial—

même	**même** le roi	*even the king*
	le **même** roi	*the same king*
	le roi **même**	*the king himself*
propre	leur **propre** chambre	*their own room*
	leurs mains **propres**	*their clean hands*
certain	un **certain** ami à moi	*a certain friend of mine*
	des nouvelles **certaines**	*authentic news*
grand	un **grand** homme	*a great man*
	un homme **grand**	*a tall man*
brave	un **brave** homme	*a worthy man*
	un homme **brave**	*a brave man*
pauvre	un **pauvre** homme	*a poor man (to be pitied)*
	un homme **pauvre**	*a poor man (needy)*

4. Watch the irregular adjectives—

blanc, blanche   *white*
frais, fraîche   *fresh*
sec, sèche   *dry*

Do not confuse **fraîche** with **la fraise**, *the strawberry.*
Translate **un homme sec** by *a lean man.*

5. Remember the translation of *most* in a superlative—

The most *beautiful garden*	**Le plus** beau jardin
A most *beautiful garden*	**Un très** beau jardin
The garden is *most beautiful*	Le jardin est **très** beau

In passages, you will often see the following ways of translating *most*—

C'est un homme des plus intéressants. *He is a most interesting man.*

C'est tout ce qu'il y a de plus intéressant. *It is most interesting.*

6. In the construction *the more . . . the more*, put **plus** only, do not put **le** or **que**—

Plus on travaille, **plus** on sait. *The more one works, the more one knows.*

Plus il est diligent, **plus** il est heureux. *The more hard-working he is, the happier he is.*

Plus on a d'amis, **plus** on a de joie. *The more friends one has, the more joy one has.*

Revise the irregular verbs **aller**, *to go*, and **envoyer**, *to send*, and note the following idioms connected with them—

Comment allez-vous?	*How are you?*
Ce chapeau lui va	*This hat suits him*
Il y va de sa vie	*His life is at stake*
Au pis aller	*At the worst*
Tout va de mal en pis	*Everything goes from bad to worse*
Allez chercher	*Go and get, bring, or fetch*
J'enverrai chercher le médecin	*I shall send for the doctor*

Il envoya le domestique à tous les diables. *He mentally consigned the servant to perdition.*

Elle renvoya le domestique. *She dismissed the servant.*

VOCABULARY FOR EXERCISE 63

l'explorateur (*m.*), *the explorer*
le journal, *the newspaper*
le président, *the president*
le pois, *the pea, dot* (*in design*)
le vertige, *the giddiness*
la responsabilité, *the responsibility*

postiche, *false* (*of hair*)
approuver, *to approve of*
errer, *to wander*
télégraphier, *to telegraph*
chatoyant, *showy, glistening*
vif, *bright, vivid, lively*
sérieusement, *seriously*

EXERCISE 63

A. *Translate into English*

1. Aimez-vous cette robe rouge vif? 2. Elle est trop chatoyante.
3. Eh bien, aimez-vous cette cravate jaune clair à pois verts? 4. Quoi!
les cravates de cette sorte me donnent le vertige. 5. Quelle couleur
préférez-vous? 6. Je préfère le bleu foncé. 7. Même le président
approuva ce qu'il avait fait. 8. En même temps il télégraphia à son
cousin. 9. Les grands hommes ne sont pas toujours des hommes grands.
10. Napoléon même était assez petit.

B. *Translate into English*

1. Elle a les dents blanches. 2. Les pommes sont fraîches, les poires
sont sèches. 3. Cet explorateur était un homme sec, aux fausses dents.
4. Elle a acheté un kilo de fraises. 5. Pourvu qu'elles soient fraîches!
(Although **pourvu que** normally means *provided that*, it is often used to
express a hope. Say, *It is to be hoped that . . .*) 6. C'est l'étudiant le
plus intelligent de la classe. 7. C'est un étudiant très intelligent. 8.
C'est un homme des plus dangereux. 9. Plus on travaille, plus on
apprend. 10. Plus on est intelligent, plus on souffre.

C. *Translate into French*

1. The more money one has, the more responsibility one has. 2. How
are you? 3. I am very well, thanks. 4. That dress suits your cousin
Marie. 5. Which dress? The dark-green dress. 6. At the worst we
shall lose only five pounds. 7. The newspapers say that things are going
from bad to worse. 8. She was wandering at random through the wood.
9. Go and fetch your uncle. 10. If she were seriously ill, we should send
for the doctor.

D. *Translate into French*

1. He dismissed the servants. 2. A bright red tie makes him dizzy.
3. Young men like yellow ties with green dots. 4. Old men prefer ties

which are not so showy. 5. That girl has light-brown hair. 6. His own father refused to give him the money. 7. A certain friend of mine wrote to us from Australia. 8. The news was false. 9. We thought that it was authentic news. 10. The maid who brought us the meal had clean hands.

LESSON 64

The Adjectives (cont.)

1. In demonstrative adjectives, remember that the plural is always **ces**—

ces fleurs   *these flowers*

2. In possessive adjectives, watch **son** meaning *his* or *her*—

son livre   *his book* or *her book*

Note the use of the masculine form **mon, ton,** etc., with a vowel, or **h** mute—

my friend (fem.)   **mon** amie

3. In the indefinite adjectives, check **tel,** meaning *such*—

un tel homme, *such a man*; plural, **de tels** hommes, *such men.*

Do not confuse with the adverb *such*, which is **si**—

un si beau jardin, *such a fine garden*; plural, **de si** beaux jardins, *such fine gardens.*
un homme **si** intéressant, *such an interesting man*; des hommes **si** intéressants, *such interesting men.*

4. Note **quel** meaning *which,* or *what a*—

quel homme?   *which man?*
quel homme!   *what a man!*

5. Observe the translation of *both* by **deux** in the following three cases—

(*a*) With the definite article,

les deux hommes   *both the men*

(b) With a demonstrative adjective,

    ces deux hommes   *both these men*

(c) With a possessive adjective,

    mes deux amis   *both my friends*

Revise the numerals, noting especially—

-ze	*-teen*	e.g. **quinze**	*fifteen*
-te	*-ty*	**cinquante**	*fifty*
-aine	*about*	**une trentaine**	*about thirty*

Check the use of **s** with **cent**—

(a) Number on the left, e.g. deux cents hommes   200 *men.*

(b) Number on the right, e.g. deux cent deux hommes, 202 *men.*

Distinguish **mille**, *thousand*, and **milles**, *miles*—

    trois **mille** soldats   *three thousand soldiers*
    trois **milles**   *three miles*

Observe the phrases—

    des centaines de marins   *hundreds of sailors*
    des milliers d'aviateurs   *thousands of airmen*

Revise the use of dates—

    le premier mai   *on the first of May*
    le deux mai   *on the second of May*

Watch the construction with age and height—

    il a vingt ans   *he is twenty*
    il a cinq pieds dix pouces   *he is five feet ten*

Revise the regular **-ir** verbs, and check the parts where the irregular **-ir** groups **sentir**, *to feel*, and **ouvrir**, *to open*, differ from the regular **-ir** group.

Note the idiomatic uses of the verb **venir**—

    Il vient d'épouser cette femme. *He has just married that woman.*

    Il **venait de** panser la blessure. *He had just bandaged the wound.*

    Elle **vint à** tomber. *She happened to fall.*

    Elle **vint à** lui. *She came to him.*

Venez me chercher à sept heures. *Come for me at seven.*
à tout venant, *to all comers.*
le nouveau venu, *the new comer.*
Il en vint des villes environnantes. *Some came from the neighbouring towns.*
Tout vient à propos. *Everything comes at the right time.*
Il vint fort mal à propos. *He came at a most awkward time.*

VOCABULARY FOR EXERCISE 64

le nord, *the north*
le prisonnier, *the prisoner*
le citoyen, *the citizen*
la citoyenne, *the citizen*
la bicyclette, *the bicycle*
la Normandie, *Normandy*

la distance, *the distance*
la promesse, *the promise*
l'exposition (*f.*), *the exhibition*
fusiller, *to shoot*
mépriser, *to despise*
ravir, *to delight*

EXERCISE 64

A. *Translate into English*

1. Ces dames sont du nord de l'Angleterre. 2. Son ancienne amie était morte. 3. De tels hommes sont dangereux. 4. J'ai vu de si belles autos à l'exposition! 5. Quelle femme accepterait une telle offre? 6. Quelle artiste! Elle chante à merveille. 7. Ces deux Français devant nous disent qu'elle chante à ravir. 8. Les deux prisonniers furent fusillés. 9. Mes deux sœurs font une promenade en auto. 10. Allons faire une promenade à bicyclette.

B. *Translate into English*

1. Mes deux amis méprisent leurs bicyclettes maintenant. 2. Leur père a acheté une motocyclette pour eux. 3. Un jour ils allèrent à Londres. 4. Quelle distance y a-t-il d'ici à Londres? 5. Il y a au moins deux cents milles d'ici là. 6. Des centaines de fermiers protestaient. 7. Des milliers de citoyens protestaient encore plus. 8. On n'y fit pas attention, puis on fit cent promesses. 9. Mon ami est né le premier août. 10. Je connais un homme qui est né le vingt-cinq décembre.

C. *Translate into French*

1. Jeanne was born on the sixth of February. 2. How old is she? She is fifteen next week. 3. How tall are you? I am six feet one. 4. My sister has opened the letters. 5. I feel tired. 6. She felt the pain

of the wound. 7. He had just heard the news. 8. She had just telephoned when he arrived. 9. He happened to fall. 10. They came to him.

D. *Translate into French*

1. An idea came to him one night. 2. Call for me at half-past six. 3. I used to sing to all comers. 4. The newcomers play tennis. 5. Some came from Normandy. 6. Everything comes at the right time. 7. She came at a most awkward time. 8. We had just finished our supper. 9. I shall come for you at five. 10. Both these men deny it.

LESSON 65

The Pronouns

Note the difference between **Il me donne un livre,** *He gives me a book*; and **Il donne un livre à moi, pas à vous.**

The conjunctive pronouns (personal pronouns) come before the verb, except in a positive command—

Donnez-le-lui. *Give it to him.*

Remember the use of **en** for *of it,* and *of them,* even though they are omitted in English—

I have some cherries. Have you? J'ai des cerises. **En** avez-vous?

Similarly, note the insertion of **y** for *there,* even though it is omitted in English—

Have you some pear trees in your garden? Yes, we have some. Avez-vous des poiriers dans votre jardin? Oui, nous **y** en avons.

In the demonstrative pronouns, remember **celui-ci** can mean *the latter,* and **celui-là** *the former*—

Ces deux hommes-là? **Celui-ci** est riche, **celui-là** est pauvre. *Those two men? The latter is rich, the former is poor.*

Note the omission of **ci** and **là** when the next word is **de** or a relative pronoun—

celui de mon frère	*my brother's*
celui qui parle	*the one who is speaking*
celui que je vois	*the one whom I see*
celui dont je parle	*the one of whom I speak*

In the possessive pronouns, watch **le nôtre**, *ours*—

Ces livres-ci sont **les nôtres**. *These books are ours.*

Observe also the idiomatic **un de mes amis**, *a friend of mine.*

In the interrogative pronouns, note the use of **qui** for *who* or *whom*, no matter what the case may be—

Qui parle?	*Who speaks?*
Qui préférez-vous?	*Whom do you prefer?*
De qui parlez-vous?	*Of whom do you speak?*

(It is possible to use a longer form, **qui est-ce qui.**)

Contrast *who* with the interrogative pronoun *what*, which changes according to the case—

Subject: **Qu'est-ce qui** tombe? *What falls?*
Object: **Que** voyez-vous?   *What do you see?*
(A longer form **qu'est-ce que** may be used.)

After any preposition, put **quoi** for *what*—

De quoi parlez-vous?	*Of what do you speak?*
Avec quoi travaillez-vous?	*With what do you work?*

Be ready for the examination favourite—

A quoi pensez-vous? *Of what are you thinking?*

Observe the use of **quel** for *what* before *is*—

Quelle **en** est la raison? *What is the reason for it?*

In the disjunctive pronouns, check their use—

After a command,   e.g. **donnez-moi**, *give me.*
After the word **que**,   e.g. plus riche **que moi**, *richer than I.*
After **c'est**,   e.g. **C'est moi**, *It is I.*
After any preposition, e.g. **avec moi**, *with me.*
For emphasis,   e.g. **Moi**, lui parler? *Do you think I would speak to him?*
With a double subject, e.g. **Vous et moi, nous** écrivons. *You and I are writing.*

Check the regular **-re** verbs, and watch the following idiomatic uses of the irregular **-re** verb **faire,** *to make* or *to do*—

1. Speaking of any phase of the weather, use **il fait**—

      Il fait beau temps   *The weather is fine*

Never say **le temps fait** . . . .
If you are given the sentence *This summer has been fine*, say **Il a fait beau cet été.**

2. Speaking of walking or going any distance, use **faire**—
    Elle **a fait** quatre milles. *She has gone four miles.*

3.

Il fait de son mieux pour réussir	*He is doing his utmost to succeed*
Cela fait mon affaire	*That is just what I want*
Qu'est-ce que cela me fait?	*What is that to me?*
Il fera son chemin	*He will make headway*
Il m'a fait un mauvais tour	*He has played me a mean trick*
Elle s'est fait faire une robe	*She has had a dress made for herself*
Il s'est fait couper les cheveux	*He has had his hair cut*
Faites comme vous voudrez	*Do as you please*
Elle fait des façons	*She makes a fuss*
On se fait à tout	*One becomes accustomed to anything*
Sur ces entrefaites	*Meanwhile*
Cela ne fait rien	*That does not matter*
Elle fit mine de s'élancer par la fenêtre	*She made as if to jump out of the window*

VOCABULARY FOR EXERCISE 65

le roman, *the novel*
l'oreille (*f.*), *the ear*
affreux, *dreadful*
sourd, *deaf*

se demander, *to wonder*
faire semblant de, *to pretend, make a pretence of*

EXERCISE 65

A. *Translate into English*

1. Le professeur donna le prix à lui et à vous. 2. Nous avons des pommiers dans notre jardin. Y en avez-vous? Oui, nous y en avons.

3. Celui qui rit vendredi, dimanche pleurera. 4. Je connais ceux dont il parle. 5. Un de nos amis nous a invités au concert. 6. Qui voyez-vous? 7. Que dites-vous? 8. A qui pensez-vous? Je pense à vous. 9. A quoi pensez-vous? Je ne pense pas, j'écoute. 10. Que pensez-vous de lui? Je ne pense jamais à lui.

B. *Translate into English*

1. Donnez-moi de l'argent. 2. Donnez-m'en. 3. Ne m'en donnez pas. 4. Elle court à moi. 5. Elle est meilleure que moi. 6. Vous et moi nous allons au cinéma. 7. Il faisait un temps affreux. 8. Il fait du brouillard. 9. Il a fait beau ce printemps. 10. Ils ont fait dix milles aujourd'hui.

C. *Translate into French*

1. She is doing her utmost to win the prize. 2. She said to her sister: "That is my business." 3. What is that to you? 4. She will make her way. 5. They played a shabby trick on him. 6. She has had a house built for herself. 7. They are going to have their hair cut. 8. Do as you like. 9. Aunt Dine is very fussy. 10. Madeleine wondered if she would become accustomed to it.

D. *Translate into French*

1. That does not matter. 2. They pretend to be working. 3. He turned a deaf ear (use **faire** for *turn*). 4. The actress made as if to jump out of the window. 5. He spent his time reading novels. 6. It is becoming dark. 7. It was windy. 8. She pretended to be ill. 9. I shall walk the five miles (add **à pied,** *on foot*). 10. "Do so," he replied.

LESSON 66

The Pronouns (cont.)

In the relative pronouns, distinguish carefully subject **qui** and object **que.**

Provided the verb is active, a simple way to remember **qui** is to note that the verb will immediately follow the relative pronoun *who, that, which*—

l'homme **qui** parle	*the man who speaks*
l'accident **qui** arrive	*the accident that occurs*
le cheval **qui** mange	*the horse which eats*

If the verb does not immediately follow the relative pronoun, use **que**—

l'homme **que** je vois	*the man whom I see*
l'accident **qu'**il observe	*the accident that he sees*
le cheval **que** je possède	*the horse which I own*

Note the use of **dont** for *of whom* and *of which*—

le soldat **dont** je parle	*the soldier of whom I speak*
l'accident **dont** je parle	*the accident of which I speak*

Remember that **dont** can translate *whose*—

la mère **dont** le fils est malade	*the mother whose son is ill*
la mère **dont** je vois le fils	*the mother whose son I see*

But if there is a preposition before the word *whose*, **dont** cannot be used—

la mère **au fils de qui** je parle *the mother to whose son I speak*

For euphony, instead of **de qui** one puts **duquel**, when **il** or **ils** follows—

le père **au fils duquel il** parle *the father to whose son he speaks*
(This is easier to say than "le père au fils de qui il parle.")

Revise the relative pronoun *what*—

Subject: **ce qui**	Je sais **ce qui** arrive. *I know what happens.*
Object: **ce que**	Je sais **ce qu'il** sait. *I know what he knows.*
With *of* or *about*: **ce dont**	Je sais **ce dont** il parle. *I know what he is speaking about.*

If **ce qui, ce que** and **ce dont** are placed first in the sentence, it is usual to put **ce** before the second verb, but not if that verb is followed only by an adjective—

Ce qui arrive est intéressant	*What happens is interesting*
Ce qu'il désire **c'**est le trésor	*What he wants is the treasure*
Ce dont il parle **c'**est l'avenir	*What he speaks of is the future*

In using the negative pronouns, remember to put **ne** always before the verb—

Personne ne vient, *Nobody comes.* **Je ne** vois personne, *I see nobody.*

Check the verbs which use **être** as an auxiliary. They are generally connected with coming or going—

Elle est allée	*She has gone*
Elle est partie	*She has gone away*
Elle est sortie	*She has gone out*
Nous sommes entrés	*We have gone in*
Vous êtes rentrés	*You have gone home*
Ils sont retournés	*They have gone back*
Je suis monté	*I have gone up*
Il est descendu	*He has gone down*
Il est tombé	*He has fallen*
Elle est née	*She was born*
Elle est restée	*She has remained*
Elle est morte	*She has died*
Je suis venu	*I have come*
Il est arrivé	*He has arrived*
Nous sommes revenus	*We have come back*
Elle est devenue	*She has become*
J'en suis convenu	*I have agreed to it*

Watch the following examination favourites—

Qu'est-elle devenue?	*What has become of her?*
Que deviendra-t-elle?	*What will become of her?*

Je ne sais pas ce qu'elle est devenue. *I do not know what has become of her.*

Je ne sais pas ce qu'elle deviendra. *I do not know what will become of her.*

Le pauvre orphelin devenait ce qu'il pouvait. *The poor orphan was left to shift for himself.*

Watch the following idioms with the irregular verb, **dire**, *to say*—

au dire de tout le monde	*according to what everyone says*
ne disant mot	*not saying a word*
Elle lui a dit son fait	*She told him off*
Je dis que oui	*I say yes*
Vous dites que non	*You say no*
A la bonne heure, dit-elle	*"All right," she said*

(Note the inversion after direct speech in the above.)

aussitôt dit, aussitôt fait   *no sooner said than done*
dites donc!   *tell me, do!*
quant aux "que dira-t-on"   *as for public opinion*
Ce ne sont que des ouï-dire   *It is only hearsay*
J'ai entendu dire qu'elle est riche.   *I have heard that she is rich.*
Écoutez! me dit-elle à l'oreille.   *"Listen!" she whispered to me.*

VOCABULARY FOR EXERCISE 66

le marché, *the market*
aveugle, *blind*
muet, *dumb*
entier, *entire*
rétif, *restive*

selon, *according to*
étonner, *to astonish*
brûler, *to burn*
brûler de, *to long to, to be impatient to*

EXERCISE 66

A. *Translate into English*

1. C'est un homme qui déteste tout le monde. 2. Le cheval qu'il me donna était rétif. 3. La femme dont nous connaissons le fils est muette. 4. Le jardinier dont le fils est sourd travaille pour nous. 5. Le boulanger au fils de qui je parlais est devenu aveugle. 6. Je sais ce qui est tombé. 7. Elle sait ce que nous savons de l'affaire. 8. Nous savons ce dont vous avez besoin. 9. Ce dont il parle c'est d'acheter la maison. 10. Ce qu'il brûle de voir c'est le trésor.

B. *Translate into English*

1. Je ne crains rien. 2. Rien n'est arrivé. 3. Personne ne les aime. 4. Ils n'aiment personne. 5. Ni l'un ni l'autre ne viennent. 6. Ils ne préfèrent ni l'un ni l'autre. 7. Il n'assiste jamais aux concerts. 8. Jamais je n'ai vu une scène si étonnante. 9. Elle est arrivée lundi, elle est restée deux jours entiers, et elle est partie jeudi. 10. Je suis allé en France.

C. *Translate into French*

1. She had gone out. 2. They had gone in. 3. We have gone back. 4. She has gone home. 5. What has become of them? 6. What will become of Marie? 7. I don't know what has become of them. 8. I don't know what will become of Marie. 9. The poor orphan was left to his own resources. 10. She has gone down.

D. *Translate into French*

1. We have come back to you. 2. She agreed to it. 3. According to what everyone says he will win. 4. She went away without saying a word. (Use the infinitive after all prepositions except **en**.) 5. They told him off. 6. Let us go to the theatre tonight. All right! No sooner said than done. 7. We have heard that it is true. 8. It is only hearsay. 9. She said: "Yes"; Marie said: "No." 10. "Have you some sugar to sell?" he whispered in the farmer's ear. "We have nothing for the black market," replied the Frenchman.

LESSON 67

The Pronouns (concluded)

In the indefinite pronouns, watch **on**.

It is used for *one* in the general sense of *people*—

> **on dit**   *people say*

Do not confuse it with the numerical **un**—

> **l'un d'entre nous**   *one of us*

It is used to convey the passive. Thus, instead of saying **Elle est louée**, *she is praised*, one can say **On la loue**.

It is better to accustom oneself to the **on** form because it must be used with dative verbs in the passive—

> *She is obeyed*   **On lui obéit**

Watch the following—
She loves and obeys her mother. **Elle aime sa mère et lui obéit.**

The main dative verbs are **obéir**, *to obey*, **désobéir**, *to disobey*, **répondre à**, *to answer*, **résister à**, *to resist*, and the "classic" nine: **dire**, *to say*, **permettre**, *to permit*, **commander**, *to command*, **persuader**, *to persuade*, **ordonner**, *to order*, **promettre**, *to promise*, **conseiller**, *to advise*, **demander**, *to ask*, **défendre**, *to forbid*—

> *He is told*, **On lui dit**, not **Il est dit**.

Observe that other words can be used for *people* besides **on**—

(*a*) **le peuple** means *the nation*—

Le peuple anglais a résisté à ses ennemis. *The English nation has resisted its enemies.*

(*b*) **gens** means a group within the nation—

Ce sont de bonnes **gens,** nos voisins. *Nice people, our neighbours.*

Watch the words of quantity taking **de** before a noun, and **à** before an infinitive—

J'ai beaucoup **de** travail **à** faire. *I have much work to do.*
J'ai trop **de** lettres **à** écrire. *I have too many letters to write.*

Note that if the English has *of the* you must put *of the* in French—

many of the books   beaucoup **des** livres

Plus de is used before a quantity, **plus que** before comparison. Numbers will not help one to decide—

Plus de trois lions attaquèrent. *More than three lions attacked.*
Le tigre mange **plus que** deux lions. *The tiger eats more than two lions (eat).*

If you find when you repeat the verb that the passage makes sense, then **plus que** is the expression you want.

When a clause follows **plus que,** one puts a **ne** before the verb—

Elle sait **plus que** vous **ne** pensez. *She knows more than you think.*

But not after a negative or a question—

Elle **ne** sait **pas plus que** vous pensez. **Sait-elle plus que** vous pensez?

nor after a time conjunction—

Elle sait **plus que lorsqu'**elle était à Aberdeen. *She knows more than when she was in Aberdeen.*

Revise the reflexive verbs and watch the position of the object
vous—

Levez-vous!	*Get up!*
Ne vous levez pas!	*Don't get up!*
Vous levez-vous?	*Are you getting up?*

Remember the use of **être,** not **avoir,** in compound tenses,
and the agreement of the past participle only with a preceding
direct object—

Nous nous sommes levés. *We rose.*

but, **Nous nous sommes envoyé des cadeaux.** *We have sent
presents to each other.*

Watch the following idioms with the irregular **-re** verb,
prendre, *take*—

à tout prendre, *all things considered.*

Il prenait bien son temps. *He was certainly taking his
time.*

Elle a pris la lettre à la poste. *She took the letter from the
post.*

cf. **Elle a porté la lettre à la poste.** *She has taken the letter
to the post.*

and **Elle a mis la lettre à la poste.** *She has posted the letter.*

Les agents l'ont pris sur le fait. *The police have caught
him in the act.*

Il est difficile de prendre le coupable en flagrant délit.
It is difficult to catch the guilty red-handed.

Il prend la balle au bond. *He seizes his opportunity.*

la prise de la ville, *the capture of the city.*

la prise de tabac, *the pinch of snuff.*

la poignée de tabac, *the fill of tobacco.*

quelle ne fut sa surprise de voir . . ., *what was her
surprise to see . . . .*

Il le fit à plusieurs reprises. *He did it several times over.*

Il se fait comprendre. *He makes himself understood.*

VOCABULARY FOR EXERCISE 67

le caporal, *the corporal*
le sergent, *the srgeeant*
l'officier (*m.*), *the officer*
le sous-officier, *the non-com-missioned officer*
le mari, *the husband*
l'assaut (*m.*), *the assault*

le partenaire, *the partner* (*in games, dancing*)
la récompense, *the reward*
malgré, *in spite of*
ironique, *ironical*
matinal, *early*
corriger, *to correct*
nager, *to swim*

EXERCISE 67

A. *Translate into English*

1. Quant aux "que dira-t-on," tout cela s'arrangera. 2. Un d'entre vous a cassé la fenêtre. 3. Non, monsieur, on est diligent dans cette classe. 4. Quand on est dans l'armée, on obéit à ses officiers et à ses sous-officiers. 5. On détestait ce caporal, mais on lui obéissait. 6. On leur ordonne de prendre la place à l'assaut. 7. On leur persuade qu'ils recevront une récompense. 8. Ce sont de bonnes gens, les Walker. Mon partenaire et moi, nous avons gagné chaque partie de tennis malgré tous leurs efforts. 9. Le peuple anglais est fier de ses héros. 10. Avez-vous autant de travail à faire que moi?

B. *Translate into English*

1. Vous n'avez que trois heures de travail à faire? 2. Vous avez de la chance, vous! Moi, j'en ai quatre à faire. 3. Beaucoup des étudiants faisaient de leur mieux pour réussir. 4. J'ai plus de livres que vous. 5. J'ai plus de vingt devoirs à corriger. 6. Le lion mange plus que trois lapins. 7. Elle étudie plus que vous ne pensez. 8. Elle étudie plus que lorsqu'elle était à Paris. 9. Mais il y a tant de choses à faire dans cette ville-là. 10. "On est matinal," dit le sergent, d'un air ironique, aux soldats.

C. *Translate into French*

1. Go to bed. 2. Don't go to bed yet. 3. Do you go to bed at midnight? 4. When do you rise? 5. You rise at seven? You are early. 6. We have caught a cold. 7. We have not spoken to each other. 8. What presents did they send to each other? 9. All things considered, these boys work hard. 10. He was certainly taking his time.

D. *Translate into French*

1. She took the letter to the post. 2. He was caught red-handed. 3. The old woman asked him for a pinch of snuff. 4. Her husband

asked him for a fill of tobacco. 5. What was her surprise to see her son in that café! 6. He tried repeatedly to swim. 7. She easily makes herself understood in Paris. 8. They were caught in the act. 9. The capture of the town surprised us. 10. The news was telegraphed at once.

LESSON 68

The Verb

Watch the agreement of the past participle.

1. After **avoir** the past participle will not agree, unless there is a *preceding direct object*—

J'ai vu les hommes	*I have seen the men*
but, Je les ai **vus**	*I have seen them*
les hommes que j'ai **vus**	*the men whom I have seen*
Quels hommes avez-vous **vus**?	*What men have you seen?*

2. After **être,** the past participle must agree with the *subject*—

Les femmes **sont louées**   *The women are praised*

3. After a *reflexive* or *reciprocal* verb, the past participle agrees with the *preceding direct object only*—

Ils **se sont vus**	*They have seen each other*
Ils **se sont parlé**	*They have spoken to each other*

4. After an *impersonal* verb, the past participle never agrees—

les pluies qu'il a **fait**   *the rains there have been*

5. After a causative verb, the past participle never agrees—

la maison qu'il **a fait bâtir**   *the house which he has had built*

6. When the past participle does not control the preceding direct object there is no agreement—

les pommes que j'avais **espéré** acheter, *the apples which I had hoped to buy.*

les pommes que j'avais **voulu** acheter, *the apples which I had wanted to buy.*

les pommes que j'avais **cru** acheter, *the apples which I thought I had bought.*

7. Watch the following—

Used *actively*, the past participles *agree*.

Used *passively*, the past participles *do not agree*—

the boys whom I have heard singing, les garçons que j'ai **entendus** chanter.

the songs which I have heard sung, les chansons que j'ai **entendu** chanter.

the girls whom I have seen dancing, les jeunes filles que j'ai **vues** danser.

the dances that I have seen danced, les danses que j'ai **vu** danser.

The Tenses

A. The *if* clauses.

Remember the following tenses after **si.**

1. The *if* clause has a present tense when the principal clause has a future tense.

Si je viens, il viendra aussi. *If I come, he will come too.*

2. The *if* clause has an imperfect tense when the principal clause has a conditional tense.

Si je venais il viendrait. *If I came, he would come.*

Do not be misled by the English words—

If only you will come, I shall come too. **Si seulement vous venez, je viendrai aussi.**

3. As in (2), but compound tenses. To make sure, put your finger over the past participle *come* and you are left with type (2).

Si j'étais venu, il serait venu aussi. *If I had come he would have come too.*

B. When **si** means *whether*, the tense in French is the same as the tense in English—

Je me demande s'il viendra. *I wonder if he will come.*
Saviez-vous s'il viendrait? *Did you know if he would come?*

C. Look out for a repeated "if" clause—

if he comes and I am ill, **s'il vient et que je sois malade.**

(Note the **que** and the subjunctive mood in the second *if* clause.)

Revise the following idioms with the irregular **mettre,** *put—*

mettant la charrue avant (or devant) les bœufs	*putting the cart before the horse*
Il a mis trois heures à écrire cela	*He has taken three hours to write that*
Il se met à travailler	*He begins to work*
Elle se mit à table	*She sat down at table*
Il se mit à genoux	*He knelt down*
Ils se mirent à la besogne	*They set to work*
la mise-en-scène	*the setting*
la mise-en-plis	*the set (for the hair)*
donner sa démission	*to resign*
Le jour promet bien	*It looks like a fine day*
Il a manqué à sa promesse	*He has not kept his promise*
Il se soumit	*He submitted*
C'est un enfant soumis	*He is a submissive child*
ne remettez jamais au lendemain	*never put off till the morrow*

VOCABULARY FOR EXERCISE 68

le ministre, *the minister (government)*
la ballade, *the ballad*

la valse, *the waltz*
absent, *absent*
extraordinaire, *extraordinary*

EXERCISE 68

A. *Translate into English*

1. Quelles fleurs avez-vous vues? 2. Les hommes se sont battus l'un avec l'autre. 3. Ils se sont méfiés l'un de l'autre. 4. Elles se sont parlé. 5. Les pluies qu'il a fait sont extraordinaires. 6. La robe qu'elle s'est fait faire est charmante. 7. Les poires que j'avais espéré acheter. 8. La maison que j'avais voulu vendre. 9. Les hommes que j'ai entendus chanter. 10. Les ballades que j'ai entendu chanter.

B. *Translate into English*

1. Les femmes que j'ai vues danser. 2. Les valses que j'ai vu danser. 3. Si elle est diligente, elle gagnera le prix. 4. Si elle était paresseuse, elle perdrait la première place. 5. Si nous avions su cela, nous ne serions pas venus. 6. Si seulement vous vouliez travailler, votre mère serait si contente. 7. Si elle vient et qu'il soit absent de la maison, envoyez-le chercher. 8. Cet enfant-là est malheureux. Il met toujours la charrue devant les bœufs. 9. Combien de temps avez-vous mis à écrire cet exercice? 10. J'ai mis une heure et demie à l'écrire.

C. *Translate into French*

1. Too late he began to work. 2. She knelt as she went into the church. 3. The setting was most beautiful. 4. They set to work at once. 5. The minister has resigned. 6. He did not keep his promise. 7. The enemy submitted. 8. She is a submissive child. 9. Postpone it till tomorrow. 10. Post the letter tonight.

D. *Translate into French*

1. What books did you buy? 2. What books did you hope to buy? 3. The books I had wanted to buy were too dear. 4. They have written some letters to each other. 5. The presents which they have sent to each other are beautiful. 6. If she had the time, she would do it. 7. If we had gone out, we should have stayed at our friend's in the afternoon. 8. I wonder if she will succeed. 9. Did you know if he would refuse? 10. If we see him and he is ready, we shall go together to the concert.

LESSON 69

The Tenses of the Verb (cont.)

THE CONCEALED FUTURES AND CONDITIONALS

| **quand** | *when* | **aussitôt que** | *as soon as* |
| **lorsque** | *when* | **dès que** | *as soon as* |

These conjunctions require careful watching, because the tense after them depends on the tense in the other clause—

A. To denote habitual action, use the same tense as in the other clause—

> *When I go to Edinburgh I always enjoy myself.* **Quand** je **vais** à Édimbourg, je m'**amuse** toujours.
>
> *When I went to Edinburgh I always enjoyed myself.* **Quand** j'**allais** à Édimbourg, je m'**amusais** toujours.

B. To denote a single action, use the future when the other clause is future, or implies the future—

> *She says that she will enjoy herself when she goes to Liverpool.*
> Elle dit qu'elle s'**amusera quand** elle **ira** à Liverpool.

Look out for this examination favourite, where the conditional is required—

> *She said that she would enjoy herself when she went to Liverpool.*
> Elle dit qu'elle s'**amuserait quand** elle **irait** à Liverpool.

C. To denote habitual action in a compound tense, use the pluperfect—

> *Every day, when he had read his letters, he used to go out.*
> **Tous les jours,** quand il **avait lu** ses lettres, il **sortait.**

To denote a single action in a compound tense, use the past anterior—

> *One day, as soon as he had read his letters, he went out.* **Un jour,** aussitôt qu'il **eut lu** ses lettres, il **sortit.**

Verbs with Prepositions

1. Remember that before an infinitive, no preposition is used with—

sembler	*to seem*	e.g. **Il semble** être vrai. *It seems to be true.*
oser	*to dare*	**Je n'ose refuser.** *I dare not refuse.*
préférer	*to prefer*	**Il préfère se taire.** *He prefers to keep silent.*
espérer	*to hope*	**J'espère accepter.** *I hope to accept.*
désirer	*to desire*	**Je désire l'obtenir.** *I desire to obtain it.*

2. **À** is used:

(*a*) By verbs suggesting eagerness to do an action—

apprendre	*to learn*	e.g. **J'apprends à lire.** *I learn to read.*
inviter	*to invite*	**Je les invite à venir.** *I invite them to come.*

(*b*) By verbs of beginning—

commencer *to begin*   **Il commence à voir.** *He begins to see.*

(*c*) By all verbs of succeeding—

réussir   *to succeed*   **Je réussis à l'obtenir.** *I succeed in obtaining it.*

(*d*) By all verbs of forcing, if two different people are involved—

forcer   *to force*   **Il nous force à étudier.** *He forces us to study.*

3. **De** is used:

(*a*) By verbs denoting emotion—

regretter   *to regret*   **Je regrette d'entendre.** *I regret to hear.*

(*b*) By verbs of trying—

tâcher   *to try*   **Il tâche de gagner.** *He tries to win.*

(*c*) By verbs of stopping—

cesser   *to stop*   **Il cesse de pleuvoir.** *It stops raining.*

(*d*) By verbs of forcing when only one person is mentioned—

forcer   *to force*   **J'ai été forcé de signer.** *I was forced to sign.*

Revise the following idiomatic uses of **savoir,** *to know*—

à l'insu de son père	*unknown to his father*
à son insu	*without his knowledge*
ne sachant que faire	*not knowing what to do*
pas que je sache	*not that I know*

Il a su qu'elle mourait. *He learned that she was dying.*

Il y a un je ne sais quoi de mystérieux dans cette chambre. *There is something mysterious about this room.*

Elle a un je ne sais quel charme. *She has an indescribable charm.*

Elle vient de je ne sais où. *She comes from somewhere or other.*

Elle le fit je ne sais comment. *She did it somehow or other.*

Cette femme sait joindre les deux bouts. *This woman can make both ends meet.*

Il ne savait sur quel pied danser. *He did not know which way to turn.*

Elle sut gré à son mari. *She was grateful to her husband.*

Elle lui sut mauvais gré de son action. *She bore him a grudge for his action.*

Je ne saurais vous le dire. *I really couldn't say.*

Je ne saurais refuser. *I really couldn't refuse.*

VOCABULARY FOR EXERCISE 69

le mystère, *the mystery*
le malheur, *misfortune*
le bohémien, *the gipsy*
la bohémienne, *the gipsy*
la vérité, *the truth*
l'aventure (*f.*), *the adventure*

la bonne aventure, *fortune, fate*
  (*as prophesied*)
épeler, *to spell*
éviter, *to avoid*
pleurer, *to weep*

EXERCISE 69

A. *Translate into English*

1. Je n'ose dire la vérité. 2. Allez chercher le médecin. 3. Venez faire une partie de tennis. 4. Courez chercher des pommes. 5. Il préférerait se taire. 6. Il semble être vrai. 7. J'espère partir bientôt. 8. Elle aime à patiner. 9. Elle les invite à jouer. 10. J'apprends à épeler.

B. *Translate into English*

1. Nous commençons à voir enfin. 2. Je cherche à éviter le malheur. 3. Elle réussit à emprunter l'argent. 4. Leur père les force à étudier. 5. Il essaie de plaire à tout le monde. 6. Il déteste écouter la radio de ses voisins. 7. Il ne cesse de neiger. 8. Elle les prie d'accepter l'invitation. 9. Elles refusent de donner un sou au bohémien. 10. Il offre de lui dire la bonne aventure.

C. *Translate into French*

1. She was compelled to sell her jewels. 2. When we go to le Havre, we always enjoy ourselves. 3. When they went to London, they always enjoyed themselves. 4. When she comes I shall tell her the

truth. 5. He said that he would tell her the truth when she came.
6. One evening, as soon as he had finished his work, he went out.
7. Every evening, as soon as he had finished his work, he used to go out.
8. He smoked a cigarette without the knowledge of his father. 9. He
was in some cinema or other. 10. Not knowing what to say, she began
to weep.

D. *Translate into French*

1. Can he play the piano? 2. Not that I know. 3. There is some
mystery or other in this matter. 4. He had an indescribable charm.
5. They came from some village or other. 6. She succeeded in doing it
somehow or other. 7. The French housewife can make both ends
meet. 8. She was grateful to her sister. 9. I really could not say what
time it was. 10. I really could not refuse.

LESSON 70

The Subjunctive Mood

Remember that the subjunctive mood follows a clause denoting—

a wish: **Je veux qu'il le fasse,** *I want him to do it;*
a command: **J'ordonne qu'on le fasse,** *I order it to be done;*
a doubt: **Je doute qu'elle le reçoive,** *I doubt whether she
will receive it;*
or an emotion: **Je regrette qu'elle soit malade,** *I regret that
she is ill.*

Note that the clauses must be joined by **que,** and that there
must be two different people involved—

Je regrette d'être en retard. *I regret that I am late.*
(One person only, so no subjunctive.)

Je suis heureux quand elle est ici. *I am happy when she
is here.*
(Clauses joined by **quand,** so no subjunctive.)

Among the emotions, watch the verbs of fearing, which take
ne as well as the subjunctive in the subordinate clause—

Je crains qu'elle ne vienne. *I fear she is coming.*

Similarly—

Ne craignez-vous pas qu'elle ne vienne? *Are you not afraid she is coming?*

but, **Je ne crains pas qu'elle vienne?** *I am not afraid she is coming* (negative).

and **Craignez-vous qu'elle vienne?** *Do you fear she is coming?* (interrogative).

Verbs of doubt and denial also take this **ne,** but only when they themselves are negative—

Je ne doute pas qu'elle ne vienne. *I don't doubt she is coming.*

Je ne nie pas qu'elle ne vienne. *I don't deny that she is coming.*

Watch for the examiner putting a clause between a verb of fearing and its object clause—

I fear that, if she comes tomorrow, she will refuse. **Je crains que, si elle vient demain, elle ne refuse.**

The student must resist the temptation to forget the subjunctive **refuse,** and remember the **ne** goes before **refuse,** not **vient.**

Watch the sequence of tenses closely—

(i) *I want him to win* **Je veux qu'il gagne** (present tenses)

(ii) *I wanted him to win* **Je voulais qu'il gagnât** (past tenses)

(iii) *I am sorry she did it* **Je regrette qu'elle l'ait fait** (present followed by past)

Number (iii) is an examination favourite.

Remember the verbs which suggest doubt when interrogative or negative—

Êtes-vous sûr qu'il soit ici? *Are you sure that he is here?*

Pensez-vous qu'elle vienne? *Do you think she is coming?*

Examiners are fond of putting an *ought* phrase after these—

Do you think I ought to do it?

This difficulty is usually surmounted by saying—

Est-ce que vous pensez que je devrais le faire?

The **est-ce que** conveys the interrogative, whereas the **vous pensez,** being affirmative, can take the indicative.

Among the virtual superlatives, **premier,** *first,* **dernier,** *last,* **rares,** *few,* **seul,** *only,* it is now quite common to see the indicative used after **premier** and **dernier,** the others still being followed by the subjunctive.

In the adverbial clauses which take the subjunctive, remember that **à moins que** is often seen with **ne,** e.g. **à moins qu'elle ne le fasse,** *unless she does it.*

Clumsy subjunctive clauses can often be avoided by using a preposition and a noun instead, e.g. **avant son départ,** *before he went away;* **jusqu'à son arrivée,** *until he arrived;* **à mon insu,** *without my knowing;* **à leur rencontre,** *to meet them.*

The Word "whatever"

THE INDEFINITE PAIR

1. Put **quoi que ce soit qui** for *whatever* if it is immediately followed by a verb—

    whatever happens   **quoi que ce soit qui arrive**

2. Put **quoi que** if a verb does not immediately follow—

    whatever you do   **quoi que vous fassiez**

Similarly—

    whoever speaks   **qui que ce soit qui parle**

    whoever you are   **qui que vous soyez**

Note why it is so important not to confuse **quoique** *although* (one word) and **quoi que** *whatever* (two words).

THE DEFINITE PAIR

1. Put **quelque(s)** for *whatever* if it is followed by a noun—

    whatever intentions he has, **quelques intentions qu'il ait.**

2. Put **quel que** (*fem.* **quelle que,** *masc. plural* **quels que,** *fem. plural* **quelles que**) if it is not followed by a noun—

    whatever his intentions may be, **quelles que soient ses intentions.**

Revise the following idiomatic uses of the irregular **-oir** verb, **pouvoir**—

Il manquait du pouvoir	*He lacked the power*
ne pouvant plus	*being exhausted*
J'aurais dû refuser	*I ought to have refused*
Il se peut qu'elle vienne	*It is possible she may come*
Cela se pourrait bien	*That might well be*
pourriez-vous?	*could you?*
il ne pouvait plus que	*he could now only*
tant que je pourrai	*as long as I am able*
quand même je pourrais	*even if I could*

VOCABULARY FOR EXERCISE 70

le fruit, *the fruit*	effrayer, *to frighten*
le menteur, *the liar*	sarcler, *to weed*
le voleur, *the thief*	guérir, *to cure, heal*
l'idée (*f.*), *the idea*	se guérir, *to recover*
accomplir, *to accomplish*	

EXERCISE 70

A. *Translate into English*

1. Je désire qu'ils fassent de leur mieux pour réussir. 2. Elle doute qu'il reçoive le prix. 3. Nous regrettons que vous soyez en retard. 4. Craignez-vous qu'elle soit malade? 5. Je crains qu'elle n'ait mal à la poitrine. 6. Je ne doute pas qu'elle ne se guérisse. 7. Elle ne nie pas qu'il ne soit voleur. 8. Je crains que lorsqu'elle le verra elle ne soit effrayée. 9. Êtes-vous sûr qu'il soit intelligent? 10. Est-ce que vous pensez que je devrais répondre à la lettre?

B. *Translate into English*

1. Je finirai mon travail avant votre départ. 2. Je sarclerai le jardin jusqu'à leur arrivée. 3. Elle a fumé une cigarette à mon insu. 4. Quoi que ce soit qui arrive, elle devrait rester ici. 5. Quoi qu'il en soit, n'ayons pas peur de dire la vérité. 6. Quoi que vous fassiez, faites-le bien. 7. Qui qu'il soit, à vrai dire j'ai peur de lui. 8. Qui que ce soit qui mente est menteur. 9. Quelques idées qu'il ait, il n'accomplit rien. 10. Quelles que soient ses idées, elles restent sans fruit.

C. *Translate into French*

1. Although she works hard, she does not succeed. 2. Whatever she does, she receives nothing. 3. She lacked the power. 4. We could have refused to come. 5. It is possible that they may come at half past seven. 6. They say she is rich. That may well be. 7. The poor woman was left to her own devices. 8. She is doing her utmost. 9. Could you tell me the way to the station? 10. Yes I can. The first street on the right.

D. *Translate into French*

1. As long as we are able, we shall continue to work. 2. Even if I could pay, I should refuse to do so. 3. Do you think he ought to come? 4. Are you sure he ought to stay? 5. I want him to stay at our house. 6. Jeanne wanted him to play at tennis. 7. She is sorry he lost every game. 8. I am not sure he went to meet them. 9. Do you believe he is telling the truth? 10. I am afraid he is telling a lie.

PASSAGES FOR TRANSLATION

Section A—Prose: French–English

1. La Classe

Les enfants sont dans la classe. La classe est grande. Le professeur est aussi dans la classe. Il est devant la classe. Les étudiants sont intelligents. Ils étudient bien. Jean est étudiant. Jean est le premier de la classe. Il travaille bien. Les étudiants préparent la leçon. Alphonse ne travaille pas bien. Il est paresseux. Alphonse est le dernier de la classe.

1. Où sont les enfants? 2. La classe est-elle petite? 2. Où est le professeur? 4. Qui est le premier de la classe? 5. Qui est le dernier? 6. Pourquoi est-il le dernier?

2. Les Amis

Pierre est un ami de Jean. Pierre est Français. Il est en France. Jean est Anglais. Il est en Angleterre. Pierre invite Jean à passer les vacances en France. Pierre a une bicyclette. Jean admire la bicyclette. Après la visite Jean retourne en Angleterre. Il parle à sa mère et à son père. "Je désire une bicyclette." La mère parle au père. "Jean est le premier de la classe. Il mérite un cadeau." Le père ne refuse pas. Il donne une bicyclette à Jean.

1. Qui est Pierre? 2. Est-il Anglais? 3. Qu'est-ce que Jean admire? 4. Que désire-t-il? 5. Qui parle au père? 6. Que donne-t-il à Jean?

3. Les Trains

Jules et Riquet aiment les trains. Les trains sont dans la gare. Jules crie à Riquet, "Je compte les trains, un, deux, trois, quatre, cinq." Un train arrive. La locomotive siffle. Riquet compte les passagers, six, sept, huit, neuf, dix, onze, douze. Le train est vide. Jules consulte sa montre. "Quelle heure est-il à votre montre?" demande Riquet. "Il est sept heures et demie! A la maison!"

1. Où sont les amis? 2. Que comptent-ils? 3. D'où arrivent les passagers? 4. Quelle heure est-il à la montre de Jules? 5. Pourquoi les amis retournent-ils à la maison?

4. Le Café

Victor et sa soeur Marie voyagent en France. Ils arrivent à Paris. Sur le trottoir devant un restaurant il y a plusieurs tables. "C'est charmant," dit Marie. "Je désire un repas ici." Victor trouve des places. Le garçon arrive. "Monsieur désire?" dit-il. Victor commande le repas. Après le repas Victor et Marie regardent les passants pour s'amuser.

1. Qui voyagent en France? 2. Où est le restaurant? 3. Que dit Marie? 4. Que dit le garçon? 5. Pourquoi Victor et Marie regardent-ils les passants?

5. Le Printemps

Au printemps la terre est très belle. Elle est couverte de fleurs. Les animaux sont contents de voir l'herbe tendre des champs. Les moutons et les agneaux quittent les plaines. Ils partent pour les collines. Un berger les garde. Les chiens du berger accompagnent les bêtes.

1. Décrivez la terre au printemps. 2. Pourquoi les animaux sont-ils contents? 3. Que font les moutons? 4. Où vont-ils? 5. Qui les garde? 6. Que font les chiens?

6. L'Hiver

En hiver il fait froid. A cinq heures, au mois de décembre, il fait nuit. Quelquefois la neige couvre la terre. Les arbres n'ont pas de feuilles. Les enfants font des hommes de neige. Ils font aussi des boules de neige. Ils sont joyeux. Mais les grandes personnes n'aiment pas la neige. Ils préfèrent rester à la maison, où il y a un bon feu.

1. A quelle heure fait-il nuit, au mois de décembre? 2. Qu'est-ce qui couvre la terre? 3. Que font les enfants? 4. Sont-ils joyeux? 5. Que préfèrent les grandes personnes? 6. Qu'y a-t-il à la maison?

7. L'ÉTÉ

En été il fait très chaud. Les grandes vacances arrivent au mois de juillet, et nous allons au bord de la mer. Cette fois nous allons en France. Nous avons déjà un passeport. Notre ami Paul était en France l'année dernière. Il a aimé les courses sur le sable. Les enfants aiment la course à l'œuf. Quelle omelette si l'œuf tombe!

1. Quel temps fait-il en été? 2. Où allons-nous au mois de juillet? 3. Pourquoi avons-nous un passeport? 4. Où fait-on les courses? 5. Pourquoi aime-t-on le sable? 6. Qu'est-ce qui arrive si un œuf tombe?

8. L'AUTOMNE

En automne les fruits sont mûrs. Les arbres sont chargés de pommes, de poires, et de prunes. Presque tous les enfants aiment les poires. Voici une anecdote d'un homme qui aimait les poires. "Mon fils," dit-il à son enfant, "apporte-moi les deux belles poires du poirier. Elles sont mûres." L'enfant va chercher les poires. Il revient à son père. Le père donne une poire au fils et commence à manger l'autre poire. Mais l'enfant prend son canif et pèle sa poire. "Comment!" dit le père. "Moi, je mange ma poire sans la peler, mais toi, tu pèles ta poire. Pourquoi cela?" "En arrivant ici," répond l'enfant, "j'ai laissé tomber une poire dans la boue, et je ne suis pas certain si c'est ma poire ou non."

1. Quels fruits sont mûrs en automne? 2. Que dit l'homme à son fils? 3. Où va le fils? 4. Que donne-t-il à son père? 5. Pourquoi prend-il son canif? 6. Pourquoi pèle-t-il sa poire?

9. L'ACCIDENT

Une femme ramasse du bois mort dans la forêt. Mais une charrette lancée au galop descend la route forestière. En faisant un effort pour se garer, elle tombe dans un trou et les deux roues de la charrette lui passent sur le corps. Le docteur arrive. Il examine la femme. Elle est très malade. Des hommes la portent à une hutte. Elle souffre; elle crie. L'hôpital est à dix kilomètres de la forêt. Enfin elle arrive à l'hôpital. Elle reste six semaines à l'hôpital. Elle marche peu à peu. Enfin elle est guérie. Elle revient à sa maison.

1. Pourquoi la femme est-elle dans la forêt? 2. Que fait la charrette? 3. Que fait la femme? 4. Qui arrive? 5. Où est l'hôpital? 6. Quand quitte-t-elle l'hôpital?

10. Le Délai

Un soir brumeux d'octobre deux personnes se trouvent dans la cuisine de leur ferme. Les animaux sont déjà aux étables. Devant le feu un chat ronronne. Les deux femmes parlent. La mère parle à sa fille.

— Huit heures! Je commence à être sérieusement inquiète. Où est ton père? Il n'est jamais rentré si tard.

— Ne t'inquiète pas, maman, répond la fille, qui s'appelle Lucie.

La mère essaie de tricoter. Le chat met la patte sur la pelote de laine. La jeune fille prépare le souper. L'horloge sonne un coup.

— Huit heures et demie! dit la mère. Décidément, ce n'est pas naturel.

A ce moment le père arrive. Il fait ses excuses à sa famille. Son auto a eu une panne.

1. Qui sont dans la cuisine? 2. Où sont les animaux? 3. Que fait le chat? 4. Quelle heure est-il? 5. Pourquoi la mère est-elle inquiète? 6. Que dit le père quand il arrive?

11. Le Boucher

Maman parle à Pierre:

— Va chez le boucher acheter des saucisses. Pierre appelle son chien Fidèle.

— Nous allons acheter des saucisses, Fidèle. Le petit chien est content. Il agite la queue. Il accompagne son jeune maître chez le boucher. Pierre met l'argent sur le comptoir. Le boucher accepte l'argent et lui donne de la monnaie, et un morceau de viande pour Fidèle. En trottant le long de la rue Fidèle observe un chat. Il le chasse. Il laisse tomber son morceau de viande. Un autre chien arrive. Il vole la viande. Fidèle n'attrape pas le chat. L'autre chien est parti avec la viande. Fidèle revient à Pierre. L'oreille basse, il lui conte l'affaire des yeux. Pierre le console. Fidèle reçoit une saucisse quand maman a entendu l'histoire.

Answer in English: 1. What does Peter buy? 2. Who goes with him? 3. What does the dog see? 4. Who steals the meat? 5. What does Peter do?

Answer in French: 1. Où va Pierre? 2. Que met-il sur le comptoir? 3. Que chasse Fidèle? 4. Pourquoi Fidèle a-t-il l'oreille basse? 5. Que fait la mère?

12. LE TEMPS

Les enfants espèrent faire un pique-nique. Maman a préparé toutes sortes de bonnes choses, du gâteau, de la gelée, de la glace, et de la limonade. Mais hélas! Quand les enfants se trouvent à la campagne, le soleil disparaît. La pluie commence à tomber. Les enfants courent s'abriter sous les arbres. Les feuilles des arbres protègent les enfants. La pluie tombe toujours. Quel dommage! Mais enfin l'eau cesse de tomber. Le soleil brille. Après quelques moments l'herbe est plus fraîche. Les enfants mangent et boivent. Après, ils jouent sur l'herbe. Même de petits lapins sortent de leur garenne. Cela amuse les enfants. Puis ils cueillent des fleurs aux doux parfums et aux belles couleurs.

Answer in English: 1. What has Mother prepared? 2. Where do the children go? 3. What starts to fall? 4. Why do the children shelter? 5. What protects them?

Answer in French: 1. Que font les enfants? 2. Décrivez l'herbe après a pluie. 3. Quels animaux apparaissent? 4. Que cueillent les enfants? 5. Décrivez quelques couleurs de fleurs.

13. LA RENCONTRE

Le jour paraît. Pierre saute du lit et va chercher l'indicateur des chemins de fer. Il désire savoir les heures des trains venant de Nantes. Il pense: "Mon télégramme est arrivé hier vers midi, peut-être avant. Marcel l'a trouvé après avoir déjeuné, sans doute, à son restaurant. Je suis sûr qu'il va s'arranger avec son directeur pour pouvoir partir tout de suite. Je suis sûr qu'il a pris le train du soir. En ce cas je le verrai à la gare dans une heure."

Pierre fait sa toilette et s'habille rapidement. Il court le long des rues désertes. Comme il arrive sur le quai, le train entre en gare. Des voyageurs descendent et, dans le premier groupe, Pierre aperçoit Marcel. Les deux amis s'embrassent.

Pierre dit à Marcel :

— Tu as l'air fatigué.

Marcel répond avec une grimace :

— Je n'ai pas dormi. Il y avait des gens impossibles dans mon compartiment.

Pierre dit :

— Nous allons déjeuner dans un restaurant tout près. Et puis nous montons chez moi.

Answer in English: 1. Why does Pierre look for the time-table? 2. What has he sent Marcel? 3. What train will Marcel take? 4. When will the train arrive? 5. Why does Peter run to the station?

Answer in French: 1. Qui descendent du train? 2. Qui est dans le premier groupe? 3. Que font les amis? 4. Pourquoi Marcel est-il fatigué? 5. Où vont les amis?

14. Le Voleur

Un nombre de visiteurs anglais à la Riviera ont été les victimes d'un jeune voleur, qui est âgé de dix-neuf ans seulement. C'est un voleur très habile. Mais il a été attrapé. Il explique à la police ses petits tours.

— Je fais mon entrée dans un des principaux hôtels de Nice par une fenêtre ouverte. Je la gagne en sautant d'un haut arbre. Une fois, en cherchant des objets de valeur dans l'une des chambres, j'entends marcher dehors. Je me glisse à la hâte dans le lit. La porte s'ouvre. 'Qu'est-ce que c'est? Je désire dormir. Ne me dérangez pas !' Ma ruse réussit. La femme de chambre se retire toute confuse.

Answer in English: 1. Who were the thief's victims? 2. How old was the thief? 3. What does he explain to the police? 4. How did he avoid detection once? 5. What did he say to the maid?

Answer in French: 1. Qui a attrapé le voleur? 2. Comment fait-il son entrée dans un hôtel? 3. Que cherche le voleur? 4. Pourquoi se glisse-t-il dans le lit? 5. Qui ouvre la porte?

15. L'Emprunt

Un soir Offenbach errait sur le Boulevard des Italiens, l'estomac vide depuis vingt-quatre heures, regardant d'un œil rageur les clients des grands restaurants. Tout à coup il se sent frapper sur l'épaule par un passant.

— N'êtes-vous pas Monsieur Offenbach?

— Heu . . . oui . . . oui.

— Voici vingt francs.

— Pardon!

— Un louis que je dois à monsieur votre frère depuis six mois et que vous allez peut-être avoir la bonté de lui donner de ma part.

— Mais . . . bien volontiers.

Et le débiteur disparaît. Offenbach reste là, son louis à la main.

— Je rêve, évidemment. J'espère ne pas me réveiller avant d'avoir dîné!

Quelques instants après il est attablé au Café Anglais devant un perdreau et une bouteille de Saint-Julien.

Answer in English: 1. To whom does the stranger owe the money? 2. How long has he owed it? 3. Why did he pay it to Offenbach? 4. Where does Offenbach dine? 5. What does he order?

Answer in French: 1. Où se trouve Offenbach? 2. Qui le frappe sur l'épaule? 3. Que lui donne l'étranger? 4. Combien d'argent lui offre-t-il? 5. Que dit Offenbach?

16. L'ARRIVÉE DE L'AVION

Onze heures cinq, l'avion New York–Paris s'immobilise sur la piste de ciment de l'aéroport. La porte du quadrimoteur s'ouvre, laissant apparaître la silhouette bleu marine de l'hôtesse de l'air.

Un à un les trente-cinq passagers descendent les marches.

Ils sont répartis par petits groupes. Les uns vont à la douane, les autres attendent leur tour.

A une jeune Canadienne qui est prête à prendre le car à 11h.45, nous demandons:

— Êtes-vous satisfaite des formalités d'accueil, Mademoiselle?

— Oui, très.

Answer in English: 1. When does the plane arrive? 2. How many engines has it? 3. Who appears at the door? 4. How do the passengers alight? 5. Why are they divided into groups?

Answer in French: 1. D'où arrive l'avion? 2. Quels sont les devoirs de l'hôtesse de l'air? 3. Pourquoi les passagers vont-ils à la douane? 4. A quelle heure part le car? 5. Que dit la Canadienne?

17. LE RAT

Un matin le docteur sort de son appartement et bute sur un rat mort, juste devant la porte. Sur le moment, il écarte la bête sans y faire attention et descend l'escalier. Mais, arrivé dans la rue, la pensée lui vient que ce rat mort n'est pas à sa place, et il retourne sur ses pas pour conter l'affaire au concierge. Quand il entend la nouvelle extraordinaire, le concierge reste d'abord stupéfait. C'est une chose impossible. Il proteste, il crie. Le docteur est surpris. La présence de ce rat paraît seulement bizarre au docteur, mais pour le concierge elle est un scandale. Il affirme qu'il n'y a pas de rats dans la maison. Le docteur l'assure en vain qu'il y a un rat sur le palier du premier étage; le concierge refuse de croire une telle chose.

Answer in English: 1. Where does the doctor find the rat? 2. What does he do with it? 3. Why does he return to the house? 4. What is the reaction of the caretaker? 5. Why does he not believe the doctor?

Answer in French: 1. Que signifie "bute sur"? 2. Pourquoi écarte-t-il la bête? 3. Que dit-il au concierge? 4. Quelle réponse reçoit-il? 5. A quel étage demeure le docteur?

18. LE NEVEU

Le neveu du pharmacien est un jeune homme de vingt et un ans. Il a l'air distingué, des yeux très bleus, une bouche fine et des manières aristocratiques. Il ne ressemble pas du tout à son oncle. Ce dernier est un homme rougeaud, courtaud et vulgaire. Le jeune homme avait déjà complété ses études à l'École de Pharmacie. Il fait maintenant son apprentissage chez son oncle. Le vieux va bientôt se retirer des affaires. Il donne la boutique à son neveu. Mais cela n'enchante pas le jeune homme. Il désire quitter la ville de province. Il désire s'établir à Paris. Naturellement l'oncle ne veut pas le voir partir. Il a élevé son neveu. Par reconnaissance Jean se résigne à son sort.

Answer in English: 1. How old is the nephew? 2. Describe his appearance. 3. Does he look like his uncle? 4. Describe the uncle. 5. Where had the young man studied?

Answer in French: 1. Que fait le jeune homme maintenant? 2. Que va faire le vieux? 3. A qui donne-t-il la boutique? 4. Quelle est la réaction du neveu? 5. Où désire-t-il aller?

19. L'Enclos

C'est un de ces endroits pour campeurs, comme on en voit beaucoup aujourd'hui, au voisinage de la Méditerranée.

Deux hommes parlaient à travers la clôture, l'un en short, l'autre en costume de ville.

— L'endroit est agréable, dit le campeur, mais il y a trop de désordre. Chacun dresse sa tente au hasard. A tout moment on se prend les pieds dans les cordes. La semaine prochaine nous tracerons des allées.

— Cela sera plus net, approuve le monsieur du dehors. Il y a un silence. Le monsieur parle encore une fois.

— Le soir, êtes-vous gêné par le bruit?

— En général, non. Tout le monde est tranquille. Quelque-fois, ceux qui viennent en voiture ont une radio et la font fonctionner jusqu'à une heure inadmissible. De temps en temps nous crions pour les faire taire. En principe ils n'ont pas le droit. Mais nous autres Français, nous n'avons pas d'organisation.

Answer in English: 1. Where is the camp? 2. How are the two men dressed? 3. What does the camper say? 4. Why do people catch their feet in the ropes? 5. What causes the noise at night?

Answer in French: 1. Pourquoi le campeur est-il fâché? 2. Que font les gens qui ont une radio? 3. Pourquoi les autres campeurs crient-ils? 4. Que traceront-ils la semaine prochaine? 5. Que dit le campeur au sujet des Français?

20. Le Guide de montagne

Les gens de la montagne, comme ceux de la mer, ont leurs héros à eux. Chaque jour, ces hommes accomplissent en silence de périlleuses tâches. La récente catastrophe aérienne survenue au sommet du Mont Blanc a démontré, une fois de plus, le courage des guides de haute montagne.

Un avion de la ligne Bombay–Londres s'écrasa, avec ses quarante-huit passagers, à peu de distance du sommet de la montagne. Des équipes de sauvetage se formèrent tout de suite afin de porter secours aux survivants.

Il faisait mauvais temps lorsque René Payot, un des meilleurs
guides de France, partit avec quatre autres montagnards pour
tenter l'ascension de la montagne.

Le vent hurlait et la neige tombait dru. Soudain le guide
perdit pied et disparut dans une crevasse profonde; en même
temps une avalanche le recouvrit. René Payot, héros de la
montagne, avait cessé de vivre.

Answer in English: 1. Where was the disaster? 2. What had happened
to the plane? 3. How many passengers were on board? 4. Why were
rescue teams formed? 5. What was the weather like?

Answer in French: 1. Comment s'appelle le héros? 2. Qu'a-t-il fait?
3. Avec qui est-il parti? 4. Pourquoi sont-ils partis? 5. Comment
a-t-il perdu la vie?

21. Napoléon à Sainte-Hélène

En 1816, la vie de Napoléon à Sainte-Hélène rentra dans la
monotonie qui ne devait guère varier jusqu'à sa mort. Ses
habitudes étaient toujours les mêmes. N'ayant qu'un sommeil
fréquemment interrompu, surtout quand il s'était couché de
bonne heure faute de pouvoir occuper ses soirées, il se levait,
lisait, dictait s'il avait Bertrand à sa portée, se recouchait, en
changeant de lit, cherchait ainsi le sommeil qui le fuyait, montait
à cheval dès que le soleil éclairait le plateau de Longwood, et
recommençait à tourner dans ce qu'il appelait "le cercle de son
enfer." Cette promenade lui devenait chaque jour plus désagréable, car pour en franchir les limites il aurait fallu traîner
après lui le malheureux officier attaché à sa garde. Le plaisir
même qu'il avait à entretenir quelques voisins était gâté par la
crainte de les compromettre en excitant les soupçons du gouverneur. A peine osait-il faire un peu de bien autour de lui de peur
d'avoir l'air de chercher des complices d'une évasion chimérique.

22. Louis Pasteur

Peu de noms sont aussi justement célèbres que celui de Louis
Pasteur. Le dix-neuvième siècle n'en a de plus grand, et je
puis dire, il n'en a pas de meilleur.

L'enfant, lorsqu'il eut l'âge d'apprendre à lire, alla à l'école
primaire d'Arbois, petite ville où son père était venu habiter.
Au lycée d'Arbois, où son père le plaça ensuite, il se montra

un élève appliqué, et que, peu à peu, la passion du travail péné-
trait. Il n'était pas dans les premiers de sa classe, mais il sentait
la puissance de sa volonté, et déjà, il se fiait à elle, comme au
plus sûr moyen de dépasser tous ceux de ses camarades qui
semblaient plus brillants que lui. L'ambition lui venait. Il se
laissait aisément persuader de se préparer pour l'université. Mais
un sentiment plus rare accompagnait cette ambition naissante.
Louis Pasteur voulait s'élever pour faire le bonheur de sa famille,
pour honorer et remercier son père, et il éprouvait une reconnaissance touchante envers ceux qui l'aidaient dans ses études.

Les découvertes scientifiques, la dignité de sa vie, son désintéressement—car Pasteur ne voulut point tirer un profit
personnel de ses inventions dont une seule eût pu faire sa fortune
—valurent au savant français une gloire incomparable.

23. Surpris par une averse

Après un quart d'heure de repos, Pierre et Guillaume avaient
repris leur promenade, gagnant le lac, allant passer au carrefour
des Cascades, pour revenir vers Neuilly, en faisant le tour, par
l'autre bord de l'eau. Mais une ondée tomba, les força de
s'abriter sous les grosses branches encore nues d'un marronnier;
et, la pluie devenant sérieuse, ils avisèrent, au fond d'un bouquet
d'arbres, une sorte de chalet, un petit café-restaurant, où ils
coururent se réfugier. Dans une allée voisine, ils avaient aperçu
un fiacre arrêté, solitaire, dont le cocher, immobile, attendait
philosophiquement sous la petite pluie d'été. Et, comme Pierre
se hâtait, il eut l'étonnement de reconnaître devant lui, pressant
également le pas, Gérard de Quinsac, qui se réfugiait là comme
eux, surpris sans doute par l'averse pendant une promenade à
pied. Puis, il crut s'être trompé, car il ne vit pas le jeune homme
dans la salle. Cette salle, une sorte de véranda vitrée, garnie de
quelques tables de marbre, était vide. Et rien ne bougeait, la
maison sortait à peine de l'hiver, on y sentait la longue humidité
des établissements que la disparition de la clientèle force à fermer
de novembre à mars.

24. Nos Excursions hebdomadaires

Aussitôt que nous sortions de Paris en chemin de fer, c'était de
chaque côté les immenses jardins pleins de légumes. Puis

venaient les vergers. Le printemps les avait fleuris de blanc et de rose. Enfin nous descendions dans un endroit choisi d'avance.

Après une matinée de marche sur les routes, nous nous arrêtions dans une petite auberge, sous une sorte de véranda ouverte à tous les vents, et construite surtout pour les Parisiens du dimanche. . . . Un moineau avait fait son nid au haut d'un pilier qui soutenait le toit. Les petits avançaient la tête sans crainte au-dessus du nid, et les parents venaient jusque sur les tables prendre les miettes de pain. Il y avait un tel silence dans la vallée que personne n'osait parler haut. Le dîner se faisait attendre, mais personne ne s'impatientait. Puis nous repartions, et en marchant sur une route en plein soleil, ou quelquefois quand nous étions assises à l'ombre d'un bois, Mlle. Hermine racontait des choses de sa jeunesse passée à la campagne. "Mon jardin à moi était plein de fleurs et de feuilles," me dit-elle un jour, "et lorsque le soleil y entrait après la pluie, les feuilles prenaient des couleurs si rares et se paraient de gouttes d'eau si étincelantes qu'elles devenaient alors plus belles que les fleurs."

Comme je m'étonnais qu'elle ait pu quitter un endroit qui lui était si cher, elle dit: "Après la mort de mes parents la maison vide m'effrayait."

25. LE PETIT TROTT ET SA SŒUR

Trott a toujours été un très bon petit garçon. Jamais on ne l'a trop gâté. Il ne se disputait jamais trop avec les autres enfants: au contraire, il était doux et cédait assez volontiers, surtout aux petites filles, parce que ce sont des demoiselles. Quant aux tout petits bébés, ils ne lui inspiraient pas grand intérêt. Mais à la maison il était bien avéré qu'il était le personnage principal. Sans doute papa et maman étaient des gens de plus haute importance. Il n'empêche pas que[1] Trott se rendait fort bien compte de la sienne; il se sentait vaguement une espèce de joujou très précieux qui était en même temps un phénomène unique. Et au fond il n'était pas sans soupçonner que l'univers avait été créé pour lui. Après tout, puisqu'il était le plus petit. . .

Mais maintenant il n'est plus le plus petit. Il y a dans la maison quelqu'un de beaucoup plus petit que lui, de bien plus

[1] Il n'empêche pas que = *For all that.*

fragile. Et ce quelqu'un-là, ce n'est pas une petite bête, un chien, un chat, qu'on caresse un moment et puis dont on ne s'occupe plus. C'est un petit enfant qui grandit, auquel on ne cesse de songer, qui est déjà une petite personne, et qui a pris une grande place dans la maison. Maintenant que Trott sait qu'on l'aime tout à fait comme on l'aimait autrefois, il n'est certainement pas jaloux, oh! pas du tout, surtout depuis qu'il sent lui-même que sa sœur a une grande place dans son cœur. Mais pourtant, il pense encore quelquefois que c'est un peu ennuyeux de n'être plus aussi important qu'autrefois.

26. Étranger en France

Figurez-vous un grand gaillard, long comme un jour sans pain, et maigre comme un bon chrétien à la fin du carême. Il s'appelait Magnus Schmoll, et ces deux vocables, étrangers l'un à l'autre, étrangers aussi à la langue qui se parlait autour de moi, ne frappaient pas moins vivement mon oreille que ses dehors fantasques ne frappaient mes yeux.

Comment Schmoll était-il venu en France? Pourquoi y restait-il? Par suite de quels événements, publics ou privés, s'était-il fixé dans la petite ville de Normandie qu'habitait alors ma famille? Autant de mystères, qu'il ne m'avait pas été donné de pénétrer! Quoi qu'il en fût, il n'avait jamais exprimé le désir de retourner dans ses foyers.

27. La Vie de fermier

Pendant notre promenade à travers champs, il me fallut subir, ce qui d'ailleurs n'avait rien d'ennuyeux, un cours complet d'agriculture. Mathieu me parla de ses angoisses pendant les gelées; sa joie, aux premiers beaux soleils de fin d'hiver, de voir les petites aiguilles d'un vert tendre pointer à travers la neige insensiblement abaissée; et comment un lapin, abusant d'une brèche de la muraille, était venu exercer d'affreux ravages dans les jeunes pousses; et comment, encore, un jour d'orage, il s'était installé, lui Mathieu, près de son champ, avec un immense parapluie rouge pour l'abriter au cas où la grêle tomberait.

28. La Vieille pauvre

Un matin, avenue de l'Opéra au milieu du public remuant et

joyeux que le soleil de mai grisait, j'ai vu passer soudain un
être innommable, une vieille courbée en deux, vêtue de loques,
coiffée d'un chapeau de paille noir, tout dépouillé de ses orne-
ments anciens. Et elle allait, traînant ses pieds si péniblement
que je ressentais au cœur, autant qu'elle-même, plus qu'elle-
même, la douleur de tous ses pas. Deux cannes la soutenaient.
Elle passait sans voir personne, indifférente à tout. Où allait-elle?
Elle portait dans un papier qui pendait au bout d'une ficelle
quelque chose. Quoi? Du pain? Oui, sans doute. Personne,
aucun voisin n'ayant pu ou voulu faire pour elle cette course,
elle avait entrepris, elle, ce voyage horrible, de sa mansarde au
boulanger. Deux heures de route au moins pour aller et venir.

29. Une Petite Vengeance

Un passager avait exaspéré par ses questions interminables le
conducteur de l'autocar qui l'emmenait à travers le désert, si
bien que celui-ci saisit l'occasion d'une petite vengeance.

Alors que le car roulait en toute sécurité, un oiseau vint à
passer, qui plana assez longtemps autour de la voiture. Et notre
passager de demander pourquoi. Le conducteur fit semblant
d'hésiter à répondre. Il déclara enfin d'un ton lugubre: "Ces
oiseaux ont un instinct extraordinaire. Ils devinent, on ne sait
comment, longtemps à l'avance, qu'il va arriver malheur au
voyageur qu'ils survolent, et dès lors ils ne quittent plus leur
victime désignée, pour être sûrs d'avoir part à la curée." Le
passager ne demanda plus rien jusqu'à la fin de l'étape. Il lui
fallut tout ce temps sans doute pour décider qu'on s'était moqué
de lui, puisqu'en fin de compte il arriva sain et sauf.

30. Une Situation tragique

Rentrée chez sa sœur, Marina lui raconta les incidents de la
soirée, car Marthe était au fait de l'histoire de Philippe. Marthe
jugea comme sa sœur la situation tragique.

— As-tu reconnu sa voix au téléphone?

— Je ne sais pas. Par moments, il me semble en être sûre;
par moments, je doute que ce soit Philippe qui m'ait parlé.
Il m'aurait fallu l'entendre plus longtemps. Si c'est lui, comme
il doit souffrir dans cet affreux logis, lui si délicat!

— Et ces hommes, que sont-ils venus faire?

— L'emmener peut-être, au loin, à l'étranger!

A cette pensée Marina se mit à pleurer. L'impuissance où elle se voyait d'arracher Philippe aux mains de ses geôliers lui était un tourment.

— Il faut partir tout de suite, dit Marthe, et tout raconter à son père.

— Tu as raison, dit Marina, je partirai demain matin.

Section B—Poetry: French-English

1

Ma fille, lève-toi; dépose là ta laine;
Le maître va rentrer; sur la table de chêne,
Que recouvre la nappe aux plis étincelants,
Mets la faïence claire et les verres brillants.
Dans la coupe arrondie, à l'anse en col de cygne,
Pose les fruits choisis sur des feuilles de vigne:
Les pêches qu'un velours fragile couvre encor,
Et les lourds raisins bleus mêlés aux raisins d'or.
Que le pain bien coupé remplisse les corbeilles,
Et puis, ferme la porte et chasse les abeilles.

2

On voit, quand vient l'automne, aux fils télégraphiques,
de longues lignes d'hirondelles grelotter.
On sent leurs petits cœurs qui ont froid s'inquiéter.

Elles sont là, perchées, pointues, faisant l'étude
de l'air, ou décrivant le vol d'un cercle doux,
pour venir repercher à l'endroit qu'elles quittent.

Ainsi l'âme qui a souffert de tant de choses,
avant de traverser les Océans divins
et de gagner le Ciel des éternelles Roses,
s'essaye, hésite, et, avant de partir, revient.

3. Chemin de fer

Près du rail où souvent passe comme un éclair
Le convoi furieux et son cheval de fer,
Tranquille, l'aiguilleur vit dans sa maisonnette.
Par la fenêtre, on voit l'intérieur honnête,
Tel que le voyageur fiévreux doit l'envier.
C'est la femme parfois qui se tient au levier,
Portant sur un seul bras son enfant qui l'embrasse.
Jetant son sifflement atroce, le train passe
Devant l'humble logis qui tressaille au fracas,
Et le petit enfant ne se dérange pas.

4. Spring Song

Sais-tu, mignonne! la pervenche
Émaille déjà les buissons,
Et les oiseaux, de branche en branche,
Disent tout joyeux leurs chansons.

Partout se réveille la vie
Sous les chauds rayons du soleil:
C'est le printemps, il nous convie
Ensemble à fêter son réveil.

Viens! nous irons, l'âme joyeuse,
Porter nos pas bien loin, bien haut,
Dans la forêt mystérieuse
Où tout chante le renouveau.

Viens! à deux il est plus facile
D'épeler au livre de Dieu,
Et si j'y suis trop inhabile,
Tu voudras bien m'aider un peu.

Tu dois comprendre bien des choses
Que seul je ne trouverais pas,
Car tes rêveuses sœurs les roses
Ont dû t'en instruire tout bas.

5

Après les feux du jour qui brûlaient le faucheur,
Voici le crépuscule apportant la fraîcheur.
Que la soirée est belle, et comme on se sent vivre!
L'herbe coupée exhale un parfum qui m'enivre;
Ces dernières lueurs qui flottent au couchant
Donnent à la campagne un aspect plus touchant,
Et mon esprit ému suit le jour qui s'achève,
Par delà l'horizon, dans le pays du rêve . . .
Oh! quand donc aurez-vous votre accomplissement,
Rêves qui m'agitez, rêves de dévoûment!

6

Elle avait l'air d'une princesse
Quand je la tenais par la main.
Elle cherchait des fleurs sans cesse
Et des pauvres dans le chemin.

A travers mes songes sans nombre,
J'écoutais son parler joyeux,
Et mon front s'éclairait dans l'ombre
A la lumière de ses yeux.

Le soir, auprès de ma bougie,
Elle jasait à petit bruit,
Tandis qu'à la vitre rougie
Heurtaient les papillons de nuit.

Les anges se miraient en elle.
Que son bonjour était charmant!
Le ciel mettait dans sa prunelle
Ce regard qui jamais ne ment.

Oh! Je l'avais, si jeune encore,
Vue apparaître en mon destin,
C'était l'enfant de mon aurore,
Et mon étoile du matin!

7. La Mort d'un chêne

O chêne, je comprends ta puissante agonie!
Dans sa paix, dans sa force, il est dur de mourir:
A voir crouler ta tête, au printemps rajeunie,
Je devine, ô géant! ce que tu dois souffrir.

Mais n'est-il rien de toi qui subsiste et qui dure?
Où s'en vont ces esprits d'écorce recouverts?
Et n'est-il de vivant que l'immense nature,
Une au fond, mais s'ornant de mille aspects divers?

Quel qu'il soit, cependant, ma voix bénit ton être
Pour le divin repos qu'à tes pieds j'ai goûté.
Dans un jeune univers, si tu dois y renaître,
Puisses-tu retrouver la force et la beauté!

8. The Poet's Retreat

Du lieu qui me retient veux-tu voir le tableau?
C'est un petit village, ou plutôt un hameau,
Bâti sur le penchant d'un long rang de collines,
D'où l'œil s'égare au loin dans les plaines voisines.
La Seine, au pied des monts que son flot vient laver,
Voit du sein de ses eaux vingt îles s'élever,
Qui, partageant son cours en diverses manières,
D'une rivière seule y forment vingt rivières.
Le village au-dessus forme un amphithéâtre;
L'habitant ne connaît ni la chaux ni le plâtre,
Et dans le roc, qui cède et se coupe aisément,
Chacun sait de sa main creuser son logement.
Ici dans un vallon bornant tous mes désirs,
J'achète à peu de frais de solides plaisirs.
Tantôt, un livre en main, errant dans les prairies,
J'occupe ma raison d'utiles rêveries:
Tantôt, cherchant la fin d'un vers que je construis,
Je trouve au coin d'un bois le mot qui m'avait fui.

9. The Sleeping Swan

Une fois, par malheur, si vous avez pris terre,
Peut-être qu'un de vous, sur un lac solitaire,
Aura vu, comme moi, quelque cygne, endormi,
Qui se laissait au vent balancer à demi.
Sa tête nonchalante, en arrière appuyée,
Se cache dans la plume au soleil essuyée;
Son poitrail est lavé par le flot transparent,
Comme un écueil où l'eau se joue en expirant;
Le duvet qu'en passant l'air dérobe à sa plume,
Autour de lui s'envole et se mêle à l'écume;
Une aile est son coussin, l'autre est son éventail;
Il dort, et de son pied le large gouvernail
Trouble encore, en ramant, l'eau tournoyante et douce,
Tandis que sur ses flancs se forme un lit de mousse,
De feuilles et de joncs, et d'herbages errants,
Qu'apportent près de lui d'invisibles courants.

10. Le Départ

Je vais donc quitter pour jamais
Mon bon pays, ma douce amie!
Loin d'eux je vais traîner ma vie
Dans les pleurs et dans les regrets.
Vallon charmant, où notre enfance
Goûta ces plaisirs purs et frais
Que donne la simple innocence,
Je vais vous quitter pour jamais!

Champs que j'ai dépouillés de fleurs
Pour orner les cheveux d'Estelle;
Roses qui perdiez auprès d'elle
Et votre éclat et vos couleurs;
Fleuve dont j'ai vu l'eau limpide,
Pour réfléchir ses doux attraits,
Suspendre sa course rapide,
Je vais vous quitter pour jamais!

Prairie où dès nos premiers ans,
Nous parlions déjà de tendresse,
Où, bien avant notre jeunesse,
Nous passions pour de vieux amants;
Beaux arbres où nous allions lire
Le nom que toujours j'y traçais,
Le seul qu'alors je susse écrire,
Je vais vous quitter pour jamais!

Section C—Prose: English–French

I

Marie likes her aunt. Aunt Lucy has given her some money
for a present. Marie hopes to buy several things in the town.
She goes into a shop. She buys gloves and handkerchiefs. But
she does not spend everything. Then she goes into a restaurant
and has an ice. She does not forget her little brother. She buys
a book and then she returns home.

2

"Someone is knocking at the door," said John. "I am going
to open the window." John calls: "Who are you?" "I am
looking for the hotel," said the man in the street. "Come into
the house and I shall give you a cup of tea. Then I shall show
you the way," said John. The man accepted the invitation and
thanked John.

3

"What a fine bicycle!" said John to his friend Peter; "I am
going to ask for it. My father will buy it." Peter said: "I shall
lend you the bicycle tonight, and your father will look at it."
"All right, Peter," said John, "I shall show your bicycle to him
tonight." John's father was pleased. John's mother spoke to
him. "John has worked all the spring in the garden. He wants
this bicycle. He deserves it."

4

"Where is your little brother?" Mrs. Brown asked. "He is in the street, Mother," said Jack. "He was patting a dog." "Why did you not stay with him?" said the mother. "He was eating his sweets," said Jack, "and he was giving some to the dog." At that moment Will arrived. He was not alone. The dog was with him. It was pleased. But Will's mother was not pleased. The dog went away sadly.

5

Three bears are entering a forest. A hunter named Bernard looks at them. He seizes his gun and hunts them. The little bears are tired after an hour. Bernard advances. At first he is going to kill the animals. But they are so young. He hesitates. Then he lowers his gun and goes away. He will not kill them.

6

The girls were playing in the garden when the sun was shining. "The roses are beautiful. I like these better than those," said Yvonne. "This one is the most beautiful," said Marie. "It has a lovely colour and a fine scent." "But it also has thorns," said Yvonne. Marie cut the roses and carried them into the house. Her mother was pleased when she looked at the lovely flowers on the table.

7

Charles and Henri are choosing some books. "Which of the books do you like?" Henri asks. "I like this one," says Charles. "It is a book of adventures." "I prefer that one," says Henri, "it is very amusing. It does not cost much. I shall buy it for my little brother." "Which one of the books will you buy?" Charles says. "I like the sea. There are many pictures of the sea in this book. I shall buy it."

8

Jacques and I are going to the theatre. He and I were at the theatre last week. Our fathers have given us the money. The actors are very good. The play is very amusing. If we like this play, we shall applaud. If we do not like it, we shall not be at the theatre next week.

9

A soldier was in a battle. He was very brave. He looked at the soldier near him. He was wounded. He did not speak. The soldier tried to save him. He carried him to a tree which was near a river. The wounded man, who was (a) captain, was soon strong again. He did not forget the brave man who helped him. He gave him a reward.

10

One day a little girl told a lie to her mother. She felt very miserable. Her mother felt very sad also. "I know all that has happened," said she. "Your father will be very angry." The little girl tried to sleep. She knew that her mother felt unhappy. She regretted what she had done. When she said that to her mother, the latter was pleased. She pardoned the fault.

11

An old legend tells us that on the fifth day of creation the animals appeared before God to thank Him for His goodness. Then God noticed that several were missing, and He asked the reason for their absence. The lion spoke, because he is the king of beasts. "Some creatures, Lord, cannot come because it is winter. The snow is too deep, and they suffer from the terrible cold. Life is very hard for them." Then the Lord answered: "I shall make life easier for them, for I pity them." That is why some animals sleep from the beginning of winter till the arrival of spring.

12

Trent looked round to make sure that they were not overheard, then faced Marlowe gravely. "There is one thing I may tell you," he said quietly, "that I don't think you know. The servant caught a few words of the conversation you had with Manderson in the garden before you started with him in the car. Do you still maintain that you do not know the object of your journey?"

Marlowe shook his head. "I know nothing, indeed. I have already told the detective what passed during that conversation. Manderson plainly said to me that he could not tell me what it was all about."

13

In the dark forests of Russia, where there is snow on the ground for eight months in the year, bands of wolves roam over the dreary plains. It is a fearful thing for travellers, especially when night is falling, to hear the howlings of these savage beasts.

A Russian nobleman, with his wife and daughter, was travelling in a sleigh. The driver was an old servant who had been born in the nobleman's castle and who loved his master so much that he had often said he would willingly give his life to save him.

The sleigh sped swiftly over the hard snow. In the moonlight the road looked like polished silver. Suddenly the little girl turned to her father and said: "What are those strange noises I heard just now?" "Nothing but the wind blowing through the trees," he answered. The child shut her eyes, and kept still. Her father listened and far away behind him, but distinct enough, he could hear a sound whose meaning he knew.

14

"Tell Rahm," my master said, "to light the lantern and bring it to me. I am going to open the window and see who is knocking."

Rahm went up with the lantern, while I stood at the bottom of the stairs, listening.

I heard the window open. Then my master called out:

"Who are you, and what do you want?"

"I have lost my way," replied a man's voice. "How far is it to Princetown, please?"

"Ten miles. But you will never get there on a night like this. Who are you?"

"A holiday-maker from London. I have walked from Okehampton today."

"How foolish!" replied my master. "Come in and warm yourself."

15

The wind still blew furiously, and the rain descended in torrents. I sat before the fire nearly asleep, but I was presently aroused by the conversation of the host. "Sir," said he, "it is now three years since I had foreigners in my house. I remember that it was just such a night as this that two men on horseback arrived here. What was unusual was that they came without any guide. I have never seen two more strange-looking persons. I shall never forget them. The one was as tall as a giant, with a yellow beard. The other was very small and looked like a hunchback. I soon found, however, that he was the master and that the big one was the servant."

16

It was Paul who told me the joyful news that Katherine was coming home with Michael for six months or so. It was seven years since he had seen his sister, and I don't suppose in all that time he had written her seven letters, being the worst correspondent in the world. But that was not a sign of forgetfulness or lack of affection. I know he thought of Katherine as the ideal woman.

Dorothy was excited about the coming of Michael and her aunt, and looked forward to it with a mixture of alarm and amusement.

"I expect Aunt Kitty is so used to being a Princess that she'll be horrified with this household! Arthur *will* leave his boots in the drawing-room, and father is the most untidy man in the world."

17

Swift was one day travelling on horseback with a servant. In the evening the two men came to an inn. Before going to bed, Swift said: "My boots are dirty; clean them, please." The servant was rather lazy; besides, he was tired; so he fell asleep without doing what his master had said. The next morning, when Swift saw what had happened, he exclaimed: "Why have these boots not been polished?" "Well, Sir, as the weather is very bad, they would soon be as dirty as before." "Very good, saddle the horses. We shall start immediately." "But, Sir, we have not had our breakfast." "Oh, never mind! If you ate now, you would soon be hungry again."

18

A police constable, young and remarkably handsome, swung himself off his bicycle and placed the machine carefully against the wall. The doctor advanced towards him.

"There's been a shocking accident," he said. "The woman either fell or threw herself off the bridge under Mr. Sutane's car. This is Mr. Sutane. The woman is dead. The body will have to be taken down to the village."

"Yes, sir."

"Meanwhile I should like to take a look at that bridge. How do you get up to it, Mr. Sutane?"

"I climbed the bank, but there's a gate a little farther along."

"Then I'll use it. Perhaps you'll be good enough to direct me."

19

The foolish noble sat down on the king's throne. His heart swelled with pride, for all men came to kneel before him and, when the feast began, he was served before anyone else.

All at once he looked up, and saw something that made him tremble with fear. There, just above his head, hanging by a single long hair from the roof of the hall, was a sword! At any moment, the hair might break and then—down would come the sword and kill him.

In dreadful fear he started up, and cried out: "Oh, let me go! I *must* go!" The king only smiled, and ordered his guards not to allow him to move. "You were very anxious to take my place," he said. "Well, I hope you have learned that a king often lives in fear of his life. If he is brave, he tries not to think of the dangers which threaten him, though he knows they are always there. Perhaps in future you will not think that the life of a king is such a fine thing."

20

The following anecdote proves that most people judge a work entirely by the author's name.

One day La Motte was being mercilessly criticized. Voltaire, growing weary of this onslaught, played the following clever trick on the company.

"Gentlemen," he said, "I am the proud possessor of one of La Fontaine's unpublished fables."

"What!" they exclaimed, "you have a fable by La Fontaine that we haven't read? Please read it to us immediately."

Voltaire read it and everyone exclaimed: "How marvellous, and how unlike the wretched fables by La Motte."

"Well, gentlemen," said Voltaire, "I am glad you like it, for it was La Motte who wrote it."

VOCABULARY

FRENCH—ENGLISH

à, to, at
abaisser, to let down, reduce
abattre, to knock down, fell
abeille, f., bee
d'abord, at first
aboyer, to bark
abri, m., shelter
à l'abri de, sheltered from
abricot, m., apricot
s'abriter, to take shelter
absent, absent
abuser de, to take advantage of, misuse
accepter, to accept
accident, m., accident
accompagner, to accompany
accomplir, to accomplish
accomplissement, m., accomplishment
accoudé, leaning (on one's elbows)
accourir, to run up to
accroupi, crouching
accueil, m., welcome, reception
accueillir, to welcome
acheter, to buy
achever, to finish, complete
acteur, m., actor
actif, active
action, f., action
actrice, f., actress
adieu, good-bye
admirer, to admire
aérien, aerial
aéroport, m., airport
affaire, f., affair, business
affirmer, to affirm, assert
affreux, frightful, horrible
afin de, in order to
afin que, in order that

âge, m., age
âgé, aged
agenouillé, kneeling
agent, m., agent, policeman
agir, to act, behave
il s'agit de, it concerns, is a question of
agiter, to shake, excite
agneau, m., lamb
agonie, f., agony
agréable, pleasant
agriculture, f., agriculture
aider, to help
aiguille, f., needle, railway point
aiguilleur, m., railway pointsman
aile, f., wing
ailleurs, elsewhere
d'ailleurs, besides
aimer, to love, like
aimer mieux, to prefer
ainsi, thus
aisément, easily, comfortably
allée, f., lane
Allemagne, f., Germany
allemand, German
aller, to go
s'en aller, to go away
alors, then, at that time
amant, m., lover, sweetheart
ambition, f., ambition
âme, f., soul, mind
amener, to bring, fetch
américain, American
ami, m., friend
amical, friendly
amie, f., friend
amphithéâtre, m., amphitheatre
amusant, amusing
amuser, to amuse

229

an, *m.*, year
ancêtre, *m.*, ancestor
ancien, old, former
âne, *m.*, donkey, ass
anecdote, *f.*, anecdote
ange, *m.*, angel
anglais, English
Angleterre, *f.*, England
angoisse, *f.*, anguish
animal, *m.*, animal
année, *f.*, year
anse, *f.*, handle (of jug or basket)
août, *m.*, August
apercevoir, to perceive
s'apercevoir, to perceive, become
    aware of
apparaître, to appear
appartement, *m.*, flat, apartment
appeler, to call, name
appliqué, diligent
apporter, to bring
apprendre, to learn, teach
apprentissage, *m.*, apprenticeship
approuver, to approve of
appuyer, to lean, support
après, after (*prep.*)
après-demain, the day after to-
    morrow
après que, after (*conj.*)
arbre, *m.*, tree
argent, *m.*, money, silver
aristocratique, aristocratic
armée, *f.*, army
arracher, to tear away, pull out
arranger, to arrange
s'arrêter, to stop, halt
en arrière, backwards
arrivée, *f.*, arrival
arriver, to arrive, happen
arrondi, rounded
article, *m.*, article
artiste, *m.* or *f.*, artist
ascension, *f.*, ascent
aspect, *m.*, aspect
assaut, *m.*, assault
s'asseoir, to sit down

assez, enough
assis, seated, sitting
assister, to be present, be a witness
assurer, to assure
atroce, atrocious, cruel
attablé, seated at table
attaquer, to attack
en attendant que, until
attendre, to wait for
attention, *f.*, attention
attrait, *m.*, attraction, charm
attraper, to catch
aubépine, *f.*, hawthorn
auberge, *f.*, inn
aujourd'hui, today
auprès de, close to, near
aurore, *f.*, dawn
aussi, as, also, and so
aussi . . . que, as . . . as
aussitôt, immediately
aussitôt que, as soon as
Australie, *f.*, Australia
autant, as much, as many
auto, *f.*, motor-car
autocar, *m.*, motor-coach
automne, *m.*, autumn
automobile, *f.*, motor-car
autour de, around
autre, other
autrefois, formerly
avalanche, *f.*, avalanche
avaler, to swallow
à l'avance, in advance, by antici-
    pation
d'avance, beforehand
avancer, to advance
avant, before
avant-hier, the day before yester-
    day
avant que, before (*conj.*)
avec, with
avenir, *m.*, future
aventure, *f.*, adventure
bonne aventure, fortune, what is
    foretold
avérer, to confirm

averse, *f.*, shower
aveugle, blind
aviateur, *m.*, aviator, pilot
avion, *m.*, aeroplane
aviser, to catch sight of, inform
s'aviser, to bethink oneself
avocat, *m.*, lawyer
avril, *m.*, April

baisser, to lower
bal, *m.*, ball, dance
balafre, *f.*, scar
se balancer, to swing, sway
ballade, *f.*, ballad
balle, *f.*, ball, bullet
bar, *m.*, bar, public-house
bas, basse, low
bas, *m.*, stocking
en bas, below, downstairs
bataille, *f.*, battle
bâtir, to build
battre, to beat
se battre, to fight
beau, beautiful
avoir beau faire quelque chose,
    to do something in vain
beaucoup, much, many
beauté, *f.*, beauty
bébé, *m.*, baby
bénin, bénigne, mild, kindly
bénir, to bless
berger, *m.*, shepherd
besogne, *f.*, work, job, task
besoin, *m.*, need
bête, stupid
bête, *f.*, beast
beurre, *m.*, butter
bibliothèque, *f.*, library
bicyclette, *f.*, bicycle
bien, well
bienfait, *m.*, kindness, benefit,
    good turn
bien que, although
bientôt, soon
bijou, *m.*, jewel
bizarre, odd, strange

blâmer, to blame
blanc, white
blé, *m.*, wheat, corn
blessure, *f.*, wound
bleu, blue
bœuf, *m.*, ox
bohémien, -ne, gipsy
boire, to drink
bois, *m.*, wood
boîte, *f.*, box
bon, good
bond, *m.*, jump, leap
bonheur, *m.*, happiness, good luck
bonnet, *m.*, cap
bonté, *f.*, goodness, kindness
bord, *m.*, edge
borner, to limit, confine
bouche, *f.*, mouth
boucher, *m.*, butcher
boue, *f.*, mud
bouger, to move, stir
bougie, *f.*, candle
bouillir, to boil
boulanger, *m.*, baker
boule, *f.*, ball, bowl
bouledogue, *m.*, bulldog
bouquet, *m.*, bunch, cluster
bouquin, *m.*, old book
bout, *m.*, end, tip
bouteille, *f.*, bottle
boutique, *f.*, shop
branche, *f.*, branch
bras, *m.*, arm
brave, brave, worthy
brèche, *f.*, breach
Brésil, *m.*, Brazil
brillant, bright, shining
briller, to shine
brouillard, *m.*, fog
brouter, to browse, graze
bruiner, to drizzle
bruit, *m.*, noise
brûler, to burn, yearn
brun, brown
bruyamment, noisily
bruyant, noisy

buisson, *m.,* bush
buter, to stumble

ça, that
çà, here
câbler, to cable
cadeau, *m.,* present, gift
café, *m.,* coffee, café
cahier, *m.,* note-book
caillou, *m.,* pebble
le Caire, Cairo
calme, calm
camarade, *m.,* comrade
campagne, *f.,* country, countryside
campeur, *m.,* camper
Canada, *m.,* Canada
canif, *m.,* penknife
canne, *f.,* cane, stick
capitaine, *m.,* captain
caporal, *m.,* corporal
car, for *(conj.)*
car, *m.,* bus
carême, *m.,* Lent
caresser, to caress, fondle
carié, decayed (of teeth)
carrefour, *m.,* cross-roads
carte, *f.,* card, map
carte postale, *f.,* postcard
cas, *m.,* case, circumstance
en cas que, in case
casser, to break
catastrophe, *f.,* catastrophe
cathédrale, *f.,* cathedral
catholique, Catholic
à cause de, on account of, because of
ceci, this
céder, to yield
cela, that
célèbre, famous
cent, a hundred
centaine, *f.,* an approximate hundred
centième, hundredth
centimètre, *m.,* centimetre
cercle, *m.,* circle

cerise, *f.,* cherry
cerisier, *m.,* cherry-tree
certain, certain
certainement, certainly
cesse, *f.,* ceasing
cesser, to cease
chacun, chacune, each one
chaise, *f.,* chair
chalet, *m.,* chalet
chambre, *f.,* room, bedroom
champ, *m.,* field
chance, *f.,* luck, chance
changer, to change
chanson, *f.,* song
chanter, to sing
chapeau, *m.,* hat
chaque, each *(adj.)*
charmant, charming
charrette, *f.,* cart
charrue, *f.,* plough
chasser, to hunt, chase
chat, *m.,* cat
châtain, chestnut-coloured, auburn
chatoyant, glistening, showy
chaud, warm
chaud, *m.,* warmth
chaumière, *f.,* cottage
chaussette, *f.,* sock
chaux, *f.,* lime
chemin, *m.,* road, way
chemin de fer, *m.,* railway
chêne, *m.,* oak
cher, dear
chercher, to look for
chérir, to cherish
cheval, *m.,* horse
cheveu, *m.,* hair
chèvre, *f.,* goat
chez, at the home of
chien, *m.,* dog
Chili, *m.,* Chile
chimérique, chimerical, visionary
chinois, Chinese
chocolat, *m.,* chocolate
choisir, to choose
chose, *f.,* thing

chou, *m.,* cabbage
chou-fleur, *m.,* cauliflower
ciel, *m.,* sky, heaven
cigarette, *f.,* cigarette
ciment, *m.,* cement
cimetière, *m.,* cemetery
ciné, *m.,* cinema
cinéma, *m.,* cinema
cinq, five
cinquante, fifty
cinquantième, fiftieth
cinquième, fifth
circonstance, *f.,* circumstance
cité, *f.,* city
citoyen, *m.,* citizen
citoyenne, *f.,* citizen
clair, clear, bright
classe, *f.,* class
classique, classic
client, *m.,* client
clientèle, *f.,* custom, customers
cloche, *f.,* bell
clocher, *m.,* steeple
clôture, *f.,* enclosure
clou, *m.,* nail
cocher, *m.,* coachman, cabman
cœur, *m.,* heart
coiffé, dressed (as to hair), wearing (on the head)
coin, *m.,* corner
col, *m.,* collar
collège, *m.,* college
colline, *f.,* hill
combattre, to fight
combien, how much, how many
combler, to fill up, heap, load
commander, to command, order
comme, as, like
commencer, to commence
comment, how
commettre, to commit
compagne, *f.,* companion
compagnon, *m.,* companion
comparer, to compare
compartiment, *m.,* compartment
complet, complete

compléter, to complete
complice, *m.* or *f.,* accomplice
comprendre, to understand
compromettre, to compromise
compte, *m.,* reckoning, account
compte: se rendre — de, to see for oneself
compte: en fin de —, in the end
compter, to reckon, expect
comptoir, *m.,* counter
concert, *m.,* concert
concevoir, to conceive
concierge, *m.* or *f.,* porter, door-keeper
condition, *f.,* condition
conducteur, *m.,* conductor, driver
confesser, to confess
confiture, *f.,* jam
confus, confused
connaître, to know
conseiller, to advise
consoler, to console
construire, to construct
consulter, to consult
contenir, to contain
content, pleased
conter, to tell, relate
continuer, to continue
au contraire, on the contrary
contre, against
contredire, to contradict
contrée, *f.,* country
convenir, to agree, suit
convier, to invite
convoi, *m.,* convoy, train
coq, *m.,* cock
coquille, *f.,* shell
corbeille, *f.,* basket
corde, *f.,* cord, rope
corps, *m.,* body
corriger, to correct
costume, *m.,* costume, dress, suit
côté, *m.,* side
à côté de, beside
côtelette, *f.,* chop, cutlet

couchant, *m.,* west
coucher, to put to bed, lay down
coudre, to sew
couleur, *f.,* colour
coup, *m.,* blow, stroke, hit
coupable, guilty
coupe, *f.,* cup, goblet
couper, to cut
courage, *m.,* courage
courageusement, bravely
courant, *m.,* current
courber, to bow, bend
courir, to run
cours, *m.,* course, stream
course, *f.,* race, running
court, short
courtaud, thickset
cousin, *m.,* cousin
cousine, *f.,* cousin
coussin, *m.,* cushion
coûter, to cost
couvrir, to cover
craindre, to fear
crainte, *f.,* fear
cravate, *f.,* neck-tie, tie
crayon, *m.,* pencil
créer, to create
crème, *f.,* cream
crépuscule, *m.,* twilight, dawn
creuser, to dig
crevasse, *f.,* crevice, crack
crier, to cry, scream
crime, *m.,* crime
croire, to believe
se croiser, to cross, pass one another
croître, to grow, increase
crouler, to crumble
cruel, cruel
cueillir, to gather, pluck
cuire, to cook
cuisine, *f.,* kitchen, cookery
cuivre, *m.,* copper, brass
cultiver, to till, cultivate
curée, *f.,* prey, booty, quarry
cygne, *m.,* swan

dame, *f.,* lady
Danemark, *m.,* Denmark
danger, *m.,* danger
dangereux, dangerous
dans, in
danse, *f.,* dance, dancing
danser, to dance
de, of, from
débattre, to debate, discuss
se débattre, to struggle
débiteur, *m.,* debtor
debout, upright, standing
décembre, December
décevoir, to deceive
décidément, decidedly
décider, to decide
déclarer, to declare
découverte, *f.,* discovery
découvrir, to discover
décrire, to describe
dédain, *m.,* disdain
défaite, *f.,* defeat
défendre, to forbid
dégeler, to thaw
dehors, *adv.,* out of doors
dehors, *m.,* outside, exterior
déjà, already
déjeuner, *m.,* breakfast, lunch
delà, beyond
délai, *m.,* delay
délicat, delicate
délit, *m.,* misdemeanour
demain, tomorrow
demander, to ask
se demander, to wonder
démettre, to dismiss
demeurer, to dwell
demi, half
démission, *f.,* resignation
demoiselle, *f.,* young lady
démolir, demolish
démontrer, to demonstrate
dent, *f.,* tooth
dentiste, *m.,* dentist
départ, *m.,* departure
dépasser, to surpass, go beyond

se dépêcher, to hasten
déposer, to lay down
dépouiller, to strip, lay bare
depuis, *adv. prep.,* since
depuis que, *conj.,* since
déranger, to disturb
dernier, last
dérober, to rob, steal
dès, from, since, as early as
dès que, *conj.,* as soon as
désagréable, unpleasant
descendre, to descend
désert, deserted
désert, *m.,* desert
désigner, to designate
désintéressement (*m.*), disinterest
désir, *m.,* desire
désirer, to desire
désobéir, to disobey
désordre, *m.,* disorder
désormais, henceforth
au-dessus de, above
destin, *m.,* destiny, fate
détail, *m.,* detail
détenir, to detain
détester, to detest, hate
détruire, to destroy
deux, two
deuxième, second
devant, before
devenir, to become
deviner, to guess
devoir, to owe, have to, be obliged to
devoir, *m.,* duty, exercise
dévouement or
dévoûment, *m.,* devotion
diable, *m.,* devil
dicter, to dictate
dieu, *m.,* God, god
difficile, difficult
dignité, *f.,* dignity
diligence, *f.,* diligence
diligent, diligent
dimanche, *m.,* Sunday
dîner, to dine

dîner, *m.,* dinner
dire, to say, tell
directeur, *m.,* director, manager
diriger, to direct
se diriger vers, to go towards, make for
disparaître, to disappear
disparition, *f.,* disappearance
disputer, to dispute, contest
distance, *f.,* distance
distingué, distinguished
divers, diverse
divin, divine
dix, ten
dix-huit, eighteen
dix-huitième, eighteenth
dixième, tenth
dix-neuf, nineteen
dix-neuvième, nineteenth
dix-sept, seventeen
dix-septième, seventeenth
docteur, *m.,* doctor
doigt, *m.,* finger
domestique, *m.* or *f.,* servant
dommage, *m.,* pity, damage
donc, therefore, so, then
donner, to give
dont, *rel. pron.,* whose, of which
dormir, to sleep
douane, *f.,* customs, custom-house
douleur, *f.,* pain, suffering, sorrow
doute, *m.,* doubt
douter, to doubt
douteux, doubtful
Douvres, Dover
doux, sweet, gentle
douze, twelve
douzième, twelfth
drapeau, *m.,* flag
dresser, to set up, raise
droit, straight
droit, *m.,* right, title
à droite, to or on the right
dru, vigorous; *adv.,* thick, fast
dur, hard
durée, *f.,* duration

durer, to last
duvet, *m.,* down

eau, *f.,* water
écarter, to set aside, avert
éclair, *m.,* flash
éclairer, to light
éclat, *m.,* burst, brightness
écorce, *f.,* bark, rind
écossais, Scottish
Écosse, *f.,* Scotland
écouter, to listen to
écraser, to crush, run over
(s') écrier, to call out, exclaim
écrire, to write
écueil, *m.,* reef
écume, *f.,* foam
écureuil, *m.,* squirrel
Édimbourg, Edinburgh
effort, *m.,* effort
effrayer, to frighten
égal, equal
également, equally, likewise
s'égarer, to lose one's way
église, *f.,* church
Égypte, *f.,* Egypt
s'élancer, to dart forth
élève, *m.* or *f.,* pupil
élever, to raise, bring up, rear
s'élever, to rise, arise
émailler, to enamel
embellir, to embellish
embrasser, to embrace, kiss
émigrer, to emigrate
emmener, to take away
empêcher, to prevent
emporter, to carry away
s'empresser, to hasten
emprunt, *m.,* borrowing, loan
emprunter, to borrow
ému, moved
en, *prep.,* in, within
en, *pron.,* of it, of them, from there
enchanter, to enchant
enclin, prone, inclined
enclos, *m.,* enclosure

encore, still, again
encourager, to encourage, cheer
encre, *f.,* ink
endormi, asleep
s'endormir, to fall asleep
endroit, *m.,* place
enfance, *f.,* childhood
enfant, *m.* or *f.,* child
enfer, *m.,* hell
enfin, at last, in short
enivrer, to intoxicate
ennemi, *m.,* enemy
s'ennuyer, to be bored, become weary
ennuyeux, tedious, boring
s'enrhumer, to catch a cold
enseigner, to teach
ensemble, together
s'ensuit, il —, it follows
ensuite, after, then
entendre, to hear
entier, entire, whole
entourer, to surround
entrée, *f.,* entrance
entrefaites, sur ces —, meanwhile
entreprendre, to undertake
entrer, to enter
entretenir, to keep up, keep in repair
envers, towards
envie, *f.,* envy, fancy, desire
envier, to envy
environner, to surround
s'envoler, to fly away
envoyer, to send
épagneul, *m.,* spaniel
épais, thick
épaisseur, *f.,* thickness
épaule, *f.,* shoulder
épée, *f.,* sword
épeler, to spell
épouser, to marry
éprouver, to test, feel, experience
équipe, *f.,* team
errer, to wander

erreur, *f.*, error, mistake
escalier, *m.*, stairs, staircase
Espagne, *f.*, Spain
espagnol, Spanish
espèce, *f.*, species, kind
espérer, to hope
esprit, *m.*, spirit, mind, wit
essayer, to try
essuyer, to wipe, endure
estomac, *m.*, stomach
étable, *f.*, stable
s'établir, to settle, establish oneself
établissement, *m.*, establishment
étage, *m.*, floor, story
étape, *f.*, stage, station
États-Unis, *m.*, The United States
été, *m.*, summer
éternel, eternal
étincelant, sparkling
étoile, *f.*, star
étonné, astonished
étonnement, *m.*, astonishment
étonner, to astonish
étrange, strange
étranger, strange, foreign
étranger, *m.*, stranger, foreigner
à l'étranger, abroad
étrangère, *f.*, stranger, foreigner
être, to be
être, *m.*, being, creature
étude, *f.*, study
étudiant, *m.*, student
étudier, to study
européen, European
évasion, *f.*, escape, flight
événement, *m.*, event
éventail, *m.*, fan
évidemment, evidently
éviter, to avoid
exactement, exactly
examen, *m.*, examination
examiner, to examine
exaspérer, to exasperate
excellent, excellent
exciter, to excite
excursion, *f.*, excursion, trip

excuser, to excuse
exercer, to exercise
exercice, *m.*, exercise
exhaler, to exhale
expirer, to expire
expliquer, to explain
explorateur, *m.*, explorer
exposition, *f.*, exhibition
exprimer, to express
extraordinaire, extraordinary

fâcher, to make angry
facile, easy
facilement, easily
façon, *f.*, make, fashion, manner
façons, *f. pl.*, fuss
facteur, *m.*, postman, railway porter
faible, weak
faïence, *f.*, earthenware, crockery
faim, *f.*, hunger
faire, to make, do
se faire à, to become used to
fait, *m.*, deed, fact
au fait de, aware of
falloir, to be necessary
famille, *f.*, family
fantasque, fantastic
farine, *f.*, flour
fatal, fatal
fatigue, *f.*, fatigue
fatigué, tired
faucheur, *m.*, reaper
faute, *f.*, fault, mistake
faute de, for want of
faux, fausse, false
favori, favourite
femme, *f.*, woman
fenêtre, *f.*, window
fer, *m.*, iron
ferme, *f.*, farm
fermer, to close, shut
fermier, *m.*, farmer
fêter, to entertain, keep (a feast or holiday)
feu, *m.*, fire

feuille, *f.*, leaf
février, *m.*, February
fiacre, *m.*, cab
ficelle, *f.*, string, twine
fidèle, faithful
fier, proud
se fier à, to trust
fiévreux, feverish
figure, *f.*, face
se figurer, to fancy, imagine
fil, *m.*, thread, wire
fille, *f.*, daughter
jeune fille, *f.*, girl
film, *m.*, film
fils, *m.*, son
fin, fine, slender
fin, *f.*, end
en fin de compte, finally
finir, to finish
fixer, to fix, fasten
flagrant, flagrant
en flagrant délit, red-handed, in the very act
flanc, *m.*, side, flank
fleur, *f.*, flower
fleurir, to flower, blossom
fleuve, *m.*, river
flot, *m.*, wave, billow
flotter, to float
fois, *f.*, time, occasion
foncé, dark, deep
fonctionner, to work, act
fond, *m.*, bottom, background
fondre, to melt
football, *m.*, football
force, *f.*, strength, might
forcer, to force, compel
forestier, forest(ed), woodland
forêt, *f.*, forest
formalité, *f.*, formality
former, to form, fashion
fort, strong
fortune, *f.*, fortune, luck
fou, folle, mad, foolish
fourmi, *f.*, ant
fourmiller, to swarm

foyer, *m.*, hearth, home
foyers, *m. pl.*, native land
fracas, *m.*, crash, din
fragile, fragile
fraîcheur, *f.*, coolness
frais, fraîche, fresh, cool
fraise, *f.*, strawberry
franc, franche, frank, sincere
français, French
France, *f.*, France
franchir, to jump or pass over
frapper, to strike, hit
fréquemment, often
frère, *m.*, brother
frire, to fry
friser, to curl, verge upon
froid, cold
froid, *m.*, cold, coldness
front, *m.*, front, forehead
fruit, *m.*, fruit
fuir, to flee
fumer, to smoke
fusiller, to shoot

gagner, to earn, gain, reach
gaieté, *or* gaîté, *f.*, merriment
gaillard, *m.*, jolly fellow
gant, *m.*, glove
garçon (petit), *m.*, boy, lad
garde, *f.*, watch, custody
gare, *f.*, station
garenne, *f.*, warren
se garer, to get out of the way
garnir, to trim, furnish
gâteau, *m.*, cake
gâter, to spoil
gauche, left
à gauche, to *or* on the left
géant, *m.*, giant
gelée, *f.*, frost; jelly
geler, to freeze
gêner, to constrain, embarrass
général, *m.*, general
genou, *m.*, knee
gens, *m. pl.*; *f. after adj.*, people
gentil, gentle, nice, noble

geôlier, *m.*, jailer
glace, *f.*, ice, ice-cream, looking-glass
(se) glisser, to slip, slide, steal
gloire, *f.*, glory, fame
golf, *m.*, golf
gorge, *f.*, throat
goûter, to taste, relish
goutte, *f.*, drop
gouvernail, *m.*, rudder, helm
gouverneur, *m.*, governor
grand, great, large, tall
grandir, to grow, increase
grand'mère, *f.*, grandmother
gré, *m.*, will, wish
grec, grecque, Greek
grêle, *f.*, hail
grêler, to hail
grelotter, to shiver
grimace, *f.*, grimace
gris, grey
griser, to intoxicate
gros, big, large, stout
grossier, coarse, rough
groupe, *m.*, group
guérir, to heal, cure
ne . . . guère, hardly, scarcely
guerre, *f.*, war
guide, *m.*, guide

habile, clever, skilful
habiller, to dress
habit, *m.*, dress
habitant, *m.*, inhabitant
habiter, to inhabit, live in
habitude, *f.*, custom, habit
haie, *f.*, hedge
haine, *f.*, hatred
haïr, to hate
hameau, *m.*, hamlet
hasard, *m.*, chance, hazard
hâte, *f.*, haste
se hâter, to hasten
haut, high
en haut, at the top, upstairs
hauteur, *f.*, height

le Havre, *m.*, Havre
hebdomadaire, weekly
hélas, alas
herbage, *m.*, pasture, herbage
herbe, *f.*, grass
héroïne, *f.*, heroine
héros, *m.*, hero
hésiter, to hesitate
heure, *f.*, hour
de bonne heure, early
heureusement, happily, fortunately
heureux, happy, fortunate
heurter, to strike, knock against
hibou, *m.*, owl
hier, yesterday
hirondelle, *f.*, swallow
histoire, *f.*, story, history
hiver, *m.*, winter
homme, *m.*, man
honorer, to honour
honte, *f.*, shame
honteux, ashamed, bashful, shameful
hôpital, *m.*, hospital
horizon, *m.*, horizon
horloge, *f.*, clock
hôte, *m.*, host; guest
hôtel, *m.*, hotel
hôtesse, *f.*, hostess
huile, *f.*, oil
huit, eight
huitième, eighth
humide, wet, damp
humidité, *f.*, dampness, moisture
hurler, to howl
hutte, *f.*, hut

ici, here
ici-bas, down here
idée, *f.*, idea
ignorer, to be ignorant of, not to know
île, *f.*, island
immense, immense
immobile, motionless

s'immobiliser, to come to a halt, stop
immortel, immortal
s'impatienter, to lose one's patience
importance, *f.,* importance
impossible, impossible
impuissance, *f.,* impotence, inability
inadmissible, inadmissible
incident, *m.,* incident
incomparable, incomparable
Indes, *f. pl.,* India
indicateur, *m.,* indicator, time-table
indifférent, indifferent
industrie, *f.,* industry, skill
inhabile, unskilful
innocence, *f.,* innocence
innommable, unmentionable, disgusting
inquiet, anxious, uneasy
s'inquiéter, to be alarmed, become uneasy
insensiblement, by imperceptible degrees
insolent, insolent
inspirer, to inspire
s'installer, to settle
instant, *m.,* instant
instinct, *m.,* instinct
instruire, to teach, instruct
à l'insu de, unknown to, without the knowledge of
intelligent, intelligent
intention, *f.,* intention
intéressant, interesting
intéresser, to interest
intérêt, *m.,* interest
intérieur, *m.,* interior
interminable, endless
interrompre, to interrupt
invention, *f.,* invention
invisible, invisible
invitation, *f.,* invitation
inviter, to invite

ironique, ironical
irriter, to irritate, provoke
Italie, *f.,* Italy
italien, Italian

jaloux, jealous
jamais, never, ever
janvier, January
Japon, *m.,* Japan
japonais, Japanese
jardin, *m.* garden
jaser, to chatter
jaune, yellow
Jean, John
jeter, to throw
jeu, *m.,* game
jeudi, Thursday
jeune, young
jeunesse, *f.,* youth
joie, *f.,* joy
joindre, to join
joli, pretty
jonc, *m.,* rush, reed
jouer, to play
joujou, *m.,* toy
jour, *m.,* day, daylight
au jour le jour, from hand to mouth
de jour en jour, from day to day
de nos jours, nowadays
journal, *m.,* newspaper
joyeux, merry, joyful
juger, to judge
juif, juive, *m., f.,* Jew, Jewess, Jewish
juillet, July
juin, June
jusqu'à, *prep.,* until
jusqu'à ce que, *conj.,* until
jusqu'ici, this far, until now
juste, *adj.,* just, rightful, exact; *adv.,* just, precisely
justement, justly, precisely

kilo(gramme), *m.,* kilogramme
kilomètre, *m.,* kilometre

là, there
là-bas, down there
là-haut, up there
lac, *m.*, lake
laid, ugly
laine, *f.*, wool
laisser, to let, leave
lait, *m.*, milk
lancer, to throw
langue, *f.*, tongue, language
lapin, *m.*, rabbit
large, broad, wide
largeur, *f.*, breadth, width
larme, *f.*, tear
las, weary, tired
laver, to wash
légume, *m.*, vegetable
lendemain, *m.*, morrow, next day, day after
lettre, *f.*, letter
lever, to lift, raise
levier, *m.*, lever
lieu, *m.*, place
au lieu de, instead of
ligne, *f.*, line
limite, *f.*, limit
limonade, *f.*, lemonade
limpide, limpid
lion, *m.*, lion
lire, to read
lis, *m.*, lily
lit, *m.*, bed
livre, *m.*, book
locomotive, *f.*, railway engine
logement, *m.*, lodgings
logis, *m.*, home, house
au loin, in the distance
Londres, London
long, long
longtemps, long, for a long time
longueur, *f.*, length
loque, *f.*, rag, tatter
lors, then
lorsque, when
louer, to praise, rent
lourd, heavy

lueur, *f.*, glimmer, light
lugubre, dismal
lundi, Monday
lune, *f.*, moon
lutter, to struggle, wrestle
lycée, *m.*, grammar-school

mai, May
maigre, lean, thin
main, *f.*, hand
maintenant, now
mais, but
maison, *f.*, house, home
maisonnette, *f.*, cottage
maître, *m.*, master
mal, *adv.*, badly, ill
mal, *m.*, evil, ill
mal à propos, at the wrong time
malade, sick, ill
malgré, in spite of
malheur, *m.*, misfortune
malheureux, unhappy
malin, maligne, mischievous, sly
maman, *f.*, mother, mamma
manche, *f.*, sleeve
manger, to eat
manière, *f.*, manner
de manière que, in such a way that
manquer, to miss, lose, be missing
mansarde, *f.*, attic
marbre, *m.*, marble
marche, *f.*, walk, walking, step
marché, *m.*, market, bargain
marcher, to walk
mardi, *m.*, Tuesday
mari, *m.*, husband
marier, to marry
marin, *m.*, sailor
marine, *f.*, navy
marron, *m.*, chestnut
marron, *adj.* (*invariable*), chestnut-coloured
marronnier, *m.*, chestnut-tree
mars, *m.*, March
massif, massive, massive

match de football, *m.,* football match

matin, *m.,* morning

matinal, early

matinée, *f.,* morning

maudire, to curse

mauvais, bad, wicked

méchant, wicked, naughty

méconnaître, to disown, not to recognize

médecin, *m.,* doctor

médire, to slander

Méditerranée, *f.,* Mediterranean Sea

se méfier, to mistrust

meilleur, *adj.,* better

se mêler, to mingle, interfere

même, *adj.,* same, self

même, *adv.,* even

ménagère, *f.,* housewife

mener, to lead, drive

menteur, menteuse, liar

mentir, to lie, tell a lie

méprendre, to be mistaken, misapprehend

mépris, *m.,* contempt, scorn

mépriser, to despise

mer, *f.,* sea

merci, *m.,* thanks

mercredi, Wednesday

mère, *f.,* mother

mériter, to deserve

merveille, *f.,* wonder

à merveille, marvellously

métal, *m.,* metal

mètre, *m.,* metre

mettre, to put

midi, *m.,* midday

miette, *f.,* crumb

mieux, *adv.,* better

mignon, delicate, dainty

mille, thousand

mille, *m.,* mile

millième, thousandth

millier, *m.,* thousand

mine, *f.,* look, aspect

ministre, *m.,* minister

minuit, *m.,* midnight

minute, *f.,* minute

se mirer, to look at oneself (in a mirror)

mise-en-plis, *f.,* set or reset (of hair-waving)

mise-en-scène, *f.,* staging (theatrical)

mœurs, *f. pl.,* manners, morals

moindre, *adj.,* smaller

moineau, *m.,* sparrow

moins, *adv.,* less

à moins que, unless

mois, *m.,* month

monde, *m.,* world, people

monnaie, *f.,* money, currency

monotonie, *f.,* monotony

monsieur, *m.,* sir, gentleman

mont, *m.,* hill, mountain

montagnard, *m.,* mountaineer, highlander

montagne, *f.,* mountain

monter, to go up, climb, ascend

montre, *f.,* watch

montrer, to show

se moquer de, to make fun of

mordre, to bite

mort, *f.,* death

mot, *m.,* word

motocyclette, *f.,* motor-cycle

mou, mol, molle, soft

mourir, to die

mousse, *f.,* moss, froth

mouton, *m.,* sheep

moyen, *m.,* means, way

moyen, moyenne, mean, medium, average

muet, dumb

muguet, *m.,* lily of the valley

mur, *m.,* wall

mûr, ripe

muraille, *f.,* wall

musique, *f.,* music

mystère, *m.,* mystery

mystérieux, mysterious

nager, to swim
naître, to be born
nappe, *f.*, tablecloth
nation, *f.*, nation
nature, *f.*, nature
naturel, natural
naturellement, naturally
né, née, born
nécessaire, necessary
neige, *f.*, snow
neiger, to snow
net, clean, clear
nettoyer, to clean
neuf, nine
neuvième, ninth
neveu, *m.*, nephew
nez, *m.*, nose
ni . . . ni, neither . . . nor
nid, *m.*, nest
nièce, *f.*, niece
nier, to deny
Noël, *m.*, Christmas
noir, black
noix, *f.*, nut
nom, *m.*, noun
nombre, *m.*, number
nonchalant, nonchalant, careless
nord, *m.*, north
Normandie, *f.*, Normandy
noter, to note, write down
nouveau, new
nouveau venu, *m.*, newcomer
nouvelles, *f. pl.*, news
novembre, *m.*, November
nu, naked
nuit, *f.*, night
nul, none, no one
nulle part, nowhere

obéir, to obey
objet, *m.*, object
obliger, to oblige, compel
observer, to observe, notice
obstrué, obstructed, blocked
obtenir, to obtain
occasion, *f.*, opportunity

occuper, to occupy
s'occuper de, to busy oneself with, attend to
océan, *m.*, ocean
octobre, *m.*, October
œil, *pl.* **yeux,** *m.*, eye
œuf, *m.*, egg
officier, *m.*, officer
offre, *f.*, offer
offrir, to offer
oiseau, *m.*, bird
ombre, *f.*, shadow, shade
omelette, *f.*, omelet
omettre, to omit
on, one, someone
oncle, *m.*, uncle
ondée, *f.*, shower
onze, eleven
onzième, eleventh
or, *m.*, gold
orage, *m.*, storm
orange, *f.*, orange
oranger, *m.*, orange-tree
ordonner, to order
oreille, *f.*, ear
organisation, *f.*, organization
ornement, *m.*, decoration
orner, to adorn
orphelin, *m.*, orphan
oser, to dare
ou, or
où, where
oublier, to forget
oui, yes
ouï-dire, *m.*, hearsay
ouvrir, to open

page, *f.*, page
paille, *f.*, straw
pain, *m.*, bread, loaf
paire, *f.*, pair
paix, *f.*, peace
palier, *m.*, landing (on staircase)
panne, *f.*, breakdown
panser, to dress, bandage
pantoufle, *f.*, slipper

papier, *m.*, paper
papillon, *m.*, butterfly
par, by
paraître, to appear
parapet, *m.*, parapet
parapluie, *m.*, umbrella
parce que, because
pardessus, *m.*, overcoat
pardessus, *prep.*, over and above
pareil, like, similar
parent, *m.*, parent, relative
parer, to adorn, array
paresseux, lazy
parfois, at times, sometimes
parfum, *m.*, perfume
parler, *m.*, speech, language
parler, to speak
part, *f.*, share, portion
de la part de, on behalf of
nulle part, nowhere
quelque part, somewhere
partager, to share
partenaire, *m.* or *f.*, partner
parti, *m.*, side, party, choice
partie, *f.*, part, game
partir, to depart, go away
pas, not, no
pas, *m.*, step, pace
passager, *m.*, passenger
passagère, *f.*, passenger
passant, *m.*, passer-by
passé, *m.*, past
passeport, *m.*, passport
passer, to pass
se passer de, to do without
passion, *f.*, passion
patience, *f.*, patience
patiner, to skate
patrie, *f.*, native land
patte, *f.*, paw, foot
pauvre, poor
pavot, *m.*, poppy
payer, to pay for
pays, *m.*, country, region
paysan, *m.*, peasant, countryman
paysanne, *f.*, country-woman

pêche, *f.*, peach
peindre, to paint
peine, *f.*, penalty, trouble, difficulty
à peine, hardly
peler, to peel, skin
pelote, *f.*, ball (of wool)
penchant, *m.*, slope, inclination
pendant, during
pendant que, while
pendre, to hang
pénétrer, to penetrate
péniblement, painfully, with
  difficulty
pensée, *f.*, thought
penser, to think
percevoir, to perceive, collect
perché, perched
perdre, to lose
perdreau, *m.*, partridge
père, *m.*, father
périlleux, dangerous
périr, to perish
perle, *f.*, pearl
permettre, to permit, allow
personnage, *m.*, personage
personne, *f.*, person
personne, no one
personnel, personal
persuader, to persuade
pervenche, *f.*, periwinkle
petit, small, little
peu, *adv.*, little
peu de, little (*sing.*); few (*pl.*)
un peu, a little
peu à peu, by degrees
peuple, *m.*, people
peur, *f.*, fear
de peur de, for fear of
de peur que, lest, for fear that
peut-être, perhaps
pharmacien, *m.*, chemist, druggist
phénomène, *m.*, phenomenon
philosophiquement, philosophic-
  ally
pianiste, *m.* or *f.*, pianist
piano, *m.*, piano

pied, *m.,* foot
pilier, *m.,* pillar
pipe, *f.,* pipe
pique-nique, *m.,* picnic
pire, worse *(adj.)*
pis, worse *(adv.)*
piste, *f.,* track, strip, runway
pitié, *f.,* pity
place, *f.,* room, space, seat, square (in a town)
placer, to place, set
plaindre, to pity
se plaindre, to complain
plaire, to please
plaisanter, to jest, joke
plaisir, *m.,* pleasure
planer, to hover, soar
plante, *f.,* plant
plateau, *m.,* tray, tableland, plateau
plâtre, *m.,* plaster
plein, full
pleur, *m.,* tear
pleurer, to weep, cry
pleuvoir, to rain
pli, *m.,* fold, crease
plomb, *m.,* lead
pluie, *f.,* rain
plume, *f.,* pen, feather
plus, more *(adv.)*
plusieurs, several *(adj. and pron.)*
plutôt, rather
poète, *m.,* poet
poignée, *f.,* handful, grip
pointer, to point
pointu, pointed
poire, *f.,* pear
poirier, *m.,* pear-tree
pois, *m.,* pea
poisson, *m.,* fish
poitrail, *m.,* breast
poitrine, *f.,* breast, chest
poli, polite, polished
police, *f.,* police
polir, to polish
polonais, Polish

pomme, *f.,* apple
pomme de terre, *f.,* potato
pommier, *m.,* apple-tree
pont, *m.,* bridge, deck
porte, *f.,* door
portée, *f.,* range, scope, reach
porter, to carry
posséder, to possess
possible, possible
poste, *f.,* post, post-office
postiche, false (of hair)
pouce, *m.,* thumb, inch
poulet, *m.,* chicken
pour, for, in order to
pour que, in order to
pour que, in order that
pourquoi, why
pourtant, yet, still
pourvu que, provided that
pousse, *f.,* shoot, sprout
pousser, to grow, push, impel
pouvoir, *m.,* power
pouvoir, to be able
prairie, *f.,* meadow
précieux, precious
prédire, to foretell
préférer, to prefer
premier, first
prendre, to take
préparer, to prepare
présence, *f.,* presence
président, *m.,* president
presque, almost, nearly
presser, press, entreat
se presser, to hasten
prêt, ready
prêter, to lend
prier, to beg, entreat
primaire, primary
prince, *m.,* prince
princesse, *f.,* princess
principal, principal
principe, *m.,* principle
printemps, *m.,* spring
prise, *f.,* capture, hold
prisonnier, *m.,* prisoner

privé, private
prix, *m.*, price, prize
prochain, next
professeur, *m.* or *f.*, professor, teacher
profit, *m.*, profit
profond, deep
profondeur, *f.*, depth
promenade, *f.*, walk, drive, ride
se promener, to go for a walk, drive, ride, etc.
promesse, *f.*, promise
promettre, to promise
à propos, to the point
mal à propos, inappropriately
propre, own, proper, fit, clean
protéger, to protect
protestant, *m.*, Protestant
protester, to protest
province, *f.*, province
prudemment, prudently
prudent, prudent
prune, *f.*, plum
prunelle, *f.*, pupil of the eye
public, public
puis, then
puisque, since
puissance, *f.*, power
puissant, powerful
puits, *m.*, well

quadrimoteur, *m.*, four-engine aircraft
quai, *m.*, quay, platform
quand, when
quand même, even though
quant à, as for
quarantaine, *f.*, about forty
quarantième, fortieth
quart, *m.*, quarter
quatorze, fourteen
quatorzième, fourteenth
quatre, four
quatre-vingts, eighty
quatre-vingt-un, eighty-one
quatre-vingt-dix, ninety

quatre-vingt-onze, ninety-one
quatrième, fourth
que, what, as, than
quel, what, what a
quelque, some
quelque chose, something
quelquefois, sometimes
quelque part, somewhere
quelqu'un, someone
queue, *f.*, tail
qui, who, whom, which
quinze, fifteen
quinzième, fifteenth
quitter, to leave
quoi, what
quoi que, whatever
quoique, although
quotidien, daily

rabattre, to pull down, lower
raconter, to tell, relate
radio, *f.*, radio
rageur, ill-tempered
rail, *m.*, rail
raisin, *m.*, grape
raison, *f.*, reason, right
avoir raison, to be right
à raison de, at the rate of
rajeunir, to make younger
ramasser, to gather, pick up
ramer, to row
rang, *m.*, row, rank, line
rapide, rapid, fast
rare, rare
rarement, rarely, seldom
rat, *m.*, rat
ravage, *m.*, ravage
ravi, delighted
ravir, to delight, ravish
rayon, *m.*, ray, spoke, shelf
réaction, *f.*, reaction
à réaction, jet-propelled
récent, recent
recevoir, to receive
réciter, to recite
recommencer, to begin again

récompense, *f.*, reward
reconnaissance, *f.*, recognition, gratitude
reconnaître, to recognize, acknowledge
record, *m.*, record
se recoucher, to go back to bed
recouvrir, to recover, cover again
redire, to repeat
réfléchir, to reflect
se réfugier, to take shelter
refuser, to refuse
regard, *m.*, look
regarder, to look at, concern
région, *f.*, region, area
regret, *m.*, regret
regretter, to regret
reine, *f.*, queen
remercier, to thank
remettre, to put back
rempli, full, filled
remplir, to fill
remporter, to carry off, win
remuer, to stir, shake
renaître, to be born again
rencontre, *f.*, meeting
rencontrer, to meet
renouveau, *m.*, renewal, spring
rentrer, to return (home)
renvoyer, to return, dismiss
répartir, to divide
repas, *m.*, meal
se repentir de, to repent of
répéter, to repeat
répondre, to reply
réponse, *f.*, reply, answer
repos, *m.*, rest
reprendre, to take back, recover
reprise, *f.*, recapture, repetition
résigner, to resign
résister, to resist
responsabilité, *f.*, responsibility
ressembler, to resemble
ressentir, to feel
restaurant, *m.*, restaurant
rester, to remain, stay

en retard, late
retenir, to hold back, retain
rétif, restive
se retirer, to withdraw, retire
retourner, to go back, turn
réussir, to succeed
rêve, *m.*, dream
réveil, *m.*, waking
se réveiller, to awake
révéler, to reveal
revenant, *m.*, ghost
revenir, to come back
rêver, to dream
rêverie, *f.*, dreaming, musing
rêveur, dreaming, musing
riche, rich
ridicule, ridiculous
rien, nothing
rire, to laugh
rivière, *f.*, river
robe, *f.*, dress
roc, *m.*, rock
roi, *m.*, king
roman, *m.*, novel
rond, round
ronronner, to purr
rose, *f.*, rose
rose, pink
rôtir, to roast
roue, *f.*, wheel
rouge, red
rougeaud, ruddy, red-faced
rougir, to redden, blush
rouler, to roll, speed along
route, *f.*, road
rue, *f.*, street
ruiner, to ruin
ruse, *f.*, ruse, trick
russe, Russian
Russie, *f.*, Russia

sable, *m.*, sand
sabot, *m.*, clog, wooden shoe
sain, healthy, sound
salé, salted
salle, *f.*, room

salle de classe, *f.*, classroom
samedi, *m.*, Saturday
sans, without
santé, *f.*, health
sarcler, to weed
satisfait, satisfied
saucisse, *f.*, sausage
sauf, safe
sauter, to jump, leap
sauver, to save
sauvetage, *m.*, rescue
savant, *m.*, scholar
savoir, to know
scandale, *m.*, scandal
scène, *f.*, scene, stage
scientifique, scientific
sec, sèche, dry
second, second
secours, *m.*, help, aid
secret, *m.*, secret
secret, secrète, secret
sécurité, *f.*, security, safety
sein, *m.*, breast, bosom
seize, sixteen
seizième, sixteenth
selon, according to
semaine, *f.*, week
faire semblant de, to pretend to
sembler, to seem
sentiment, *m.*, sentiment, feeling
sentir, to feel, smell
sept, seven
septembre, *m.*, September
septième, seventh
sergent, *m.*, sergeant
sérieusement, seriously
sérieux, serious
serpent, *m.*, serpent, snake
servir, to serve
se servir de, to use
seul, alone
seulement, only
short, *m.*, shorts, short trousers
si, so, such, if, whether
siècle, *m.*, century

sifflement, *m.*, whistling, hiss
siffler, to whistle, hiss
signer, to sign
signifier, to signify, mean
silence, *m.*, silence
silhouette, *f.*, figure, silhouette
simple, simple, plain
sitôt, as soon
situation, *f.*, situation
situer, to situate
six, six
sixième, sixth
sœur, *f.*, sister
soif, *f.*, thirst
soir, *m.*, evening
soirée, *f.*, evening, evening party
soixante, sixty
soixante-dix, seventy
soixante-dixième, seventieth
soixantième, sixtieth
soldat, *m.*, soldier
soleil, *m.*, sun
solide, solid, strong
solitaire, solitary, lonely
sommeil, *m.*, sleep
sommet, *m.*, summit, top
songe, *m.*, dream
sonner, to ring
sonnette, *f.*, bell
sort, *m.*, fate, lot
de sorte que, so that
sortir, to go out
sot, sotte, silly, foolish
soudain, sudden
souffrant, suffering, patient, ill
souffrir, to suffer, bear
soulier, *m.*, shoe
soumettre, to submit
soupçon, *m.*, suspicion
soupçonner, to suspect
soupe, *f.*, soup
souper, *m.*, supper
souper, to sup
sourd, deaf, muffled
sous-officier, *m.*, non-commissioned officer

soutenir, to support, maintain
se souvenir de, to remember
souvent, often
sport, *m.*, sport
stupéfait, dumbfounded
stupide, stupid
stupidement, stupidly
subir, to undergo
subsister, to subsist
sucer, to suck
sucre, *m.*, sugar
suite, *f.*, rest, result
par suite de, through, owing to
tout de suite, at once
sur, on
sûr, sure
surprendre, to surprise
surtout, chiefly, above all
survenir, to arrive, occur
survivant, *m.*, survivor
survoler, to fly over
suspendre, to hang up, suspend
suspendu, hanging, suspended
sympathie, *f.*, sympathy

tabac, *m.*, tobacco
table, *f.*, table
tableau, *m.*, picture
tableau noir, *m.*, blackboard
tache, *f.*, stain, blot
tâche, *f.*, task
tâcher, to try
taille, *f.*, height, size
se taire, to keep silent
tandis que, while, whereas
tant, so much, so many
tant que, as long as
tante, *f.*, aunt
tantôt . . . tantôt, now . . . now
tapis, *m.*, carpet
tapisser, to carpet
tard, *adv.*, late
taxi, *m.*, taxi
tel, such
télégramme, *m.*, telegram

télégraphier, to telegraph
télégraphique, telegraphic
téléphone, *m.*, telephone
téléphoner, to telephone
télévision, *f.*, television
temps, *m.*, time, weather
à temps, in time, soon enough
tendre, tender
tendresse, *f.*, tenderness
tenir, to hold
tennis, *m.*, tennis
tente, *f.*, tent
tenter, to attempt, tempt
terre, *f.*, earth, ground
tête, *f.*, head
thé, *m.*, tea
théâtre, *m.*, theatre
tiens! look here! hullo!
tigre, *m.*, tiger
tirer, to draw, pull, shoot
toilette, *f.*, dress
toit, *m.*, roof
tomber, to fall
tonnerre, *m.*, thunder
tort, *m.*, wrong
tôt, soon
toucher, to touch
toujours, always
tour, *m.*, turn, trick, walk
tour, *f.*, tower
tourment, *m.*, torture
tourner, to turn
se tourner, to turn round
tournoyer, to wheel, whirl
tout, *adj.*, all
tout, *pron.*, everything
tout, *adv.*, quite
tout à coup, suddenly
tout à fait, quite, completely
toutefois, yet, nevertheless
tracer, to trace
tragique, tragic
train, *m.*, train
traîner, to drag, trail
tranquille, quiet, still
tranquillement, quietly, calmly

transmettre, to transmit
transparent, transparent
travail, *m.,* work
travailler, to work
à travers, across, through
treize, thirteen
treizième, thirteenth
trentaine, *f.,* about thirty
trente, thirty
trente et un, thirty-one
trentième, thirtieth
très, very
trésor, *m.,* treasure
tressaillir, to start, be startled
tricoter, to knit
triste, sad
trois, three
troisième, third
tromper, to deceive
se tromper, to be mistaken
trop, too, too many, too much
trotter, to trot
trottoir, *m.,* pavement
trou, *m.,* hole
troubler, to unsettle, make muddy
troupeau, *m.,* flock, herd
trouver, to find
tuer, to kill
turc, turque, Turkish

un, une, a, one
unique, unique
univers, *m.,* universe
université, *f.,* university
utile, useful

vacances, *f.,* holidays
vacarme, *m.,* uproar
vache, *f.,* cow
vaguement, vaguely
valeur, *f.,* value
vallée, *f.,* valley
vallon, *m.,* vale
valoir, to be worth
valse, *f.,* waltz

velours, *m.,* velvet
vendre, to sell
vendredi, *m.,* Friday
vengeance, *f.,* revenge
venir, to come
vent, *m.,* wind
véranda, *f.,* veranda
verger, *m.,* orchard
vérité, *f.,* truth
verre, *m.,* glass
vers, *m.,* verse, line
vers, *prep.,* towards, about
vert, green
vertige, *m.,* dizziness
vêtir, to clothe
viande, *f.,* meat
victime, *f.,* victim
victoire, *f.,* victory
vie, *f.,* life
vieux, vieil, vieille, old
vif, vive, quick, lively
vigne, *f.,* vine
vilain, ugly
village, *m.,* village
ville, *f.,* town
vin, *m.,* wine
vingt, twenty
vingt-deux, twenty-two
vingt et un, twenty-one
vingt et unième, twenty-first
vingtième, twentieth
violette, *f.,* violet
violon, *m.,* violin
visite, *f.,* visit
visiteur, *m.,* visitor
vite, quickly
vitre, *f.,* pane of glass
vitré, glass, made of glass
vivement, quickly, briskly
vivre, to live
vocable, *m.,* vocable, word, term
voici, here is, here are, behold
voilà, there is, there are, behold
voir, to see
voisin, *m.,* neighbour
voisinage, *m.,* neighbourhood

voiture, *f.,* carriage, car
voix, *f.,* voice
vol, *m.,* flight, theft
voler, to fly, steal
voleur, *m.,* thief
volonté, *f.,* will
volontiers, willingly
vouloir, to wish, will
voyage, *m.,* journey
voyager, to travel

voyageur, *m.,* traveller
voyant, showy, gaudy, loud
vrai, true
vraiment, truly, indeed
vulgaire, vulgar, common

y, *adv.,* there
y, *pron.,* to it, of it

zéro, *m.,* nought

VOCABULARY

ENGLISH—FRENCH

able, to be, pouvoir
above, au-dessus de
about, what is it —?, de quoi s'agit-il?
absence, absence, *f.*
accept, accepter
accident, accident, *m.*
account, on — of, à cause de
accustomed, grow —, s'accoutumer
act-or, -ress, acteur, actrice
admire, admirer
admit, admettre
advance, avancer
adventure, aventure, *f.*
advise, conseiller
affection, affection, *f.*
afraid, to be, avoir peur
after, après
again, encore (une fois); de nouveau
against, contre
age, -d, âge, *m.*, âgé
ago, il y a
agree, convenir
alarm, alarme, *f.*; alarmer; effrayer; faire peur à
alas, hélas
all, tout
allow, laisser; permettre
alone, seul
already, déjà
also, aussi
although, quoique
always, toujours
amuse, amuser
amusement, amusement; divertissement, *m.*
anecdote, anecdote, *f.*

angry, fâché; en colère
angry, to grow, se fâcher
animal, animal, *m.*
answer, réponse, *f.*; répondre
anxious, to be — to, tenir à
anyone else, tout autre
appear, paraître; apparaître
applaud, applaudir
apple, -tree, pomme, *f.*, pommier, *m.*
April, avril, *m.*
apricot, abricot, *m.*
arouse, réveiller; exciter
arrival, arrivée, *f.*
arrive, arriver
as, aussi; que; comme; puisque
ashamed, to be, avoir honte
ask, demander
asleep, to fall —, endormi, s'endormir
at, à
attend, assister à
August, août, *m.*
aunt, tante, *f.*
Australia, Australie, *f.*
authentic, certain
author, auteur, *m.*
awkward, gauche

baby, bébé, *m.*
bad, -ly, mauvais, mal
baker, boulanger, *m.*
ball, bal, *m.*; balle, *f.*
band, bande, *f.*
bank, berge; rive, *f.*
battle, bataille, *f.*
be, être
bear, ours, *m.*
beard, barbe, *f.*

beast, bête, *f.*
beat, battre
beaut-iful, -y, beau, beauté, *f.*
because, parce que
become, devenir
bed, lit, *m.*
bed, to go to, se coucher
before, avant; avant de; avant que
beg, prier
begin, commencer
beginning, commencement, *m.*
behind, derrière
believe, croire
bell, cloche, *f.*
beside, auprès de
besides, d'ailleurs
better, *adj.* meilleur; *adv.* mieux
bicycle, bicyclette, *f.*
big, gros
bird, oiseau, *m.*
bite, mordre
blackbird, merle, *m.*
blame, blâmer
blow, coup, *m.*; souffler
blue, bleu
body, corps, *m.*
book, livre, *m.*
boot, botte; bottine, *f.*
born, to be, naître
borrow, emprunter
both, tous deux
bottom, pied, *m.*
boy, garçon, *m.*
brave, courageux; brave
bravely, courageusement
bread, pain, *m.*
break, briser; casser; rompre
breakfast, déjeuner, *m.*
bridge, pont, *m.*
bright, clair; vif
bring, apporter
brother, frère, *m.*
brown, brun
build, bâtir
business, affaires, *f. pl.*

but, mais
butter, beurre, *m.*
buy, acheter

call, appeler
Canada, Canada, *m.*
captain, capitaine, *m.*
car, automobile, *f.*
carefully, soigneusement
carry, porter
case, cas, *m.*
castle, château, *m.*
cat, chat, *m.*
catch, attraper
Catholic, catholique
chair, chaise, *f.*
charm, charme, *m.*
cheese, fromage, *m.*
chemist, pharmacien, *m.*
cherish, chérir
cherry, -tree, cerise, *f.*, cerisier, *m.*
chestnut, châtaigne, *f.*; marron, *m.*
chestnut, *adj.* châtain
chicken, poulet, *m.*
child, enfant, *m.* or *f.*
chill, rhume, *m.*
chirp, pépier
chocolate, chocolat, *m.*
choose, choisir
Christmas, Noël, *m.*
Christopher, Christophe
church, -yard, église, *f.*, cimetière, *m.*
cicada, cigale, *f.*
cigarette, cigarette, *f.*
cinema, cinéma, *m.*
circumstances, circonstances, *f. pl.*
city, cité, *f.*
class, -room, classe, *f.*, salle de classe, *f.*
clean, propre; nettoyer; cirer (shoes)
clever, intelligent
climb, grimper; monter
clog, sabot, *m.*
coat, habit, *m.*

cock, coq, *m.*
coffee, café, *m.*
cold, rhume, *m.*; froid, *noun* and *adj.*
college, collège, *m.*
colour, couleur, *f.*
Columbus, Colomb
come, -back, venir, revenir
coming, arrivée, *f.*
company, compagnie, *f.*
compel, forcer
concert, concert, *m.*
constable, agent de police, *m.*
continue, continuer
conversation, conversation, *f.*; entretien, *m.*
copper, cuivre, *m.*
correspondent, correspondant, *m.*
cost, coûter
cottage, chaumière, *f.*
count, compter
country, pays, *m.*
course, of —; in the — of, naturellement; en
course, cours, *m.*
cousin, cousin, *m.*, cousine, *f.*
cover, couvrir
cow, vache, *f.*
cream, crème, *f.*
create, créer
creation, création, *f.*
creature, créature, *f.*
criticize, critiquer
crow, corbeau, *m.*
cry, s'écrier
cup, tasse, *f.*
cut, couper
cutlet, côtelette, *f.*

dance, danse, *f.*
daily, quotidien
danger, -ous, danger, *m.*, dangereux
dark, obscur
daughter, fille, *f.*
day, jour, *m.*

deaf, sourd
dear, cher
debate, débat, *m.*
deceive, tromper
December, décembre, *m.*
decision, parti, *m.*
deep, profond
defeat, défaite, *f.*
delighted, enchanté
demolish, démolir
deny, nier
descend, descendre
deserve, mériter
desire, désirer
detective, détective, *m.*
determine, déterminer
Devonshire, Devonshire, *m.*
die, mourir
difficult, difficile
diligent, diligent
din, vacarme, *m.*
dine, dîner
dinner, dîner, *m.*
direct, indiquer le chemin
dismiss, renvoyer
distinct, distinct; net
do, faire
doctor, médecin, *m.*
dog, chien, *m.*
donkey, âne, *m.*
door, porte, *f.*
Dover, Douvres
down, — there, bas, là-bas
drawing-room, salon, *m.*
dreadful, affreux; redoutable
dreary, triste; morne
dress, robe, *f.*
drink, boire
driver, conducteur, *m.*
dry, sec, *m.*, sèche, *f.*
during, pendant
dwell, demeurer

each, *adj.* chaque; *pron.* chacun
eager, impatient
ear, oreille, *f.*

easy, facile
eat, manger
Edinburgh, Édimbourg
effort, effort, *m.*
eight, huit
either . . . or, ou . . . ou
embellish, embellir
emigrate, émigrer
empty, vide
encourage, encourager
end, bout, *m.*
England, Angleterre, *f.*
English, anglais
enjoy oneself, s'amuser
enough, assez
enter, entrer
entirely, entièrement
equal, égal
error, erreur, *f.*
especially, spécialement; surtout
even, même
evening, soir, *m.*
event, événement, *m.*
everyone, tout le monde
everything, tout
excite, exciter
exclaim, s'écrier
expect, s'attendre à
eye, œil, *m.*, yeux, *pl.*

fable, fable, *f.*
face, faire face à; affronter
fall, — asleep, tomber, s'endormir
false, faux
family, famille, *f.*
far away, loin; au loin
farmer, fermier, *m.*
fast, vite
father, père, *m.*
fault, faute, *f.*
fear, for — of, peur; crainte, *f.*,
    craindre; avoir peur; de peur de
fearful, craintif
feast, fête, *f.*, festin; régal, *m.*
February, février, *m.*
feel, sentir

fetch, apporter; chercher
few, peu
few, a —, quelques
fifth, cinquième
fight, combattre; se battre
fill, poignée, *f.*
film, film, *m.*
find, trouver
fine, beau
finish, finir
fire, feu, *m.*
first, premier
flower, fleur, *f.*
fog, brouillard, *m.*
follow, -ing, suivre, suivant
foolish, sot; bête
foolishly, stupidement
foot, on —, -ball, pied, *m.*, à
    pied, football, *m.*
for, pour; car
foreigner, étranger, *m.*, étrangère,
    f.
forest, forêt, *f.*
forget, oublier
forgetfulness, oubli, *m.*, inatten-
    tion, *f.*
franc, franc, *m.*
France, France, *f.*
freeze, geler
fresh, frais
Friday, vendredi, *m.*
friend, -ly, ami(e), amical
from . . . till, dès . . . jusqu'à
full, plein
furiously, furieusement
fussy, to be, faire des façons
future; in —, avenir, *m.*; à
    l'avenir

gain, gagner
game, jeu, *m.*
garden, jardin, *m.*
gate, porte; barrière; grille, *f.*
general, général, *adj. and noun, m.*
gentleman, monsieur, *m.*
German, allemand

get up, se lever
ghost, revenant, *m.*
giant, géant, *m.*
girl, jeune fille, *f.*
give, donner
glad, content; heureux
glove, gant, *m.*
go, — away, — back, aller, s'en aller, retourner
go, — home, — in, — out, — up, rentrer, entrer, sortir, monter
goat, chèvre, *f.*
God, Dieu, *m.*
gold, or, *m.*
golf, golf, *m.*
good, -bye, bon, adieu
good, to be — enough, avoir la bonté de; vouloir (bien)
goodness, bonté, *f.*
grass, l'herbe, *f.*
gravely, gravement; sérieusement
Greek, grecque
green, vert
grey, gris
ground, terre, *f.*; sol, *m.*
grow, devenir; croître
guard, garde, *f.*
guide, guide, *m.*
gun, fusil, *m.*
gurgle, glou-glou, *m.*

hair, cheveu, *m.*
half, moitié, *f.*
hall, salle, *f.*, vestibule, *m.*
hand, main, *f.*
handkerchief, mouchoir, *m.*
handsome, beau
hang, pendre
hanging, suspendu
happen, arriver
happy, heureux
hard, dur; ferme
hat, chapeau, *m.*
hate, détester
have, avoir
head, tête, *f.*

health, santé, *f.*
hear, -say, entendre, ouï-dire, *m.*
heart, cœur, *m.*
heaven, ciel, *m.*
hedge, la haie
help, aider
here, ici
hero, le héros
hesitate, hésiter
high, haut
hold, tenir
holiday-maker, personne en vacances, *f.*; touriste, *m. or f.*
home, -land, chez soi, patrie, *f.*
home, to go or come —, rentrer
hope, espoir, *m.*; espérer
horrify, épouvanter
horse, cheval, *m.*
horseback, on —, à cheval
host, hôte, *m.*
hotel, hôtel, *m.*
hour, l'heure, *f.*
house, -wife, maison, *f.*, ménagère, *f.*
household, maison, *f.*, ménage, *m.*
how, -about? comment, et?
however, cependant; pourtant
howling, hurlement, *m.*
hunchback, bossu, *m.*
hungry, to be, avoir faim
hunt, chasser
hunter, chasseur, *m.*
hurry, se dépêcher
hush! chut!

ice, glace, *f.*
ideal, idéal
if, si
immediately, immédiatement; tout de suite
in, -to, dans
inclined, enclin
indeed, vraiment
India, Indes, *f. pl.*
ink, encre, *f.*
inn, auberge, *f.*

insist, insister
insolent, insolent
instead, au lieu
intelligent, intelligent
interesting, intéressant
invit-e, -ation, inviter, invitation, *f.*
iron, fer, *m.*
irritate, irriter

January, janvier, *m.*
jealous, jaloux
jewel, bijou, *m.*
join, joindre
joke, plaisanter; plaisanterie, *f.*
journey, voyage, *m.*
joy, joie, *f.*
joyful, joyeux
judge, juger; estimer
July, juillet, *m.*
jump, sauter
June, juin, *m.*
just now, tout à l'heure

keep, garder; rester
kill, tuer
kindly, aimable
king, roi, *m.*
kneel, s'agenouiller
knock, frapper
know, savoir; connaître
knowledge, savoir, *m.*; connaissance, *f.*

lack, manquer; manque; besoin, *m.*
lady, dame, *f.*
lantern, lanterne, *f.*
large, gros
last, dernier
late, en retard
lazy, paresseux
lead, mener
learn, apprendre
leave, laisser; partir; quitter
legend, légende, *f.*

lend, prêter
lesson, leçon, *f.*
letter, lettre, *f.*
lie, mentir
life, vie, *f.*
life-time, vivant, *m.*
lift, lever
light, clair, *m.*; lumière, *f.*; allumer
lightning, éclair, *m.*
like, aimer
like, comme
lily, lis, *m.*
lion, lion, *m.*
listen to, écouter
little, a —, peu; petit; un peu
live, vivre
loaf, pain, *m.*
London, Londres
long, long
look, — at, — out! avoir l'air, regarder, gare!
look for, chercher
look forward to, s'attendre à; attendre avec impatience
look up, lever les yeux
lose, perdre
love, aimer
lovely, beau
low, bas
lower, baisser

machine, machine, *f.*
maid, bonne, *f.*
maintain, maintenir
make, faire
make + *adj.*, rendre
man, homme, *m.*
manner, manière, *f.*
many, beaucoup de
marry, marier
marvellous, merveilleux
master, maître, *m.*
matter, I have something the —, j'ai quelque chose
May, mai, *m.*

meal, repas, *m.*
meaning, signification, *f.*; sens, *m.*
meanwhile, en attendant
meat, viande, *f.*
meet, rencontrer
mercilessly, sans pitié
metal, métal, *m.*
metre, mètre, *m.*
midnight, minuit, *m.*
mile, mille, *m.*
milk, lait, *m.*
mind, never —, esprit, *m.*; n'importe
minister, ministre, *m.* (*political*); pasteur *or* prêtre, *m.* (*clergyman*)
mirror, miroir, *m.*
miserable, misérable; malheureux
missing, to be, manquer; être absent
mistake, erreur, *f.*
mistaken, to be —, se tromper
mixture, mélange, *m.*
moment, moment, *m.*
Monday, lundi, *m.*
money, argent, *m.*
month, mois, *m.*
moon, lune, *f.*
more, plus
morning; next —, matin, *m.*; le lendemain matin
most, la plupart
mother, mère, *f.*
motor-cycle, motocyclette, *f.*
move, bouger; remuer
much; so —, beaucoup; tant
music, musique, *f.*
mysterious, mystérieux
mystery, mystère, *m.*

name, nom, *m.*; nommer
named, nommé
near, près de
necessary, to be, falloir
need, avoir besoin
neither, ni
nephew, neveu, *m.*

never, jamais
new, –comer, nouveau, nouveau-venu
news, nouvelle(s), *f.* (*pl.*)
newspaper, journal, *m.*
next, *adv.*, ensuite; *adj.*, suivant; prochain
night, nuit, *f.*
no, non
nobleman, gentilhomme; seigneur, *m.*
noise, bruit, *m.*
noisily, bruyamment
nor, ni
Normandy, Normandie, *f.*
not, ne . . . pas
nothing, rien
notice, remarquer
novel, roman, *m.*
now, maintenant

object, but, *m.*
of, de
offer, offrir
often, souvent
old, vieux
omit, omettre
on, sur
once, une fois; all at —; tout d'un coup; sur-le-champ
only, seulement; ne . . . que
onslaught, attaque, *f.*; assaut, *m.*
open, ouvrir
or; — so, ou; à peu près
orange, orange, *f.*
order; in — to, ordre, *m.*; pour
order, ordonner; commander
orphan, orphelin(e)
other, autre
overhear, entendre par hasard; saisir
owe, devoir
owl, le hibou
ox, bœuf, *m.*

pace, pas, *m.*
page, page, *f.*

pain, douleur, *f.*
paint, peindre
pardon, pardonner
Paris, Paris
pass, passer; se passer
past, passé, *m.*
pat, caresser
patient, patient
pay, payer
pear, -tree, poire, *f.*, poirier, *m.*
pen, plume, *f.*
pencil, crayon, *m.*
people, gens, *m.*
perceive, apercevoir
perhaps, peut-être
perish, périr
permit, permettre
person, personne, *f.*
persuade, persuader
Peter, Pierre
piano, piano, *m.*
pick up, ramasser
picture, tableau, *m.*
pinch, prise, *f.*
pink, rose
pity, pitié, *f.*; plaindre; avoir pitié de
place, place, *f.*
place; take the — of, placer; remplacer
plain, plaine, *f.*
plainly, franchement; évidemment
plant, plante, *f.*
play, jouer
play, pièce de théâtre, *f.*
play a trick on, faire un tour à
please, s'il vous plaît
pleased, content
police constable, agent de police, *m.*
polish, polir
poor, pauvre
poppy, pavot, *m.*
possessor, possesseur, *m.*
possible, possible

post, mettre à la poste
post-card, carte postale, *f.*
postpone, remettre
potato, pomme de terre, *f*
pound, livre, *f.*
power, pouvoir, *m.*
precious, précieux
predict, prédire
prefer, préférer
prepare, préparer
present, cadeau, *m.*
presently, tout à l'heure
pretend, faire semblant de
pretty, joli
pride, orgueil, *m.*
prince, prince, *m.*
princess, princesse, *f.*
prize, prix, *m.*
promise, promettre; promesse, *f.*
protect, protéger
protest, protester
Protestant, protestant
proud, fier
prove, prouver, se montrer
provided that, pourvu que
put, mettre

quarter, quart, *m.*
quiet, tranquille
quietly, tranquillement

radio, radio, *f.*
rain, pluie, *f.*; pleuvoir
random, at, au petit bonheur
rap, heurter
rapid, rapide
rather, un peu; assez; plutôt
read, lire
ready, prêt
really, vraiment
reason, raison, *f.*
receive, recevoir
recognize, reconnaître
refuse, refuser
regret, regretter
relate, raconter

remain, rester
remarkably, remarquablement
remember, se rappeler, se souvenir
repeatedly, à plusieurs reprises
replace, remplacer; replacer
reply, répondre
resign, donner sa démission
resources, to be left to one's own; devenir ce qu'on peut
responsibility, responsabilité, *f.*
restaurant, restaurant, *m.*
return, revenir
reveal, révéler
reward, récompense, *f.*; récompenser
rich, riche
right; all-, raison, *f.*; droit, *m.*; bien entendu
right, be, avoir raison
ring, sonner
rise, se lever
river, rivière, *f.*
road, route, *f.*; chemin, *m.*
roam, errer; rôder
roast, rôti
roof, toit, *m.*
room, chambre, *f.*
rose, rose, *f.*
ruin, ruiner
run, — up, courir, accourir
Russia, Russie, *f.*
Russian, russe
rustle, frou-frou, *m.*

sad, triste
saddle, seller
sadly, tristement
sand, sable, *m.*
satisfy, satisfaire
Saturday, samedi, *m.*
savage, sauvage; féroce
save, sauver, épargner
say, dire
scent, parfum, *m.*
Scotsman, -woman, Écossais(e)
scream, crier

sea, -side, mer, *f.*, bord de la mer, *m.*
secret, secret, *m.*
see, voir
seek, chercher
seem, sembler
seize, saisir; s'emparer de
seldom, rarement
sell, vendre
send, envoyer
sense, sentir
September, septembre, *m.*
seriously, sérieusement
servant, domestique
serve, servir
set, mettre
setting, décor, *m.*
several, plusieurs
shabby, vilain
shake, secouer
shell, coquille, *f.*
shine, briller; luire
shocking, affreux
shoe, soulier, *m.*
shop, boutique, *f.*
show, montrer
shut, fermer
sign, signe, *m.*
silver, argent, *m.*
since, puisque
sing, chanter
single, seul
sir, monsieur
sister, sœur, *f.*
sit, s'asseoir; être assis
situated, situé
sleep, dormir
sleeve, manche, *f.*
sleigh, traîneau, *m.*
small, petit
smile, sourire, *m.*; sourire
smoke, fumer
snow, neige, *f.*
so, si; aussi; donc
so much, tant
soldier, soldat, *m.*

someone, quelqu'un
something, quelque chose
sometimes, quelquefois
son, fils, *m.*
soon, bientôt
Spain, Espagne, *f.*
speak, parler
speed, vitesse, *f.*; aller à la hâte
spend, passer (time); dépenser (money)
sport, sport, *m.*
spring (season), printemps, *m.*
stairs, escalier, *m.*
stand, se tenir
start, partir
start up, tressaillir
station, gare, *f.*
stay, rester
stealthy, furtif
step, pas, *m.*
still, tranquille
stop, s'arrêter, cesser
story, histoire, *f.*
straight, droit
strange, étrange
strange-looking, à la mine bizarre
stranger, étranger, *m.*
street, rue, *f.*
strike, frapper
strong, fort
student, étudiant, *m.*
study, étudier
submissive, soumis
submit, soumettre
succeed, reússir
such, tel
suddenly, tout à coup
suffer, souffrir
sugar, sucre, *m.*
suit, aller (à)
summer, été, *m.*
sun, soleil, *m.*
Sunday, dimanche, *m.*
supper, souper, *m.*
suppose, supposer

sure; to make —, sûr; s'assurer
surprise, surprendre
surround, envahir
swallow, avaler
swarm, fourmiller
sweet, *adj.* doux; bonbon, *m.*
swell, enfler; gonfler
swiftly, vite
swim, nager
swing oneself off, s'élancer de
sword, épée, *f.*

table, table, *f.*
take, prendre
tall, grand
tea, thé, *m.*
teacher, professeur, *m. or .*
telegraph, télégraphier
telephone, téléphoner
tell, dire; raconter
tennis, tennis, *m.*
terrible, terrible; formidable
thank, remercier
thanks, merci
that, qui, que, cela, ce
the, le, la, les
theatre, théâtre, *m.*
their, leur
then, puis; alors
there, là
thick, épais
thin, mince
thing, chose, *f.*
think, penser
thirsty, be, avoir soir
this, ce
thorn, épine, *f.*
though, quoique
threaten, menacer
throat, gorge, *f.*
throne, trône, *m.*
through, à travers; au travers de
throw, jeter
thunder, tonnerre, *m.*
Thursday, jeudi, *m.*
tie, cravate, *f.*

time, temps, *m.*
tired, fatigué
to, à
today, aujourd'hui
together, ensemble
tomorrow, demain
tone, ton, *m.*
tonight, ce soir
too, trop; aussi
tooth, dent, *f.*
torrent, torrent, *m.*
touch, toucher
towards, vers
town, ville, *f.*
transmit, transmettre
travel, voyager
traveller, voyageur, *m.*; voyageuse, *f.*
tree, arbre, *m.*
tremble, trembler
trick; play a — on, tour, *m.*; faire un tour à
trouble, peine, *f.*
true, vrai
trust, se fier à
truth, vérité, *f.*
try, essayer
Tuesday, mardi, *m.*
Turkish, turc, turque
turn, tourner; se tourner

ugh! ouais!
uncle, oncle, *m.*
uncover, découvrir
under, sous
understand, comprendre
undertake, entreprendre
unhappy, malheureux
unknown to, à l'insu de
unless, à moins que; à moins de
unlike, différent de
unpublished, inédit; non publié
untidy, en désordre
until, jusqu'à
unusual, rare; peu commun
use, se servir de

used, to be — to, avoir coutume de
useful, utile

very, très
victory, victoire, *f.*
village, village, *m.*
violin, violon, *m.*
visit, visiter, rendre visite à
voice, voix, *f.*

wait, — for, attendre
walk, marcher
walk, go for a —, se promener
wall, mur, *m.*
wander, errer
want, désirer
warm, chaud, *adj.*; chauffer
watch, guetter; regarder; montre, *f.*
water, eau, *f.*
way, route, *f.*
weariness, fatigue, *f.*
weary; grow —, las; s'ennuyer
weather, temps, *m.*
Wednesday, mercredi, *m.*
week, semaine, *f.*
weep, pleurer
well, puits, *m.*; bien; eh bien
what! comment!
what a! quel!
wheat, blé, *m.*
when, quand, lorsque
where, où
whether, si
which, qui; quel; lequel; ce qui
while, pendant que, tandis que
whisper, chuchoter
white, blanc
who, qui
whole, tout
why, pourquoi
wide, large
width, largeur, *f.*
wife, femme, *f.*
willingly, volontiers

win, gagner
wind, vent, *m.*
window, fenêtre, *f.*
wine, vin, *m.*
winter, l'hiver, *m.*
wipe, essuyer
wish, vouloir
with, -out, avec, sans
wolf, loup, *m.*
woman, femme, *f.*
wonder, se demander
wood, bois, *m.*
word, mot, *m.*

work, travail, *m.*; travailler
world, monde, *m.*
wound, blesser
wretched, malheureux; infortuné
write, écrire
wrong, be, avoir tort

year, an, *m.*
yell, hurler
yellow, jaune
yes, oui
yesterday, hier
young, jeune